MW01289191

Hot Straight and Normal

There is a port of no return, where ships
may ride at anchor for a little space
And then, some starless night, the cable slips,
leaving an eddy at the mooring place…
Gulls, veer no longer. Sailor, rest your oar.
No tangled wreckage will be washed ashore
Leslie Nelson Jennings

It is the practice of submariners everywhere, when thinking of a parting shipmate, to use the phrase "rest your oar." With that sentiment in mind, this volume is dedicated to the crews and families of all submarines lost in war or peace of all nations.

Copyright-Ron Martini-Sheridan, Wyoming
First Edition-1997 and Second Edition-2001

Hot Straight and Normal

A Submarine Bibliography

Ron Martini

Writer's Showcase
San Jose New York Lincoln Shanghai

Hot Straight and Normal
A Submarine Bibliography

All Rights Reserved © 2001 by Ron Martini

No part of this book may be reproduced or transmitted in any form
or by any means, graphic, electronic, or mechanical, including
photocopying, recording, taping, or by any information storage
retrieval system, without the permission in writing from the
publisher.

Writer's Showcase
an imprint of iUniverse, Inc.

For information address:
iUniverse, Inc.
5220 S. 16th St., Suite 200
Lincoln, NE 68512
www.iuniverse.com

ISBN: 0-595-20825-8

Printed in the United States of America

From the Control Room of the "USS Observation Island" 20 July, 1960

"LOOKS GOOD X STATINGGXX STAGING
LOOKS GOOD ON TV AND T/M (TELEMETRY) LOOKS GOOD
LOOKS GOOD X STILL GOOD
N IP (IMPACT PREDICTOR) HOT STRAIGHT AND NORMAL
IP STILL GOOD STILL GOOD ON TV
STILL GOOD X IP MOVING ON OUT
STILL LOOKS GOOD EVERYTHING LOOKS GOOD
IT
LOOKS REAL GOOD
LOOKS REAL GOOD IN IP X RITE IN THE PICKLE BARREL AG
LOOKS LIKE WE HUNG ON TO THE TIGER'S TAIL
/ALL THE WAY/"

Communications from the Observation Island to Building M in Washington D.C. on the day of the first firing of the Polaris missile from the submarine, USS George Washington SSBN 598.

Acknowledgments
and Thanks

My apologies have to be extended to my family who have tolerated this passion of submarine books for the past five years. Thanks to my wife Shirley who rode in the After Torpedo Room for the whole cruise but made many trips forward to the Mess Hall in my behalf. Thanks to the thousands of people who have checked into my Internet pages, be they Diesel Boats Forever/DBF, Nuclear Boats Forever /NBF or simply fans of submarines for making the memories of my days aboard both diesel and nuclear submarines a joy to remember and relive on a daily basis. Thanks to Jim Mandelblatt of Rockville, MD; author of "Rebirth of a Submarine/Requin" and "Albacore" who helped in the publication of the first edition. Thanks to the kind staff of the Nimitz Library at Annapolis and their listing of the Thomas Paine Special Collection on-line. Thanks to Captain Jim Hay of Naval Submarine League for his help, review and use of article index in Appendix II. Also thanks to Fred Rainbow (Editor-in-Chief) for his help with the U.S. Navy Institutes Naval Proceedings magazine Index from 1874-1977, and others from the staff at Naval Institute. My gratitude to the University of Wyoming and it's associated American Heritage Center and the staff there for the information on Appendix X on the Clay Blair collection. Thanks to Steve Smith for sending me the Lockwood Papers listing. I must thank my father who instilled in me the desire to read and who said the real key to life is the library card and the real key to knowledge is not the amount you have, but the knowledge of where to find it. He would have loved the Internet world from where 35% of this book is derived.

Enjoy the work and I hope you find it useful, either as a research tool or as a method of adding to or cataloguing your submarine book library. Please remember that the hatch is always open on my cyber Submarine Base at: http://www.rontini.com where you can find over 2000 links to all things submarine.

Ron Martini Sheridan, WY 1997 & 2001

Terms, abbreviations and notes

I attempted to eliminate pamphlets, magazine articles or trade publications unless I felt the information was important to the world of submarines or that it was consolidated. The use of the Naval Submarine League's Submarine Review which is a quarterly publication containing articles and an index of early articles from Naval Proceedings are examples. There are other publications available which do a great job in listing periodicals and miscellaneous publications.

Quite a few of the non-fiction works, especially those in the last twenty years do a very good job of listing magazine sources in their bibliographies. I did not list any books as sources of this bibliography as that seemed redundant.

I tried diligently to record only books whose content was significant in the submarine history world. Obviously some more than others. Some books, because of their contribution to the Naval history of World War II, were included. Examples include all of Samuel Morison's volumes on the History of United States Naval Operations in World War II and the 13 page Cruise Book from 1945 of the USS Sperry. Also, the world of diving and other submersibles and commercial submarines is not included with but very few exceptions.

ISBN NUMBER (International Standard Book Number) is a worldwide identification system which has been in use since the late 60's. There is a different ISBN number for each edition and binding for each book. I made no attempt to identify which edition/hardcover/soft-cover the ISBNs I make reference to in this bibliography are associated with. Meaning of numbers: ex. 0-915516-21-7 (0-Book originated in English speaking country, 915516-Identifies publisher, 21-Identifies particular title and edition (hard or soft cover) of book. 7-Check digit. Mathematical function to check accuracy of other digits).

Obtaining ISBN Number: Publishers now can assign the numbers or write RR Bowker Co., 121 Chanlon Road, New Providence, NJ 07974.

The letter "p" indicates the page count.

USNIP indicates United States Naval Institute Press-Annapolis
USGPO or GPO is the United States Government Printing Office
HMSO Her Majesty's Stationary Office

Some standard rules of bibliographies were not used in this publication because of personal preference.

This is the only bibliography of it's type in which the title appears as the main field and not the author. This may hinder some researchers who key on authors, but it will appeal to more of the casual reader and collector. Author's names were not italicized as a matter of personal preference. The page count information is given with a single 'p' and not the 'pp' found in others. Again, my preference. Titles of foreign language books also included, where known, the translated title in English.

"The Submarine is always in a fog." Sir Charles Beresford

Contents

Nonfiction

10 Jahre und 20 Tage-by Doenitz, Karl-Anthenum-Frankfort-1958
100 Best True Stories of World War II-Wise & Co-1945
100 Lat Okretow Wojennych-by Supi, Witold-Warsaw-1968-201p
100000 zeemijl per onderzeeboot-by Comitee Onze Marine-de Boer, V.H.C & Helder, Den-1939-The submarine voyages of professor Vening Meinesz
2000 Fathoms Down-by Houot, Georges-Dutton, NY-1955
20000 Rupie di Taglia-by Ferretti, CM-Danesi, Rome-1948-20,000 Rupee Reward
22 Cells in Nuremberg-by Kelley, DM-NY-1947-One chapter on Doenitz
24 Torpedoes & 13 Buttons-by Dishong, Howard B-Self Published 75 and revised in 1981-252p-USS Cod

30 years service to submarines: USS Sperry AS-12, 1942-1972-1973-98p
300000 Tonnen Versenkt!-by Valentiner, Max-Ullstein, Berlin-1917-154p
40 Fragen an Karl Doenitz-40 Questions to Karl Doenitz-by Doenitz, Karl-Bernard & Graefe-1979
40 Great Submarine Simulator War Adventures-by Sheffield, Richard G-Compute-1989-
5 Days to War: April 2-6, 1917-DuPuy, R Ernest-Stackpole Books, Harrisburg, Pa-1967
50 North-An Atlantick Battleground-by Easton, Alan Herbert-Eyre, London-1963 & Ryerson, Toronto-1964-287p

54-S-by Office of Naval Intelligence-1943

60 Jahre Deutsche Uboote 1906-1966-by Herzog, B-Lehmann-Munich-1980-324p-

66 Tage unter Wasser. Atom U-Schiffe und Raketen-by Rohwer, Jurgen-Stalling, Hamburg-1962-88p

73 North-by Pope, Dudley-Wiedenfeld & Nicolson-1958-Battle of the Barents Sea Dec-1942

80 Foot Elco Submarine Chaser: Instructions, Care and Operation-by Macintyre, Donald-Norton, NY-1957-239p

A

A Battle History of the Imperial Japanese Navy (1941-45)-by Dull, Paul S-USNIP-1978

A Bloody War-by Lawrence, Hal-Macmillan-1979-One mans memories of the Canadian Navy 1939-45

A Brief History of Mine Warfare-by Patterson, Andres-National Academy of Sciences-1970-49p

A Brief History of U.S. Navy Torpedo Development-by Jolie, EW-Naval Underwater Systems Center-1978

A Buvarnaszad Haboru-by Julier, Ferenc-Victorisz, Budapest-1940-52p-WW I submarine operations

A Careless Word-A Needless Sinking-by Moore, A-American Merchant Mar. Museum 1983

A Case of Too Much Accuracy-by Voge, Richard-USNIP-1950

A Century of Barrow Built Boats-by Dancer, Alec-The Submariners Association, Barrow-2001 60p

A Century of Naval Construction-by Brown, DK-London-1983

A Century of Spies, Intelligence in the Twentieth Century-by Richelson, Jeffrey T-Oxford U. Press-1995

A Century of U.S. Naval Intelligence from 1882-by Packard, Wyman-USGPO-1996-498p-Intended as a reference work, this is a topical chronology. A history of the origins, development and organization of naval intelligence from the Civil War to 1960.

A Colby Book About Submarines-by Colby, CB-1953

A Concise Project for Equalizing and Conquering the Submarine Menace-by Claflin, Wilbur A-1917

A Damned Un-English Weapon-by Gray, Edwyn A-Seeley, London-1971-The British submarine service in WW I

A Dictionary of General Dynamics-General Dynamics-1967-63p

A Different Kind of Victory: A Biography of Adm Thomas Hart-USNIP-1981

A Guide to Archives and Manuscripts in the United States-Edited by Hamer, Philip-Yale Univ. Press-1961-775p

A Guide to Submarine Insignia-by Phillips, Allen-Bainbridge Is., WA-1994 (Revised)-56 page booklet

A Guide to the Sources of United States Military History-by Higham, Robin-Archon Books-1975-559p-Supp. #1 1975 300p, Supp. #2 1986 332p

A Guidebook to Nuclear Reactors-by Nero, Anthony-U. of CA. Press-1979

A History of Russian and Soviet Sea Power-by Mitchell, Donald W-Macmillan, NY-1974-657p-Includes photos of submarines

A History of Shipbuilding at Fore River-by Sarcone, Anthony F & Rines, Lawrence F-1975

A History of the French Navy-by Jenkins, EH-Macdonald and Jane's, London-1973-364p

A History of the United States Atomic Energy Commission-The New World-Vol 1-by Hewlett, Richard G & Anderson, Oscar E-1972

A History of the United States Atomic Energy Commission-Atomic Shield-Vol 2-by Hewlett, Richard G & and Duncan, Francis-1972

A History of the Unites States Navy-by Knox, Dudley W-G.P. Putnam's Sons-1935

A Legacy of Pride; A Future of Promise-by Bath Iron Works-Bath, ME-1984

A Long Line of Ships-by Lott, Arnold S-USNIP-1954-268p-Mare Island's Century of Naval Activity in California-1854 to 1954

A Man Called Intrepid-by Stevenson, William-Harcourt, Brace, Jovanovich-1976-The Secret War

A Marinha do Brazil, No Segunda Guerre Mundial-by de Gama, Saldanha, Arthur O-Grafica, Brazil-1982

A Matter of Risk-by Varner, Roy D-Random House-1978, 21 photos-The inside story of the CIA's Hughes Glomar Explorer mission to raise a Russian submarine

A Modern Submarine Boat-by Danrit-1912

A Naval History of the War, 1914-1918-by Newbolt, Sir Henry John-Hodder, London-1920 350p

A Naval History of World War I-by Halpern, Paul G-USNIP-1994

A Navy Maverick Comes of Age-1939-1945-by Moffat, Alexander-Wesleyan U. Press-1977 152p

A Navy Second to None-by Davis, George-Harcourt, Brace & Co.-1940

A New Propulsion System for Submarines-by Siemens & Reuter, Karl-Erich-1995

A Night Before Christmas-by Sanders, Joachim Sanders-Putnam-1963-230p-U-486 attacks a troop ship

A Night of Terror-by Caulfield, Max-Muller-1958-222p-The Story of the Athenia examines the controversy caused by the U-Boat attack and sinking of the unescorted British liner, Athenia, within hours of war being declared

A Note on the History of Submarine War-Newbolt, Sir Henry John-1916-26p

A Perspective on Anti-Submarine Warfare-by McGrath, Thomas D-Washington Data Publications-1966-132p

A Pictorial Account of the Crossin' the Line-1945-13p-Cruise book of Sperry AS12

A Pictorial History of Oceanographic Submersibles-by Sweeney, James B-Crown, NY-1971

A Professional's Story-by Eadie, Thomas-Houghton, NY-1929

A Race on the Edge of Time; Radar-by Fisher, Davie E-McGraw-Hill-1987

A Sailor's Odyssey-by Cunningham, Andrew B-Hutchison-1951

A Selected and Annotated Bibliography of American Naval History-by Coletta, Paolo E-University Press of American, MD,-1988-523p

A Statistical Summary of Shipbuilding Under the U.S. Maritime Commission During WW II-by Fisher, Gerald J-U.S. Maritime Commission-1949

A Submarine at War-by Cooke, Bruce SR-RA Cunningham, Plymouth, UK-1992-1942-44 action of HMS Taurus

A Submariner Remembers-by Jones, Gilbert Hackforth

A Submariners' War-by Wilson, Michael-Although not a major battle-field, the Indian Ocean was the only ocean where all the countries submarines came to fight. This is that story.

A Survey Report on Human Factors in Undersea Warfare-by National Research Council-1949 541p-Supplement in 1954, 92p

A Train of Powder-by West, Rebecca-Viking-1955

A World at Arms-by Weinberg, Gerhard L-Cambridge U. Press-1994

A World War Two Submarine-by Humble, Richard-P Bedrick Books-1991-48p-ISBN 0872263517

Abandon Ship-by Newcomb, Richard F-Holt, NY-1958-305p-Death of the USS Indianapolis

ABC's of Stress, The-Praeger-1992-220p-A submarine psychologist's perspective

About Submarines-by Carlisle, Norman V-Melmont Pubs, Chicago-1969-47p-For the very young

Above Us the Waves-by Warren, Charles ET & Benson, James-Harrap, London-1964-176p-The story of midget submarines, and human torpedoes. Includes the important Tirpitz attack

Abruzzo sul Fondo-by ANMI-ANMI, Montesilvano-1991-Abruzzo on the Bottom

Aces of the Reich-by Williamson, G-Arms & Armour-1989

Acoustic Triangulation and its Applications to Submarine Signaling -by Mundy, Arthur-Millet, Boston-1900-16p

Acqua Salata-by Caporilli, P-Ardita, Rome-1962-Salt Water

Action Imminent-by Smith, Peter-Kimber, UK-1980-352p-Three studies of the Naval War in the Mediterranean during the most critical days of 1940, giving a new perspective to the war at sea in this vital period of WW II

Action In Submarines-by Widder, Arthur-Harper & Row-1967-213p-Younger audiences

Administration of the Navy Department in World War II-by Furer, Julius A-GPO-1960-1042p

Admiral Arleigh Burke-by Jones, Ken & Kelly, Hubert-USNIP-232p, 21 photos-ISBN 1557500185-Previously published

Admiral Dan Gallery-by Gilliland, C. Herbert & Shenk, Robert-by USNIP-1999-332p-ISBN 1557503370

Admiral Dan Gallery Papers-Special Collections Section, Nimitz Library, Annapolis, MD

Admiral Harold R. Stark 1939-1945-Simpson, BM-U of SC Press-1989

Admiral Rickover and the Nuclear Navy-by David, Heather M-Putnam, NY-1970-233p

Admiral's Lobby, The-by Davis, Vincent-U of NC Press-1967

Admiral's Wolf-Pack, The-by Noli, Jean-Doubleday, NY-1974-396p-U-Boat War 1939-1945

Admiralty Brief-by Terrel, Edward-Geo. G Harrap, UK-1958-The Story of Inventions that contributed to victory in the Atlantic

Admiralty Regrets, The-by Warren, Charles E.T.-1958-223p-Story of HMS Thetis & Thunderbolt. The submarine Thetis failed to surface on June 1st, 1939. She was eventually salvaged, refitted, and re-launched as the Thunderbolt, before finally being sunk by an Italian warship

Adolph Hitler and the Secrets of the Holy Lance-by Buechner, Howard A & Bernhart, Wilhelm Thunderbird Press Inc.-1988

Advance Force Pearl Harbor-by Burlingame, Burl-Pacific Monograph -1992-Concerns the 5 Japanese Midgets that hit Pearl Harbor

Advanced Submarine Technology and Antisubmarine Warfare-USGPO-1990-72p-Hearing before the Sea power and Strategic and Critical Materials Subcommittee and the Research and Development Subcommittee of the Committee on Armed Services, House of Representatives, One Hundred First Congress, first session, hearing held, April 18, 1989

Advances in Soviet Underwater Capability and Weapons-by Corlett, Roy-Maritime Defense-1987

Adventures in Depth-by King-Putnam-1975-250p

Adventures in Partnership-by Various authors-Private Publication-1960-96p-Story of the Polaris. Sponsored collectively by contractors involved in production of the Fleet Ballistic Missile Weapon System and given to libraries and individuals who played a significant role in the development of the FBM System

Adventures of the U202-by Spiegel & Peckelsheim-Century, NY-1917-202p

Affare Laconia-See **The Laconia Affair**

Afloat In a Sunken Forest-by Senarens, Luis-Garland Publishing-1979-ISBN 082403547X

After Fifteen Years-by Jaworski, Leon-1961-154p-Author was in charge of the war crimes trials in the US-occupied section of Germany and prosecuted most of those trials.

Against All Odds-by Gallagher, Thomas M-1971-170p-Midget Submarines against the Tirpitz

Against All Odds-by McKee, Alexander-USNIP-1991-272p-ISBN 1557500258-16 photos Battles At Sea 1591-1949

Against the Odds-Holmes, WJ-Zebra-1979-350p-A story of the early years in the submarine war in the Pacific

Air Power Versus U-boats-USGPO-1999-24p-Prepared by Air Force History and Museums Program

Aircraft & Submarines-by Abbot, Willis-Putnam-1918-388p-The Story of the Invention, development, and present-day uses of war's newest weapons

Aircraft versus Submarine-by Price, Alfred-William Kimber, UK-1973-268p-ISBN 718304128-The evolution of the Anti-submarining Aircraft 1912-1980

Alarm Schnellboote-by Mayen, Jan-G. Stalling, Oldenburg-1961-227p-Alarm Torpedo Boats

Alarm! Tauchen!! U-Boot im Kampf und Sturm-by Furbringer, Werner-Ullstein, Berlin-1933 257p

Alan Turning: The Enigma-by Hodges, Andrew-Simon & Schuster, NY-1983-A biography of the Father of computers including his work at Bletchley Park

Aleutians Campaign, June 1942-August 1943-GPO-1993-143p-ISBN 0160418011-Discusses the reoccupation by the United States of the islands of Attu and Kiska, the only United States territory in the Western Hemisphere to fall to the enemy (Japan) during World War II. Includes black and white maps and photographs, footnotes, and appendices

Ali Cremer-by Brustat-Naval, Fritz-Ullstein-Verlag, Berlin-1994-400p-ISBN 3548354238-A first-person story of the career of a famous U-Boat commander of U-333

Allied Claims and Enemy Confirmation of Damage to Japanese Ships-by CNO Pacific Strategic Intelligence Section, SRH 184, Record Group 457, National Archives-Declassified records of so-called Ultra intercepts available at the National Archives and Naval Historical Center

Allied Intelligence Bureau: Our Secret Weapon in the War Against Japan-by Ind, Allison-David McKay-1958

All the Drowned Sailors-by Lech, Raymond-Stein & Day-1982-USS Indianapolis Sinking-

All the World's Fighting Ships-1947-1982-by Friedman, Norman-Conway Press, UK-1983

Allegations About Trident Submarine Program Matters-GAO-1986-33p-Briefing report to the Vice Chairman, Subcommittee on Economic Resources, Competitiveness, and Security Economics, Joint Economic Committee, Congress of the United States / United States General Accounting Office

Alles wel....K XVIII- by Angenent, A.W.P.-N.V. Het Nederlandse Boekhuis, Tilburg-1936-The voyage around the world of the Dutch submarine "K XVIII"

Allied Coastal Forces of WW II-by Lambert, John & Ross, Al-USNIP-1994-256p-ISBN 1557500347-Fairmile Designs and US Submarine Chasers

Allied Escort Ships of World War II-by Elliott, Peter-USNIP-1977

Allied Submarine Attacks of World War Two-European Theater-by Rohwer, Jurgen-USNIP-1997-288p-ISBN 155750038X

Allied Submarine Successes of World War Two: European Theatre of Operations, 1939-1945-by Rohwer, Jurgen-USNIP-1997-252p-ISBN 155750038X-Includes Index of Commanding Officers and an Index of Ships Attacked and an Index of Submarines

Allied Submarines-by Watts, Anthony J-Arco Publishing Co-1977-64p-ISBN 0668041712

WWII Fact Files and names all the Allied boats used

Allied Submarines of World War Two-by Poolman, Kenneth-Arms & Armour-1990-160p-ISBN 0853689423

Almanac of Seapower 1996-by Thomas, Vincent-Navy League-1996

Als das Eich brach-by Lochner, RK-Heyne Verlag, Munich-735p, maps, photos-**When the Ice Broke-**ISBN 3453016904

Als Führer der U-Boote im Weltkriege-by Bauer, Herman-Leipzig, Koehler & Amelang-1942-470p-**As Commander of U-Boats in WW II**

Als U-Boots-Kommandant gegen England-by Forstner, Georg-Ullstein, Berlin-1916-221p-
A U-Boat commander fighting England

Amazing Adventure-by Chatterton, Edward K-Hurst & Blackett, London & Ryerson, Toronto-1935-285p-Narrating the career of Cdr Godfrey Herbert

Amazing Boats-by Lincoln, Margaret-Alfred Knopf, NY-1992-Youth oriented

America's Entry in WW I-by Bass, Herbert J-1964-122p

America's Military Revolution-by Odom, Lt. Gen William-American University Press-1993-Strategy and Structure After the Cold War

America's Nuclear Powered Submarines-CNO

America's Use of Sea Mines-by Duncan, Robert C-GPO-1962-173p

America's Wars and Military Excursions-by Hoyt, Edwin-McGraw-Hill-1987-539p

American Anti-Submarine Operations in the Atlantic-May 1943-May 1945-by Lundeberg, Philip 1953

American Command of the Sea: Through Carriers, Codes and the Silent Service-by Boyd, Carl-Mariner's Museum, Newport News, VA-1995-WW II and Beyond 80p-ISBN 0917376439

American Industry in the War-by Baruch, Bernard M-GPO-1921

American Magic, The-by Lewin, Ronald-Farrar Straus Giroux, NY-1982-War in the Pacific

American Military Patch Guide-From WW I to Today-by Morgan, Pete & Thurman, Ted-1997 96p

American Navy, 1918-1941: A Bibliography-by Smith, Myron-Metuchen, NJ-1974-429p

American Navy in Europe, The-by Leighton, John L-Holt-1920-169p

American Secretaries of the Navy-by Coletta, Paolo E-2 volumes-USNIP-1980

American Submarine-by Polmar, Norman-Nautical and Aviation Pub Co-1981 (2nd in 1983)-170p

American Submarine Operations in the War-by Alden, Carroll Storrs-USNIP-1920

American Submarines-by Lenton, HT-Doubleday-1973-128p-ISBN 0385047614-Navies of the Second World War

American War with Japan, The-by Spector, Richard-NY-1985

An Affair of Chances-by McGeoch, Ian-A Submariner's Odyssey 1939-44

An alle Wolfe: Angriff-by Kurowski, Franz-Podzun-Pallas-Verlag, Friedberg-1986-525p, 145 photos-ISBN 3860708538-**To all wolves: Attack!**

An Administrative History of the Bureau of Ships during World War II-by Dept. of the Navy-1952

An Annotated Bibliography of Submarine Tech. Lit., 1557-1953-National Research Council, Committee on Undersea Warfare-Washington-1954-261p-2 copies at Navy Dept. Library

An Annotated Literature Survey of Submarines, Torpedoes, Anti-Submarine Warfare, Anti-Submarine Weapons 1941 to 1962-by Bryant, Barbara-Autonetics-LA-1962-485 entries

An Appetizing Extravaganza-by Officer's Wives' Club, San Diego-1991-A cookbook

An Bord: Kriegserlebnisse bei den See-und Luftflotten-by Fendrich, Anton-Franckhlche, Stuttgart - 1916-140p

An Evaluation of the U.S. Navy's Extremely-Low-Frequency Submarine Communication-by National Resource Council-NAAC-1997-240p-ISBN 0309055903-Paperback

An Illustrated Guide to Modern Naval Warfare-by Walmer, Max-Prentice Hall, NY-1989-117p

An Illustrated Guide to Modern Submarines-by Miller, David-Arco Publishing-1982-159p ISBN 0668054956

An Illustrated Guide to Modern Warships-by Lyon, Hugh-Arco Pub., NY-1980-159p

An Illustrated History of the Navies of the World War II-by Preston, Antony-Hamlyn, NY-1976-224p

An Investigation of Hydrodynamic Characteristics of Bow Shapes-by DeNuto, John Victor-USNIP-1986

Analysis of Japanese Submarine Losses to Allied Subs in WW II-by Miller, Vernon J-Bennington, VT.: Weapons and Warfare Press-1984

Analysis of Risks Associated With Nuclear Submarine Decommissioning, Dismantling, and Disposal by Ashot A. Sarkisov and Alain Tournyol Du Clos-Dordrecht ; Boston: Kluwer-1999-443p

Anatomy of the Nuremberg Trials-by Taylor, Telford-Alfred A. Knopf, NY-1992

Anatomy of the Ship-HMS Alliance-by Lambert, John & Hill, David-USNIP-1986-120p

And I was There-by Layton, Edwin & Pinean, Roger-Morrow, NY-1985-ISBN 0688048838

Angriff, Ran, Versenken!-by Alman, Karl-Pabel Verlag, Rastatt-328p, 50 photos-Title was Doenitz's motto: **Attack, go in and sink!**

Annail della Vasca Naz per le Esperienze di Archit. Navale-by Zannoni, CVF-Ist Polit Stato, Rome, 1939-**Annals of the National Towtank relating to Naval Architecture**

Annual Report of the Navy Department: 1914-1940-U.S. Department of the Navy

Annual Report on the Present Status of Chemical Research in Atmospheric Purification and Control on Nuclear Submarines-by USN-Off. of Naval Research-1965-60p

Anti-Submarine Handbook, The-Rector Press-1994

Anti-Submarine Operations-by Bacchus, Wilfred A-Naval War College, Newport-1966

Anti-Submarine Warfare-by Baker, David

Anti-Submarine Warfare-by Gardner, WJR-Brassey's-1996-160p-ISBN 1857531205

Anti-Submarine Warfare-by Heppenheimer, TA-Arlington, Va.: Pasha Publications-1992-150p

Anti-Submarine Warfare-by Hill, JR-USNIP-1989, 1990 2nd Edition-112p-ISBN 0870210815

Anti-Submarine Warfare-Meeting the Challenge-by CNO-1990-72p

Anti-Submarine Warfare and Superpower Strategic Stability-by Daniel, Donald C-U. of Illinois Press-1986-222p

Anti-Submarine Warfare in World War II-by Sternhell, Charles M & Thorndike, Alan M-Navy Dept., Wash DC-1946-Report #51

Anti-Submarine Warfare on the Continental Shelf-by Brunson, Bruce-Air War College-1989-49p

Anti Submarine Warfare Task Group, The-Tokyo: Daito Art Print. Co-1962-324p-Mostly Illus

Approaches Are Mined, The-by Langmaid, Kenneth JR-Jarrolds, London-1965-256p

Approaching Storm, The-by Chewning, Alpheus-Aquarius Tailliez-1964-U-Boats off Virginia

Archaeology of Boats and Ships-by Greenhill, Basil-Conway Maritime Press-1996-288p-ISBN 0851776523

Arctic Convoys-by Woodman, Richard-John Murray, London-1994-496p

Arctic Submarine, The-by Mclaren, Alfred-Center for Arctic Studies-1983-46p-Evolution and scientific and commercial potential

Argonaut-by Poluhowich, John-College Station: Texas A&M University Press-1999-224p

Arms Control: The Interwar Naval Limitation Agreements-by Hoover, Robert A-Grad. School of International Studies, Denver-1980

Arms of Krup-by Manchester, William-Little, Brown and CO-1968

Around the World, Around the Clock, Always Ready: U.S. Navy Submarine Force-Washington, DC, Navy Dept-1992-22p

Around the World Submerged-Beach, Captain Edward-Holt, Rinehart & Winston, NY-1962-293p-The author was directed to take the newly commissioned USS Triton SSRN-586 on an 36,000 mile underwater circumnavigation to prove the reliability of the Rickover conceived submarine. Also republished by USNIP 2001 in trade paperback.

Art Of Naval Warfare-by Bridge Adm Sir Cyprian-Smith Elder and Co., London-1907

Assault of a Queen-by Finney, Jack-Simon & Schuster-1959

ASW: Anti-Submarine Warfare-CNO-1959-38p

ASW In World War II-by Sternhell, CM-Navy Dept-1946

ASW: Meeting the Soviet Threat-by Holcomb, Staser-USNIP-1987-34p

ASW Versus Submarine Technology Battle-by Gerker, Louis-Chula Vista, CA, American Scientific Corp-1986-753p-ISBN 0961716304

At Dawn We Slept-by Prange, Gordon W-McGraw-Hill-1981 and Viking Penquin in 1991-889p-The Untold Story of Pearl Harbor-ISBN of 1991 edition: 0140157344

At War At Sea-by Spector, Ronald H-Viking-2001-ISBN 0670860859-The most important Naval Battles of the Twentieth Century are reviewed in detail

Atakuyut Podvodniki-by Dmitriyev, VI-Ministry of Defense, Russia-1973-**The Submariners Attack**

Atlante delle Uniformi-by Vittorio, Elioe-Ermano Albertelli Editore, Parma-1984

Atlantic Campaign, The-U-Boat War 1939-45-by van der Vat, Dan-Hodder & Stoughton-1988-ISBN 0060159677

Atlantic Star 1939-45, The-by Thomas, David A-WH Allen & Co-1990-ISBN 1852271477-The Battle of the Atlantic

Atlantic Torpedo-by Hawkins, Doris M-Gollancz, London-1943-48p

Atlantic Turkey Shoot, The-Cheatham, James T-1990-U-Boats off the Outer Banks in WW II

Atlantik 1943-by Gretton, Peter-Stalling Verlag, Oldenburg-160p, 20 photos-ISBN 3797918569-An account, by the escort commander involved, of Convoy HX 231, during which six escorts fought off 20 U-boats.

Atlantik-U-Boote-by Boeckhein, Gunther-1977-Atlantics U-boats

Atlantikschlacht-by Costello, John & Hughes, Terry-See **The Battle of the Atlantic**

Atlantis, Kaperfahrt under zehn Flaggen-by Mohy, Ulrich & Sellwood, Arthur-Koehlers, Hamburg 1960-233p-Atlantis, raider under ten flags

Atomic Shield-by Hewlett, Richard G & Duncan, Francis-Penn. State U-1969

Atomic Submarine and Admiral Rickover-by Blair, Clay-Henry Holt, NY-1954-277p

Atomic Submarine and Polaris, The-Anderson, Barr & Howard-1961

Atomic Submarine, The-by Lewellen, John B-Crowell, NY-1954-134p

Atomic Submarine, The-by Hoban, Russell-Harper, NY-1960-For the very young-A Practice Combat Patrol

Atomic Submarines-by Ewart, William D-Weidenfeld & Nicolson, London-1963-143p-Young Engineer Series

Atomic-powered Submarine Design-by Bukalov, VM & Narusbayev, AA-Proyektirovaniye atomnykh podvodnykh lodok in Russian

Atomic Submarines-by Anderson, William R-1968

Atomic Submarines-by Polmar, Norman-Van Nostrand-1963-286p

Atomnye Podvodnye Lodki-by Bykhovsky, Izrail A-Leningrad-1957-176p-Atomic Submarines

Attack & Sink-by Edwards, Bernard-New Era Writers Guild, UK-1995-199p-ISBN 1899694404-The Battle for convoy SC42

Attack on Pearl Harbor-by Kimmett, Larry & Margaret-Navigator Publications-1992

Attack Submarine, The-A Study in Strategy-Kuenne, Robert E-Yale U. Press-1965-215p

Attack Submarines-Alternative For a More Affordable SSN Force-GAO-1994

Attack Submarines-by Graham, Ian-Gloucester Press-1989-32p-Youth-Design, construction and maintenance and also describes weapons, communications and evasion tactics

Attivita in Mar Nero e Lago Ladoga-by Lupinacci, PF-USMM, Rome-1993-Activity in the Black Sea and lake Ladoga

Auch Kleine igen haben Stacheln-Enders, Gerd-Koehler Verlag, Herford-1984-240p, 60 photos ISBN 3782203348-German U-Boats in the Black Sea

Auf allen Meeren-by Kurowski, Franz-Heyne Verlag, Munchen-1986-446p, 63 photos-ISBN 3453023943-In All Seas

Auf Gefechtsstationeu:U-Boote im Einsatz gegen England-by Hardegen, Reinhard-Boreas-Leipzig-1943-227p, 119 photos-Action Stations: U-Boats Against England & America written by a famous U-Boat commander

Auftauchen! Kriegsfahrten von U-53-by Rose, Hans-Essen-1939-315p-20 photos-WW I submarine operations-Drawings by Claus Bergen

Augelaufen Westwarts: U-Boots-Schicksale von Ruben und Druben-by Ramlow, Gerhard-Voggenreiter, Potsdam-1937-143p

Augen Durch nacht und Nebel-by Bekker, Cajus (pseud)-Stalling, Hamburg-1964-284p-Story of Radar-Translates to Eyes Through Night and Fog

August Piccard: Captain of Space, Admiral of the Abyss-by Field, Adelaide-Houghton Mifflin, Boston-1969-150p-The story of the bathyscaphe and it's inventor

Aus dem Logbuch des I. Wachoffiziers, U66-by Kramsta, Joachim-Verlag, Hanover-1931-189p-From the logbook of the first officer of the U-66

Australia's Navy: Past, Present and Future-by Gillett, Ross-Brookvale, New South Wales, 1986

Australian Submarines-by White, Michael WD-1992-284 p-ISBN 066424397X-A History

Australians in Nine Wars, The-by Firkins, Peter-Sydney-1982

Austro-Hungarian Warships of World War I-by Allen, Ian-1976

Authors At Sea-by Shenk, Robert-USNIP-1996-336p-1557507996-35 photos-7 Pulitzer Winners who served in WW II-

Autumn of the U-Boats-by Jones, Geoffrey-1984-224p-ISBN 0718305345-In 1943 the U-boats had an acoustic homing torpedo to sink escorts. Yet 34 U-Boats were sunk in 44 days

Aux Sous-Marins de Calais et de Brest, 1916-1918-Anonymous-1986

Axis Submarine Manual-by ONI-1942-32p

Axis Submarine Successes of World War Two-1939-1945-by Rohwer, Jurgen-USNIP-1983-386p-Offers the most extensive and reliable tabulation available of Axis submarine victories during the war of German, Italian and Japanese Successes

Axis Submarines-by Watts, Anthony John-Arco Pub Co-1977-ISBN 0668041595-Technical data is given, and a brief note on the fate of each submarine

B

Back From the Deep-by Lavo, Carl-USNIP-1994-226p-Squalus & Sculpin

Badges and Insignia of the British Armed Forces-A.C. Black, London-1974

Badges and Insignia of World War II-by Rosignoli, Guido-1983-363p-Details Allied-Axis air force, naval and marine insignia of WW II. Color Photos. 363 p

Badges and Tokens of the Russian Imperial Navy, 1696-1917-by Dotsenko, VD-St. Petersburg, 1993 in Russian

Badges of the Soviet Armed Forces, The 1918-1991-by Borisov, VA-St. Petersburg, 1994 in Russian

Ballistic Missile-Carrying Submarines-by Glasser, Robert D-UCLA-1989

Baltic Assignment-by Wilson, Michael-Leo Cooper, UK-1985-ISBN 0436578018 British Submarines in Russia 1914-1919-244p

Bamboo and Bushido-by Allbury, AG-Robert Hale Ltd.-1955

Barrier and the Javelin-by Willmott, HP-USNIP-1983-Japanese and Allied Strategies Feb-June, 1942-

Base Exterior Architecture Plan, Naval Submarine Base, San Diego, California / Western Division,

Naval Facilities Engineering Command-San Bruno, Calif.: The Division-1984

Basic Enlisted Submarine Text-NavPers 10490-1963-Revised version of NavPers 16160

Basic Theory of Submarines-by Bol'shakov, Yu I-Voyenizdat-1977

Bateaux Sous-marins a Grande Vitesse Sous l'Eau-by Proposto, C-Merttens, Brussels-1910-107p

Batfish-by Lowder, Hughston E-Prentice Hall-1980-232p-ISBN 0130665630-The Champion submarine-killer submarine of WW II

Bath Iron Works: The First One Hundred Years-by Snow, Ralph L-Maine Maritime Museum-1987

Battle at Sea-by Keegan, John-1993-From Man-of-War to Submarine

Battle Below-by Casey, Robert J-Bobbs-Merrill Co-1945-380p-Informal narrative of a war correspondent.

Battle for Inner Space, The-by Domville-Fife, Charles W-1920-Undersea Warfare and Weapons

Battle for Innerspace-by Stambler, Irwin-1962-1962-USN nuclear submarines and undersea warfare

Battle for the Pacific-by MacIntyre, Donald-WW Norton & Co-1966

Battle History of the Imperial Japanese Navy-by Dull, Paul S-USNIP-1978

Battle of Britain, The-by Hough, Richard & Richards, Denis-WW Norton & Co-1989

Battle of Leyte Gulf-by Cutler, Thomas J-Harper Collins, NY-1994-343p

Battle of the Atlantic-1939-1943-by Morrison, Samuel E-Atlantic, Brown, Little-1947-432p Vol 1 of 15 of Naval Ops in WW II

Battle of the Atlantic-by Pitt, Barrie and editors of Time-Life-Time-Life, Chicago-1977-208p

Battle of the Atlantic 1939-1945-by Howarth, Stephen-USNIP-1994

Battle of the Atlantic, The-by Hughes, Jerry & Costello, John-Dial Press, NY-1977-479p-200 photos-War in the Atlantic 1939-1945. Includes U-Boat actions and engagements by surface vessels

Battle of the Atlantic, The-by Macintyre, Donald-BT Batsford-1961-208p

Battle of the Atlantic, The-H.M. Stationery Office, UK-1946-103p

Battle of the Atlantic, The-by Pitt, Barrie-Time Life Books-1977

Battle of the Atlantic, The and Signals Intelligence: U-Boat situations and Trends, 19414-1945-by Syrett, D, Clayton, JW & Winn, R-Ashgate-1999

Battle of Leyte Gulf-by Hoyt, Edwin P-Weybright and Talley, NY-1972

Battle of Stonington: Torpedoes, Submarines, and Rockets in the War of 1812-by De Kay, James T USNIP-1990-ISBN 0870212796

Battle of the Seaways-by Johnston, George Henry-Angus and Robertson, Sydney, London-1941-240p

Battle Report-by Karig, Walter-Rinehart & Co, NY-1944+-6 Volumes

Battle Report: The Atlantic War-by Karig, Burton, & Freeland-Farrar and Rinehard-1946

Battle Report: The End of an Empire-by Karig, Harris & Manson-Rinehart-1948-532p

Battle Stations Submerged-by Benitez, Ralph C-USNIP-1948

Battle Stations!-by Hudson, Alec (pseud)-Macmillan-1940-71p

Battle Submerged-by Cope, Harley & Karig, Walter-WW Horton-1951-244p-Submarine Fighters of WW II-Written by an Admiral, a Captain and an official Naval historian, the book describes the saga of the U.S. submarine service in vivid and authentic detail.

Battle Surface-by Jenkins, David-Random House, Australia-1993-Japan's Submarine War Against Australia 1942-1944

✓**Battles of the Philippine Sea**-by Lockwood, Charles & Adamson, Hans-Thomas Y Crowell, Co.- 967

Beating the U-Boats-Chatterton, Edward K.-Hurst, London-1943-172p-WW I Submarine war-sequel to "Fighting the U-Boats"

Before the Deluge-by Friedrich, Otto-Harper & Row-1972

Beginning of Modern Submarine Warfare Under David Bushnell-by Abbot, Henry L-Archon Books-1966-69p-A facsimile reproduction of the rare 1881 pamphlet

Belona Report #2-by Nilsen, Thomas & Kudrik, Igor & Nikitin, Alexander-Oslo, 1996-The Russian Northern Fleet, Sources of Radioactive contamination

Below the Belt-by Winton, John-Conway Maritime Press, London-1981-192p-Novelty, subterfuge, and surprise in naval warfare

Below the Surface-Chatterton, Edward K-Hurst & Blackett, London-1934-286p

Below the Surface-Hazeltine, Alice I-Abingdon Press, Nashville-1958-223p

Bemannte Torpedos und Klein-U-Boote im Einsatz 1939-1945-by Kemp, Paul-Motorbuch Verlag, Stuttgart-1999-279p-ISBN 3913019361-Manned Torpedoes and Midget U-boats in Action

Beneath the Waves-by Evans, AS-W Kimber, London-1986-A History of HM Submarine Losses 1904-1971

Berlin Diary-by Shirer, William L.-Alfred A. Knopf-1941

Beruhmte Schiffe des Zweiten Weltkrieges-by Ellis, Chris-Orell Fussli-1978-189p-ISBN 328000988X-Famous Ships of WWII

Bias Buoy Measurement and Depth Control Instrumentation-by Singleton, Robert J-David Taylor Dev. Center, Bethesda, MD-1975-36p

Bibliographic Guide to the Two World Wars: An Annotated Survey of Reference Materials-by Bayliss, Gwyn-Bowker, NY-1977-578p

Bibliographical Source Book of Compressed Air, Diving, and Submarine Medicine-by Hoff, EC Wash, D.C.: Research Division, Project X-427, Bureau of Medicine and Surgery, Navy Dept

Bibliography-by ISB-Internationale Submarine Bibliographie-Germany-1954

Bibliography of Submarine Warfare-by Imperial War Museum, London-1953-16p

Bibliography of the Literature of Submarines, Mines and Torpedoes -by Rushmore, David-GE-1917

Bibliography of the Submarine-1557-1953-National Research Council, Committee on Undersea Warfare-1954

Bibliography Source Book of Compressed Air, Diving and Submarine Medicine-by Hoff, Ebbe C Navy Bur. of Med. and Surg.

Big Book of Real Submarines, The-by McCoy, Jack-Grossett & Dunlap -1955-Young

Big Red-By Waller, Douglas-Harper Collins-2001-336p-ISBN 0060194847 -Three Months on a Trident Nuclear Submarine-The author rode for sea trials and interviewed crew and families. 32 interior photos of the Nebraska's crew

Biographical Dictionary of World War II-Boatner, Mark-Presido-1996-736p

Biographies of Naval Officers-Naval Academy Alumni Assoc.-Yearly

Birth and Development of American Submarine, The-by Cable, Frank T-Harper & Bros.-1924 337p

Biz Zum Letzten Flaggenchuss-Trapp-1935

Biz Zur Letzten Stunde-by Ernst, Georg-Mittler & Sohn Verlag, Berlin-1999-224p-ISBN 3828903452-To the Last Hour-A book about the common sailor in the U-Boat arm at the end of the war. The author survived the surrender of the U-1109.

Black May-by Gannon, Michael-Dell War-1999-Hardback-1998-514p-ISBN 0440235642 The story of the Allies defeat of the German U-Boats in May 1943

Black Saturday-by Mckee, Alexander-New English Library, UK-1972-Tragedy of the Royal Oak

Black Sea Fleet, The-by various authors-Military Publishing House, Moscow-1987-in Russian

Blimps & U-Boats-by Vaeth, J Gordon-USNIP-1992-205p

Blind Eye-by Langmaid, Kenneth JR-Jarrolds, London-1972-166p

Blind Fight-by Steward, CM-Self Published, Altus, OK-72p-Written by a crew member/author from diaries kept during his time aboard the USS Cobia SS 245 in WW II

Blind Man's Bluff-by Sontag, Sherry & Drew, Chris-PublicAffairs /Perseus Books Group-1998-352 pages-ISBN 1891620088-The book lifts the lid on some of the most secret submarine operations of the Cold War. Blue Bells, Glomar Explorer, Bump in the Dark, Gudgeon's near capture and more. Pocketbook edition by Harper in Oct of 1999 also contains a listing of awards to submarines from 1958 forward.

Blood, Tears and Folly-by Deighton, Len-Harper Collins-1993

Bloody Winter-by Waters, John M-USNIP-1984-ISBN 0870210912-War Memoir of a Coast Guard Officer

Blow All Ballasts!-by Barrows, Nathaniel A-Dodd, Mead, NY-1940-298p-Also by Court Book Co in 1941-The Story of the Squalus by a reporter on the scene

Bluejacket's Manual-USNIP-The 1950 issue is the 14th edition of this Navy handbook issued to every person entering the US Navy. The book was first published in 1902 and authored by Lt Ridley McLean

Blutiger Winter-by Waters, John M-See Bloody Winter

Boarding Party-by Leasor, James-Houghton Mifflin, Boston-1979-203p

Boats, Ships, Submarines and other Floating Machines-by Graham, Ian-Grieswood & Dempsy, London-1993-Youth oriented

Bodyguard of Lies-by Brown, Anthony Cave-Harper & Row-1975

Boevoi put Sovetskogo Voenno-Morskogo Flota-by Pitersky, N-Moscow-1964-Also in German: Die Sowjet-Flotte im Zweiten Weltrieg

Book of Submarines, The-McCoy, HJ-Grosset & Dunlap, NY-1966

Boot Greift Wieder An: Ritterkreuztrager Erzahlen-by Luth, Wolfgang & Korth, Claus-Erich Klinghammer, Berlin-1944-320p-U-Boat Strikes Again: Tales of the Knight's Cross

Bowfin-by Hoyt, Edwin Palmer-Van Nostrand Reinold-1983-234p-1998 edition by Buford Books, Inc, Short Hills, NY-One of the most successful submarines to survive the war.

Boy Allies with the Navy-by Hayes, Clair Wallace-Burt, NY-1915-A series of books

Boys Book of Submarines, The-by Collins, Archie F-Stoke, NY-1917-220p

Brassey's Naval Annual-Brassey Macmillan-Various years starting in 1903-405p

Breaking the Ring-by Barron, John-Houghton Mifflin-1987-The Rise and Fall of the Walker family spy network

Bridge of Magpies-by Jenkins, Geoffrey-1974-Fiction

Brief History of U.S. Navy Torpedo Development-by Jolie, EW-Newport: Naval Underwater Systems Center-1978

Britain's Clandestine Submarines 1914-1915-by Smith, Gaddis-Yale U. Press, 64 & Archon, 75-155p-Scholarly study of Britain's purchase of submarines in Canada

Britain's Sea War: A Diary of Ship Losses 1939-1945-by Young, J-Patrick Stephens

British Escort Ships-by Lenton, HT-Doubleday & Co-1965-2 vols

British Intelligence in the Second World War-by Hinsley, FH-Doubleday-1966-3 vols

British Seapower-by Schofield, BB-Batsford-1967

British Shipbuilding Yards-by Middlemiss, Norman I-1995-3 Volumes

British Submarine-by Lenton, HT-Doubleday-1972-160p

British Submarine in Being, The-by Blackburn, JA & Watkins, K-Gieves, London-1920-191p

British Submarine Policy, 1918-1939-by Henry, David-Hodder & Stoughton-1977

British Submarine, The-by Lipscomb, FW-Conway Maritime Press-1975-284p-44 plates-Covers history of British submarines from their beginnings through WW II, with speculation on the future

British Submarines-by Lenton, Henry T-Doubleday, NY-1972-160p-Navies of the Second World War

British Submarines at War 1939-1945-by Mars, Alistair-USNIP-1971-256p-ISBN 0870218115

British Submarines in WW II-by Kemp, Paul J-Sterling Pub. Co.-1987-64p ISBN 0853687781

British Submarines of WW I-by Kemp, Paul J-Arms & Armour-1990-24 leaves

British Vessels Lost at Sea 1939-1945-by Stephens, Patrick-HMSO-1948

British Warships 1914-1919-by Dittmar, FJ & Colledge, JJ-Ian Allen, London-1973

British Warship Losses in World War Two-by Lenton, HT & Colledge, JJ-Ian Allen, London-1976

Brittany Patrol-Rose-1937-The Story of the Suicide Fleet -

Broken Seal, The-by Farago, Ladislas-Random House, NY-1967-Japanese diplomacy, codes and Magic with emphasis on the Pearl Harbor attack

Brute Force: Allied Strategy and Tactics in the Second World War-by Ellis, John-Viking-1990

Builders For Battle-Dutton & Co-1946-415p-Construction of Pacific Naval Bases

Building American Submarines 1914-1940-by Weir, Gary E-USGPO-1991-166p ISBN 0945274041-40 photos

Building the Kaiser's Navy 1890-1919-by Weir, Gary E-USNIP-1991

Building the Navy's Bases in World War Two-USGPO-1947

Building U.S. Submarines in WW II-by Davis, HFD-USNIP-1946

Bull of Scapa Flow-by Frank, Wolfgang-G Stalling-1958

Business in Great Waters U-Boat Wars 1916-1919-by Terraine, John-Leo Cooper-1989-842p-ISBN 0850527600-The foremost history of the two unrestricted U-Boat wars of 1916-1918 and 1939-1945. Unparalleled for its exhaustive account, this massive volume covers every aspect of the conflict from submarine tactics and design through the evolution of defense measures such as the convoy system, anti-submarine weaponry, and the full story of the in cracking German communications

By Guess and by God-by Carr, William Guy-Hutchinson, London-1930-288p-The story of British subs in WW I-Also Doubleday, NY edition in 1930

By Sea and by Stealth-by Wilkinson, Burke-Coward-McCann, NY-1956-218p-Details Allied-Axis surprise naval attacks during WW II

C

C The Secret Life of Sir Steward Graham Menzies-by Brown, Anthony Cave-Macmillan-1987

Call of Duty, The-by Strandberg, John-Bender, RJ-384p-960 photos-1782-1961-Military Awards & Decorations

Cammell Laird-by Roberts, David-ISBN 0952102021-The Story of a Shipyard in England

Camouflage of the WW II Era-Floating Drydock-1988-ISBN 094405501X

Campaign in the Marianas-by Dept of Army-1960

Campaigns of the Pacific War-by Ofstie, RA-USGPO

Can Our Nation's Security Survive a Disappearing Submarine
       Force: 1999 communications guide-
Pearl Harbor, Hawaii: Naval Submarine Base-1999-27p
Canada's Submarines 1912-1923-by Perkins, Dave-The Boston Mills
       Press-1989-226p ISBN 1550460145
Canadian Directorate of History, National Defense Headquarters
       (NDHQ)
       Naval Board Minutes
       Naval Staff Minutes
       'Summaries of Naval War Effort'
       C-in-C, CAN War Diary
       Naval Historian's Files
       Ship's Movement Cards
       Naval Historian's Narrative A: 'Canadian Participation in the
       North Atlantic Convoy Operations,
       June 1941 to December 1943'
       Naval Historian's Narrative: 'Modernization of Armament and
       Equipment'
       Monthly Anti-Submarine Reports
       US Fleet Anti-Submarine Bulletin
       RCN-RCAF Monthly Operational Review
       PW Nelles papers
       Interviews by H. Lawrence
       Canadian Confidential Naval Orders
       Confidential Admiralty Fleet Orders
       Defeat of the Enemy Attack on Shipping
       Handbooks for the Type 147B Asdic
Canadian Nuclear Powered Attack Submarine Program-by O'Rourke,
       Ronald-LOC-1988
Canadian Submarine Service in Review-by Perkins, David J-Vanwell
       Press-2000-208p-ISBN 1551250314
Captain and Submarine CSS Hunley, The-by Duncan, Ruth-SC U of-
       1965-110p

Captain Gilbert Roberts, RN and the Anti-U-Boat School-by Williams, M-Cassell, UK-1979

Captains of War-by Gray, Edwyn-Cooper, UK-1988-275p-The author examines then careers of some seventeen submarine captains, British, their Allies and the Axis powers

Captured German and Related Records-by Wolfe, Robert-Ohio U. Press-1974

Cargo Aircraft and Cargo Submarines-by US Congress-Washington-1942-131p

Casabianca-by L'Herminier, J-Fredrick Muller-1953-243p-The Secret Mission of a Famous Submarine

Case Against the Nazi War Criminals, The-by Jackson, Robert H.-G.P. Putnam's Sons-1965

Cento Sommergibili non sono Tornati-by Meneghini, T-CEN, Rome-1980-One Hundred Submarines have Not Returned

Central Blue-by Slessor, John C.-Cassell, UK-1956

Century of U.S. Naval Intelligence-1996-USGPO-1996-520p

Challenge of the Seafloor-by Field, Adelaide-Houghton Mifflin, Boston-1970-133p

Challengers of the Deep-by Cross, Wilbur-William Sloane Assoc-1959-258p-The Story of Submarines

Changing Enemies-by Annan, Noel-256p-The Defeat and Regeneration of Germany

Changing Interpretations and New Sources in Naval History-by Love, Robert William-Garland-1980

Changing Soviet Navy, The-by Blechman, Barry-Brookings Institution -1973-51p

Chancileer-GPO-1941-241p-Sub Rescue Vessel-Building Specs

Charleston Navy Yard-USGPO-80p

Chechichte des U-Boot Krieges 1939-1945-by Peillard, L-Wilhelm Heyne-Munich-1974

Chester Lincoln Soners Collection of Submarine Books-Nimitz Library/Annapolis-1991

Chiefs of Naval Operations, The-by Love, Robert W ed.-USNIP-1980

China's Strategic Seapower-by Lewis, John W & Litai Xue-Stanford
     U. Press-1994-
Christie Papers-Admiral Christie's letters and diaries-Unpublished
Chronik des Seekrieges 1939-1945-by Rohwer, Jurgen-G. Stalling,
     Oldenburg-1968-655p Chronicle of the War at Sea 1939-1945-
     This is a study of all naval actions worldwide
Chronology of the War At Sea-1939-1945 2 Vol-by Rohwer, J-USNIP-
     1992-650p-Revised edition
Chronology of US Navy Submarine Operations in the Pacific 1939-
     1942-Kimble-1988
Churchill & Roosevelt: The Complete Correspondence-3 Vols-by
     Kimball, Warren F-Princeton U. Press-1984
Churchill and the Admirals-Roskill, Stephen-William Morrow & C,
     NY-1977-by Winters, John D-LSU Press-1963
Claus Bergen: Leben und Werk des Grossen Marinemalers-by
     Herzog, Bobo-Ruhl, Krefeld-1963-117p-Bergen's paintings are
     hanging at Subase, New London and Norfolk
Clean Sweep-by Davenport
Cinderellas of the Fleet-by Nutting, William W.-Standard Motor
     Const. Co, Jersey City-1920-178p-Story of anti-submarining in
     WW I
Clash of Titans-by Boyne, Walter J-Simon and Schuster-1995
Clear the Bridge!-by O'Kane, Richard H.-Rand McNally or Bantam
     1977-337p-ISBN 0553281615-The USS Tang submarine's com-
     manding officer relives the events of each of five WW II
     patrols, including the rescue of Navy fliers off Truk and stalk-
     ing enemy convoys off Japan
Clear the Decks-by Gallery, Daniel V-1951-242p-Capture of the U-505
     and other tales of the baby flattop's campaign in the Atlantic
     against U-Boats
Coastwatchers-by Feldt, Eric A-Nelson Doubleday, NY-1979
Cock Sparrow-by Bernard, Oliver P-Jonathan Cape, London-1936
Cockleshell Heroes-by Phillips, CE Lucas-Heinemann, London-1956

Code Book, The-by Singh, S-Doubleday-1999-The Evolution of secrecy from May, Queen of Scots to Quantum Cryptography with coverage of German Enigma code in WWII

Code Breakers-Hinsley, FH-Oxford U. Press-1993

Codebreaker-The Inside Story of Bletchley Park-by Hinsley, FH-Oxford, UK-1993

Codebreakers, The-by Kahn, David-Macmillan-1967

Codebreaking and Signals Intelligence-by Andrew, Christopher-Frank Cass & Co Ltd, UK-1986

Coffin Boats, The-Warner, Peggy & Seno, Sadao-Leo Cooper, UK-1986-ISBN 0436563304 Japanese Midget Submarines

Colts Submarine History-The Secret and the Enigma

Combat Beneath the Sea-by Brou, Willy C-Crowell, NY-1957-240p-Same as "War Beneath the Sea-Muller, London-1958-239p

Combat Fleets of the World 1993-by Baker, AD-USNIP-1993

Combat Medals of the Third Reich-by Ailsby, Christopher-Patrick Stephens LTD, Norhthamptonshire, 1987

Combat Patrol-by Blair, Clay-Bantam War Book-1978-382p-Adapted from Silent Victory.

Combined Fleet Decoded-by Prados, John-Random House-1995-ISBN 0679437010-The secret history of American Intelligence and the Japanese Navy in WW II

Command At Sea-by Warner, Oliver-Cassell-ISBN 0304296678-Great fighting admirals from Hawke to Nimitz

Command Decisions-by Greenfield, KR-Harcourt, Brace & Co.-1959

Command of the Sea-by Reynolds, Clark G-Krieger Pub Co-1983-ISBN 0898746469-Comes with Atlas Workbook-The History and Strategy of Maritime Empires

Command of the Seas-by Lehman, John F-Charles Schribner & Sons, NY-1988-400p-ISBN 1557505349-The story of the 600 ship Navy from President Reagan's SecNav

Commander in Chief-F.D. Roosevelt, His Lts. and Their War-by Larrabee, Eric-Harper & Row-1987

Commando The M/Z Unit's Secret War Against Japan-by Feuer, AB-Praeger, Westport, CT-1996-172p-ISBN 0275954080

Commandos From the Sea-by Strekhrin, Iurii-USNIP-1996-ISBN 1557508321-Soviet Naval Spetsnaz in WW II

Comparative Naval Architecture of Modern Foreign Submarines-by Stenard, John K-MIT-1988-Thesis

Compendium of Available WW II Italian Submarine Messages-Translations-1943-49p

Compilation of Intelligence Data-by Snedberg, William R-1945-Japanese Submarine Forces

Complete Book of Submarines, The-by Rush, CW & Chambliss, WC-World Publishing-1958-159p

Complete History of World War II-by Miller, Francis T-Readers Service Bureau, Chicago-1945

Concepts in Submarine Design-by Burcher, R & Rydall, L-Cambridge U. Press-1994-314p ISBN 0521416817

Conduct of the War at Sea, The-by Doenitz, Karl-1947-57p-Essay written by the German naval commander detailing the operations of the German Navy in WW II

Confederate Privateers, The-by Robinson, William M-Yale U. Press-1928-372p

Confederate Submarines-by Kelln, Albert-Virginia Historical Society-1953-293p

Confederate Underwater Warfare-by Schafer, Louis S-1996-An Illustrated History

Conference on the Limitation of Armament 1921-1922-Canada-1922-222p

Conflict of Duty-by Dorwart, Jeffrey M.-USNIP-1983-The US Navy's Intelligence Dilemma 1919-1945

Conflict Over Convoys-by Smith, Kevin-Ball State U-1996-320p-Logistic Diplomacy in World War II

Conflict Over the Bay (of Biscay)-by Franks, Norman LR-William Kimber-1986

Conqueror Diary, The-by Sethia, Lt. Nyrena-51p-Diary kept by a Lt
    on HMS Conqueror
during the Falklands Incident and the sinking of the Begrano
Convoy-by Middlebrook, Martin-Morrow-1976-378p-The Battle for
    Convoys SC122 & HX229
Convoy-by Winton, John-Michael Joseph, UK-1983-The Defense of Sea
    Trade-1890-1990
Convoy Escort Commander-by Gretton, F, ADM Sir Peter-P. Davis,
    London-1974
Convoy is to Scatter-by Broome, Jack-William Kimber, UK-1972
Convoy Protection-Kemp, Paul-Arms and Armour Press, London-
    1993
Convoy! Drama in Arctic Waters-by Kemp, Paul-Arms & Armour
    Press, UK-1993-256p
ISBN 1854091301-100b/w illustrations
Conway's All the World's Fighting Ships 1860-1905-Conway-1979-
    440p-ISBN 087021912X
Conway's All the World's Fighting Ships 1906-1921-Conway-1984-
    439p-ISBN 0870219073 950 illustrations
Conway's All the World's Fighting Ships 1922-1946-Conway-1980-
    456p-ISBN 0878021913 994 illustrations
Conway's All the World's Fighting Ships 1947-1982-2vol-Conway-
    298p (part1)
ISBN 0870219189-Part2 509p. Part1(Western Powers), 2 (Warsaw)
Coral Sea, Midway and Submarine Actions-by Morison, Samuel E-
    Little, Brown-1949-307p
Cordon of Steel: The U.S. Navy and the Cuban Missile Crisis-by
    Utz, Curtis A-1993-USGPO
Corvette and Submarine-by Shean, Max
Corvette Navy, The-by Lamb, James B-Macmillan
Cost Growth and Delivery Delays at Electric Boat-USGAO-1982-33p
Coastal Command-by British Air Ministry-Macmillan-1943-143p
Count Not the Dead-by Hadley, Michael-USNIP-1995-253p-The
    Popular Image of the German Submarine

Couples Satisfaction with Navy jobs-Masters Theses-Conn. College-
    1988-57p
Cradle of American Shipbuilding-by Portsmouth Naval Shipyard-
    1978
Crash Dive-by Leyland, Eric-Edmund Ward-1961
Crazy Ivan-by Reed, W. Craig & Reed, William-iUniverse-2000-241p-
    ISBN 0595006132-Cold War Espionage
Crisis in the Pacific-by Aston, Gerald-Donald Fine-1996-496p-The
    Battles of the Philippines
Crisis of the Naval War, The-by Jellicoe, John R-Cassell, UK-1920
Critical Convoy Battles of March 1943-by Rohwer, Jurgen-Ian Allan,
    UK-1977 ISBN 0711007497-The convoy control systems are
    examined, as well as U-Boat operations.
Chronology of the Cold War at Sea 1945-1991- by Polmar, Norman-
    Wertheim, Eric-Bahjat, Andrew-Watson, Bruce-USNIP-1997-
    312 p-ISBN 155750685X
Chronology of the U.S. Navy in World War II-by Cressman, Robert J-
    USNIP-2000-367p-ISBN 1557501491
**Chronology of U.S. Navy Submarine Operations in the Pacific, 1939-
    1942**-by Kimble, David L-International Graphics Inc, Bennington,
    VT-1982
Cold War Submarines: U.S. and Soviet Design and Construction-by
    Polman, Norman & Moore, KJ-Brassey's, Inc-2001-ISBN 1
    5774883666-366p
Cross and the Ensign: A Naval History of Malta-by Elliott, Peter-
    USNIP-1980-217p
Cruelest Night, The-by Dobson, Christopher & Miller, John & Payne-
    Stodder & Houghton-1979 Germany's Dunkirk and the
    Sinking of the Wilhelm Gustloff
Cruise Book-USS Nautilus
Cruise Book-USS Scorpion
Cruise Books of the U.S. Navy in WW II-- by Mawdsley, Dean-
    USGPO-1993-162p-A Bibliography of 800 books and their
    locations

Cruisers for Breakfast-by Mansfield, John G-Media Center Publishing-1997-302p-The War Patrols of the USS Darter and USS Dace

Curriculum for Officers Class, Sub School New London-- NavPers 16469-1945-70p-24 Week course

D

Da Matapan al Golfo Persico la MMI dal fascismo alla repubblica-by Giorgerini G-A Mondadori, Milano-1989-From Matapan to the Persian Gulf, The Italian navy from Fascism to the Republic

Damn the Torpedoes-by Hellyer-McClelland & Steward-1990-ISBN 077104061X

Damn the Torpedoes-by Macdonnell, JE-Horwitz-ISBN 0725501308

Damn the Torpedoes: A Short History of U.S. Naval Mine Countermeasures, 1777-1991-by Melia, Tamara Moser-Naval Historical Center-1991-ISBN 0945274076

Damn the Torpedoes: Naval Incidents of the Civil War-by Hoehling, AA-John F. Blair Pub-1989-207p-ISBN 0895870738

Damned Don't Drown, The-by Sellwood, AV-USNIP-159p-A reconstruction of the events that led up to and accompanied the tragic sinking of the German liner Wilhelm Gustloff, whose decks were packed with over 6,500 refugees on that fateful day in January 1945, when it was hit by torpedoes twelve miles off shore, with the resulting loss of more than 6,000 lives.

Danger Beneath the Waves-by Kloeppel, James E-Sandlapper Pub.-1992-A History of the H.L. Hunley

Danger Zone-Chatterton, Edward, K-Little, Brown, Boston-1934-437p-The story of the Queenstown command-40 plates and 3 maps

Danger!-by Doyle, A. Conan-AL Burt, NY-1911-310p-

Dardanelles Patrol-by Shankland, Peter & Hunter, Anthony-Scribner's, NY-1964-192p

Dark Invader, The-by Rintelen

Dark Seas Above-by Gibson, John F-Blackwood, London-1947-286p

Das Bildbuch der deutschen Kriegsmarine 1939-1945-by Bekker, Cajus-Heyne Verlag, Munchen 1991-239p-ISBN 3453009169-**Pictorial book of the German Navy 1939-1945**

Das Buch der deutschen Kriegsmarine 1935-1945-by Showell, Jak-Motorbuch Verlag, Stuttgart-1992-ISBN 3879438803-**The German Navy in WWII**

Das Deutsche Bild der Russischen und Sowjetischen Marine-by Rohwer, Jurgen-Frankfurt-1962

Das Ende der Franzosischen Flotte im Zweiten Welkkrieg-by Koward, Hannsjorg-Mittler & Sohn Verlag, Berlin-1998-207p-280 photos-ISBN 3813205487-**Hitler and the French Fleet, Toulon 1940-1944**-The scuttling of the French Fleet at Toulon and the development of a U-boat base at that city

Das Geheimnis um U-110-by Roskill, SW-Bernard & Graefe, Frankfurt-1960-147p-**The Secret of U-110**-The events surrounding the boats capture

Das Geister U-Boot-U-31-by Laar, Clemens/ Koebsell, Eberhard-Wehrmacht Verlag, Berlin-1939-187p

Das Kampfschicksal der Deutschen Flotte im Weltkreig-by Forstner, Georg-Seemann, Leipzig-1937-423p

Das Kreuz-600+ Postcard Photos of Knight's Cross Recipients-320p-**The Cross**

Das Letzte Book: Atlantik Farewell-Hirschfeld, Wolfgang-Universitas-Munich-1989-**The Last Boat-Atlantic Good-bye**

Das U-Boot Bei der Arbeit-by Kirchner, Johann-Mittler, Berlin-1917-86p

Dati Statistici-by USMM-USMM, Rome-1972-**Statistical Data**

David Bushnell and his American Turtle-by Tomlinson, E-Akron & Chicago, NY-1899

David Bushnell and His Turtle-by Swanson, June-McMillan-1991

Day of Deceit-by Stinnett, Robert B-Free Press-2000-386p-ISBN 0684853396-The truth about FDR and Pearl Harbor

Day the Admirals Slept Late, The-by Hoehling, A.A.-Zebra War Book-1978-283p-The day of the Pearl Harbor attack   ·

De Ijzeren Zeehond-by Thies, Hans Arthur-Westland, Amsterdam-1943-355p

De Nederlandse Onderzeedienst 1906-1966-by Stok, A.D. M.C.-Zuid-Hollandse Uitgevers Maatschappij, The Hague-1966-**The Dutch Submarine Service 1906-1966**

De Onderzeeboten van de Koninklijke Marine-by Kubatz, FJ-Ten Brink Maritiem, Meppel-1987-ISBN 0905123001-General technical info about Dutch submarines

De wereldreis van H.M. K XVIII-Holdert & Co, Amsterdam-1935-**The Voyage Around the World of the Dutch Submarine K XVIII**

Dead Reckoning-by Klaxon-London-1939-269 p-WWI submarine actions

Deadly Seas-Duel between the St. Croix and the U305-by Bercuson, David J & Herwig, Holger H-Toronto-1997-356p-includes photos

Death in the Irish Sea-by Stokes, R-Collins Press-1999-The sinking of the RMS Leinster in the First World War

Death of a Navy-by d'Albas, Andrieu-Devin-Adair, NY-1957-363p-Japanese Naval action in WW II

Death of the Thresher-by Polmar, Norman-Chilton Books-1964-148p

Death of the U-Boats, The-by Hoyt, Edwin P-McGraw Hill-1988-248p-ISBN 007030629X

Death on All Seas-by Freyer, Paul H-Militari-Verlag-1971

Death on the Hellships-by Michno, Gregory F-USNIP-2001-344p, 20 photos-ISBN 1557504822

Decima Flottoglia Mas-by Borghese, Junio V-See "Sea Devils"-Tenth Torpedo Boat Flotilla

Decision at Sea-by Kemp, Peter-Elsevier-Dutton-1978 &1984-The convoy escorts

Decisive Battles of World War II-by Jacobsen, HA & Rohwer, J-G.P. Putnam's-Sons-1965 The German View

Decline and Fall of Nazi Germany and Imperial Japan-by Dollinger, Hans-Bonanza Books-1965

Defeat of the Wolfpacks-by Jones, Geoffrey-Presidio-1987-223p-ISBN 0718305892-The story of the loss of 35 U-Boats during the winter of 1943/44

Defensively-Armed merchant Ships and Submarine Warfare-by Higgins, Alexander P-1917-32p

Deficiencies of the United States Submarine Torpedo in the Pacific Theater: World War II, The-Luther Gates Ingram, Jr.-1978-110 leaves

Der Andere Auftrag-by Gellermann, Gunther-W-Bernard & Graefe Verlag, Koblenz-1997-240p-ISBN 3763759719-The other mission: German U-boats in special operations in Second World War)

Der Bau von Unterseebooten auf der Germaniawerft-by Techel, H-Berlin-1922-103p

Der Brandtaucher-by Bethge, Hans-Georg-Delius, Klasing-1968-173p-Story of Wilhelm Bauer and Germany's first submarine

Der Deutsche Unterseeboot-krief-by Pohl, Heinrich-Enke, Stuttgart-1925-54p-International Law and the submarine

Der Fall Laconia-by Brennecke, Hans J-Biberach and er Riss-1959-158p-**The Laconia Incident**-About the sinking of the line Laconia by U-156 and the rescue operation

Der Handelskrieg mit U-Booten-by Spindler, Arno-ES Mittler 32-44/Cassel 1966-**Trade War with Submarines** 5 Vols-Also translated into Italian and French

Der Krieg in der Nordsee-by Groos, Oto-Mittler, Berlin-1920-1937-7 Vol

Der Lusitania-fall und die Deutsche Wissenchaft-by Becker, Willi-Abel, Greifswald-1919-86p

Der Mord Versuch on Oberleutnant-by Bischoff, Ernst-1917

Der Perlentaucher-by Berge, Victor-Rutten & Loening-1932-317p-Artist and painter Bergen, Claus of German submarines at sea and in port

Der Schrecken der Meere-by Valentiner, Max-Amalthea-Verlag, Zurich-1931-327p-Memoirs of WW I U-Boat ace

Der Seekrieg-by Brennecke, Jochen & Durk, Dieter & Farber, Mathias-Verlagsunion Pabel-Moewig KG, Rastatt-1994-ISBN 3811842218 **-The War at Sea**

Der Seekrieg-by Ruge, Vice Admiral Fredrich-USNIP-1957

Der Tod auf Allen Meeren-by Freyer, Paul H-Militar, Berlin-1972-390p-**Death on all the Oceans**-East German viewpoint of WW II U-Boat warfare

Der U-Boot Kommandant Wolfgang Luth-by Vause, Jordan-Motorbuch Verlag, Stuttgart-1999 68p-ISBN 361301937X-A study of the WWII **U-Boat Commander Wolfgang Luth**

Der U-Bootkrieg als Weg zum Endsieg-by Bacmeister, Walter-Duncker, Weimar-1917-30p

Der U-Bootkrieg -1914-1918-by Michelsen, Andreas-Hase & Koehler, Leipzig-1942-207p-Also a 1925 first edition

Der U-Bootkrieg-1939-1945-by Busch, Rainer & Roll, Hans J-Mittler & Sohn, Berlin-1996-344p-There is 3 Volumes in this series and volume 3 has not been published as of 2001.

Der U-Bootkrieg 1939-1945 in der Literatur-by Schlemm, Jurgen-Elbe Spree Vig, Hamburg-2000-212p-ISBN 3931129241-A bibliography in German by Uboat.net's master researcher and covers many hundreds of book, articles and pamphlets relating to the U-Boat war.

Der U-Bootskrieg 1914-1918-Koehler-1925

Der Weltkrieg-3 Vols-Helfferich-1919

Der Wolf im Atlantik-by Robertson, Terrence-Munich-1955-ISBN 3893506950-German version of The Golden Horseshoe-Kretschmer's career in the U-Boats and as a POW in England and Canada.

Des U-Boot als Kriegs-und Handelsschiff-by Kuester, Julius-1918-166p

Description and Photographs of Japanese Midget Sub. No 19-1940?-(Rare)-29p

Design & Construction of British Warships 1939-1945-by Brown, DK.-Conway Maritime Press-1996-160p-ISBN 0851776744-Vol II-Submarines, Escorts, and Coastal Forces

Design, Developments & Tactics-by Breemer, Jan-Janes-1989

Design of Manned Submersibles-by Dimitriyev, AN-Sudostroyeniye, Leningrad-1978

Design of Nuclear Submarines-by Bukalov, VM & Narusbayev, AA-Russian

Destination Dardanelles-by Wilson, Michael-Cooper UK-1988-193p

Destroyer Killer-by Hoyt, Edwin P-Pocket Military-222p-1989-History of Sam Dealy and the USS Harder

Destruction of Convoy PQ17-by Irving, David-Simon & Schuster-1968-337p

Det Norske Ubatvapen 1909-1959-by Ronneberg, Harald-Eides, Bergen-1959-127p-History of the Norwegian submarine force

Detail specifications for building submarine rescue vessels nos. 7 to 11 incl. for the United States Navy: including specifications for the installation of ordnance and ordnance outfit-Navy Department, Bureau of Ships-Washington: U.S. G.P.O-1941-241p

Detail specifications for building submarine tender no.11 Fulton for the United States Navy: including specifications for the installation of ordnance and ordnance outfit and specifications for the installation of outfit and equipment: under the cognizance of the Bureaus of Medicine and Surgery, Navigation, Supplies and Accounts/Navy Department, Bureau of Construction and Repair.-USGPO-1938-476p

Determining the Future of the US Submarine Force-by Brian, Thomas Howes-1992-119p

Deutsche Strategie zur See im zweiten Weltkrieg-by Doenitz, Karl-Bernardo Graefe-Munich-1969

Deutsche U-Bootbunker gestern und heute-by Schmeelke, Karl-Heinz-Podzun-Pallas-Verlag, Friedberg-1996-48p-ISBN 3790905763 **-German U-boat Bunkers Yesterday and Today**

Deutsche U-Boote 1939-1945-by Brennecke, Jochem-Heyne, Munich-1991

Deutsche U-Boote-by Mason, David-Moewig Verlag, Rastatt-1992-160p-ISBN 3811872761

German U-Boats. A general overall view of U-boats in WWII. ½ of the book is photos.

Deutsche U-Boote geheim-by Lakowski, Richard-Brandenburgisches Verlagshaus, Berlin-1997-207p-ISBN 3894880309-**U-Boat Secrets**-An illustrated work with many U-boat pictures, taken in construction or shortly there after

Deutsche U-Boote von 1906-1966-by Herzog, Bodo-Pawlak Verlag, Herrsching-1993-324p-ISBN 3860700367-German U-Boats-Many maps and drawings

Deutsche U-Boote Zum Schwarzen Meer-by Enders, Gerd-240p-Type II-B Subs

Deutsche Uniformen 1939-1945-by Lagarde, Jean de-Motorbuch Verlag, Pietsch-1998-127p-ISBN 3613018691-Covers uniforms and equipment of the Wehrmacht, including the U-Boat arm, for various theatres of the war, climates and times of year. Also covers rank insignia and decorations. **German Uniforms 1939-1945**

Deutschen U-Boote, 1939-1945 Ihr Verblieb, Tech. Daten, Typenliste, Namen der Kommandaten, etc-by Mielke, O-Munich-1959-112p

Deutschland, The-Atherly-Jones, Llewellyn Archer-London-1918

Deutschlands U-Boote-by Kiel, Kurt-Wilhelm Kohler Verlag, Minden-1940-80p, 90 photos-**Germany U-Boats**. A overview but some prewar photos showing daily life aboard a U-boat

Development and History of the Hunley-by Aliano, Samuel E-1964-88p

Development of Foreign Submarines and Their Tactics-by Khiyaynan, LP-Voyenizdat-Moscow 1988

Development of the German U-Boat Arm-Thesis-U. of Washington-1963

Development of the Lake Type Submarine Torpedo Boats-by Lake Torpedo Boat Company-CT-1913-27p

Development of the Torpedo-Bethell, P-Engineering, London-Articles in Vol 159-161-1945-1946

Devil's Device, The-by Gray, Edwyn-USNIP 1975-253p-ISBN 0870212451 -Robert Whitehead and the History of the Torpedo-1991 edition revised and updated

Diary While on Board USS Sailfish SS-192 December 1941 Manila-by Doritty, R.E.

Dictionary of Admirals of the U.S. Navy-Cogar, William B-2 vols-USNIP-1991-Vol 1 (1862-1900), Vol 2 (1900-1916)

Dictionary of American Fighting Ships in 8 Volumes by Name-USGPO-500+names-Vol 8 includes a series guide-Cost $29-56 each

Dictionary of American Naval Fighting Ships Vol 1-5(Vol 6&7 unpublished)-USGPO

Dictionary of Military Abbreviations-by Polmar, Norman, Warren, Mark, Wertheim, Eric-USNIP 1994-307p-ISBN 1557506809

Dictionary of Ships of the Royal Navy of WW II-by Young, John-Patrick Stephens-1975 192p

Die Abenteurliche Fahrt der Nautilus-by Anderson, William R with Blair, Clay-Desch, Munich 1959-198p-German translation of Nautilus 90 North

Die Bekanntmachungen des U-Boot-Handelskrieges-by Hubernagel, Wilhelm-Hartmann, Greifswald-1927-89p-**Submarines and International Law**

Die Boote in Netz-by Boddeker, Gunther-Bergisch, Gladbach-1983-492p ISBN 3404650573-**Caught in the Net**

Die Bundeswehr und ire Uniformen-by Horman, Jorg-M-Podzun-Pallas, Freiberg-1987

Die Deutsche Kriegsflotte und Ihre Verbundeten-by Mittler, Jost-ES Mittler, Berlin-1915-22 5 volumes-Covers four years of sea warfare

Die Deutsche Kriegsmarine 1939-1943-by Lohmann, Walter-Hildebrand, Hans Podzun 1956+-3volumes-Vol 1 includes U-Boats, Vol 3 is a listing of German Naval Officers

Die Deutsche Kriegsmarine im Zweiten Weltkrieg-by ˙ Von der Porten, Edward-Motorbuch Verlag, Stuttgart-1994-302p, 40 photos-ISBN 3613011484-The German Navy in World War II

Die Deutsche Marine 1920-1945-by Giese, Fritz-Bernard & Graefe-1956-The German Navy 1920-1945

Die Deutsche Marine-Funkaufklarung 1914-1945-by Bonatz, Heinz-Wehr und Wissen Verlag, Darmstadt-1970-174p-German Naval Radio Reconnaissance

Die Deutsche Seekriegsleitung 1939-1945-by Salewski, Michael-Bernard & Graefe-Munich-1970+-Director of German Sea War 1939-45 3 Vols

Die Deutschen Kreigsmarine-Band3-by Beyer, Siegfried-Podzun-Pallas-Verlag, Friedberg-1987 192p, 263photos and maps-ISBN 3790903205-The German Navy-Volume 3

Die Deutschen Kriegsschiffe 1815-1945 Bd. 3 U-Boot-by Groner, Erich-Bernard & Graefe Verlag, Koblenz-1985-298p-ISBN 3763748024-The German Warships 1815-1945, Volume 3: U-boats

Die Deutschen Kriegsschiffe 1939-1945-by Ciupa, Heinz-Moewig Verlag, Rastatt-1988-175p ISBN 3811814095-The German Warships 1939-1945. Originally published in 1979

Die Deutschen U-Boat Kommandanten-by Busch, Rainer-Roll, Hans-Joachim-1992

Die Deutschen Ubootbunker und Bunkerwerften-by Neitzel, Sonke-Bernard & Graefe Verlag, Koblenz-1991-ISBN 3763758232

Die Deutschen Ubootbunker und Werften-by Neitzel, Sonke-Bernard & Graefe Verlag, Koblenz-1991-340p, 140 photos-U-boat pillboxes and shipyards

Die Deutschen U-Boote 1906 bis 1945-Herzog, Bodo-JF Lehmanns, Munchen-1959-234p-German Submarines 1906-1945

Die Deutschen U-Boote 1939-1945-by Mielke, Otto-Pabel Verlag, Rastatt-1991-98p-First published in 1959

Die Deutschen U-Boote in Iher Kriegfuhrung, 1914-1918-by Gayer, Albert-Mittler, Berlin-**Vol 1**-Outbreak of war to Feb 1915, **Vol 2**-Feb to Oct 1915, **Vol 3**-Oct 1915 to Apr 1916, **Vol 4**-May 1916 to Feb 1917-These volumes only cover action against warships

Die Deutschen U-Boote und ihr Verbleib 1939-1945-by Grutzemacher, Carl-Wilhelm-Karlsruhe-1952-The German U-boats and their fates 1939-1945

Die Deutschen Uboote und Ihre Werften-by Rossler, Eberhard-Bernard & Graefe-1990-ISBN 3763758798-The complete data for each U-boat, when ordered, laid down, launched and commissioned and some technical information

Die Deutschen und Osterreichischen U-Boot-Verluste in Beiden Weltkriegen-by Kemp, Paul-Urbes Verlag, Munchen-1998-303p-ISBN 33924896437 German and Austrian U-boat losses in both World Wars based on the most current information

Die Deutschen Waffen und Geheimwaffen-by Lusar, Rudolf-Lehmann, Munich-1964-379p-Describes German weapons and secret weapons of WW II, including submarines

Die Eisernen Sarge-by Werner, Herbert-Heyne-Munich-1984-ISBN 3453005155-**Iron Coffins**-A U-boat commander on the U-415 and U-953 and of his life also on the U-557 and U-230-

Die Entstehundsgeschichte der U-Boote-by Lawrenz, Hans-Joachim-JF Lehmanns-Germany-1968-147p-History of submarines from earliest times to the present

Die Entwicklung der Antriebe von Unterwasser fahrzeugen-by Moler, Eberhard-Berlin-1989

Die Fahrt der Deutschland: das Erste Untersee-Frachtschiff-by Koenig, Paul-1916-254p-**The Voyage of the Deutschland**-The skipper of the U-boat tells of his first journey to Baltimore in 1916

Die Farhtender Breslau im Schwazen Meer-Doenitz, Karl-Ullstein, Berlin-1917-The Voyages of the Breslau in the Black Sea

Die Feldpostnummern der Deutsche Unterseeboote 1939-1945-by Steckel, Olaf-Self Published-1987-117p-German U-boat ship cancellations

Die Festung-by Buchheim, Lothar-Gunther-Hoffmann und Campe-1997-1469p-ISBN 3442438225-The author's account of the last days of the war at Brest-**The Fortress Die Frage der Minen im Seekrieg vor Ihrer Beandlung auf der II**-by Rocholl, Erich-Leipzig-1910-47p-Submarine Mining and International law

Die Gefangenen; Leben U. Uberleben-by Boddeker, Gunther & Schmidt, Paul-Frankfurt-Prisoners; Life and Survival

Die Hollenmaschine im U-Boot-by Sauer, Herbert-Scherl, Berlin-1928-145p

Die Kriegsmarine-Uniforms & Traditions Vol 1 of 3-by Angolia, John & Schlicht, Adolph-Bender 1991-416p

Die Juhne Fahrt der Deutschland-by Braehmer, Artur-B Siegmund, Berlin-1916-96p

Die Letzte Feindfahrt: Mai 1943-by Alman, Karl-Rastalt, Baden-1973-The Last War Patrol

Die Manner von U96-by Wiebicke, Karl-Koehler, Leipzig-1934-208p

Die Manner von U-995-by Hess, Hans Georg-Stalling Maritime-1979-The Men of U-995

Die Ritterkreuztragen der Deutschen Wehrmacht by Dorr, Manfred-Biblio-Verlog-1988-The Knight's Cross Holders in the German Military

Die Schiffe der Deutschen Kriegsmarine und Luftwaffe, 1939-1945-by Groener, Erich-86p

Die Seeminen in Krieg-by Berg, Ernst-Frankernthal-Gohring-1910

Die Sowjetische U-Bootswaffe in der Ostsee 1939-45-by Rohwer, Jurgen-Frankfurt-1956-Soviet submarine warfare in the Baltic

Die Torpedos der deutschen U-Boote-by Rossler, Eberhard-Koehlers Verlags, Herford-1984-Entwicklung, Herstellung and Eigenschaften der deutschen Marine-Torpedos

Die U-Boot-Faher: die Boot, Die Bestazungen und ihr by Buchheim, Lothar-Gunther-Bertelsmann-1985-Admiral The Submarines: The boat, The crews, and their Admiral

Die U-Bootserfolge der Achsenmachte, 1939-1945-by Rohwer, Jurgen-1968-376p-The submarine successes of the Axis

Die U-Bootswaffe-by Doenitz, Karl-Mittler, Berlin-1939-65p-Document outlining strategy and tactics for the German U-Boat forces prior to the beginning of WW II

Die Unterseeische Schiffahrt-by Hauff, Louis-Munich-1915-78p

Die Verluste der kreigsflotten, 1914-1918-by Rehder, Jacob-JF Lehmanns, Munchen-1969-199p

Die Wende im U-Boat-by Brennecke, Hans Jochen-Weltbild-Verlag, Augsburg-1959-573p-Turnabout in the U-Boat War-also 1991 issue ISBN 3453036670

Die Wolfe-by Vause, Jordan-Motorbuch Verlag, Stuttgart-1999-255p-ISBN 3613020025-U-Boat commanders in WWII

Die Wolfe und der Admiral-by Frank, Wolfgang-Lubbe Verlag Bergisch, Gladbach-1992-746p-ISBN 3404650255-The wolves and the Admiral-A very good personal account of U-Boat action in WWII. The author attended several staff meetings with Donitz and also served aboard several U-Boats in the war

Dienstverpflichtet-by Malisius, Richard-Lohse-Eissing-1981-184p, 27 photos-ISBN 3920602250-Duty Bound-An engineer tells of U-boat construction during WWII

Diesel-electric Submarines and Their Equipment: an International defense review editorial supplement Cointrin-Geneva, Switzerland: Interavia, 1986-70p

Diplomatic Correspondence Between the United States and Belligerent Governments Relating to Neutral Rights and Commerce-US Dept. of State-Oxford, NY-1917-393p

Diplomatic Ramifications of Unrestricted Submarine Warfare 1939-1941-by Manson, Janet M Greenwood Press-1990-215p-Details the origins of the Allied-Axis decisions to adopt unrestricted submarine warfare tactics during WW II

Disabled Submarines-US Naval Sea Systems Command-US Dept of Navy-1978

Disaster at Sea-by Marriott, John-Hippocrene-176p-Riveting accounts of 16 dramatic real-life sea disasters, from the Titanic to the Andrea Doria to the tragedy of the submarine Thresher, chosen for the useful questions of navigation and seamanship they raise.

Disaster in the Deep-USS Thresher-Washington Star-1963-Newspaper article-27p

Discharged Dead-by Hart, Sydney-Odhams Press-1956-208p-True story of Britain's submarines at War

Discoveries and Inventions of the 19th Century-by Routledge, Robert G-Routledge, UK-1896

Dishes From the Deep-1996-Cookbook from USSVI Perch Base

Disposal of Decommissioned Nuclear Submarines-GPO-1983-166p

Dissertations on Submarine Navigation-by Wilkins, John-1948

Distintivi e Medaglie della RSI-Sparachino, Fausto-Editrice Militare Italiana, Milan, 1988

Dive and Attack-A submariner's Story-by King, W-Kimber-1983-224p

Dive Into History Vol 3: U-Boats-by Keats, Henry C.-George C. Faar-1986 -2nd Edition by Pisces Books

Dive!-by Harris-Warren, Cmdr-Harper, NY-1960-130p-The Story of the Atomic Submarine

Divine Thunder-by Millot, Bernard-McCall-1970-243p-Kamikaze subs in WW2

Diving Into Darkness-by Johnson, Rebecca L-A Submersible Explores the Sea

Diving Into Dolphin History-by Dolphin Scholarship Foundation-A cookbook-1999-360p

Diving the U-85 German Submarine-by Brunch, Jim-May 86-79p

Diving With & Without Armor-Diving exploits of JB Green-Green, JB-1990

Dix Ans et Vingt Jours-by Doenitz, Karl-Plon, Paris-1959

Dix-Neuf Histoires de Sous-Marins- by Frank, Bernard-Payot, Paris-1918-233p

Do Trzech Razy Sztuka-by Nowak, Jan-Wydawn, Gdynia-1960-63p

Doenitz and the Wolf packs-by Edwards, Bernard-Arms & Armour-1996-240p-An up-to-date study of how Doenitz evolved the wolf-pact strategy, why it was so successful, and how it came close to crippling allied resistance. The book contains a great deal of information of the actual battle-by-battle workings of the system as well as how it fitted into a grand strategy, and why, in the end, the Allies overcame it.

Doenitz at Nuremberg: A Reappraisal-by Thompson, HK & Strutz, Henry-Amber Pub. Corp-1976

Doenitz, The Last Fuhrer-by Padfield, Peter-Gollancz, UK-1984-Also Panther Books, UK-1985-Also in German as ISBN 355007956 608p. The author is British and biased.

Dolphin Delicacies-by Pearl Harbor Submarine Wives-circa 1980

Dolphin Dips and Sips-New London, CT-1971-A recipe book

Dolphin Dishes-Collected by Submarine Cook Book Committee /Submarine Officer's Wives' Club, New London-Teagle & Little-1959-284p

Dolphin Tales-by Various authors-A collection assembled by the Dolphin Scholarship Fund-Teagle & Little Printers, Norfolk-144p-The book is 144 pages of submarine tales (and some family grams) submitted by officers and enlisted personnel. A few of the articles are from 1942. Several of the authors went on to make Admiral etc. A few of the submitters are: Ken Carr, Ed Beach, E P Wilkinson and many others.

Donitz, The Last Fuhrer-by Padfield, Peter-Harper & Row-1984

Donitz and the Wolf Packs-by Edwards, Bernard-1997-240p

Double-Edged Secrets-by Holmes, WJ-USNIP-1979-ISBN 0870211625-US Naval Intelligence in WW II by one of the intelligence officers that worked on Ultra-Also republished as a Bluejacket Book by USNIP in 1998

Dover Patrol, The-by Bacon, Reginald HS-Hutchinson, London-1919-2 vols-

Down in Davey Jones Locker-by Door, WT-Charlie Noble Press-1943-426p

Down the Hatch-by Winton, John-St Martins, NY-1962

Down to the Sea In Subs-by Charles A. Lockwood-WW Norton-1967-376p-Memoirs

Down to the Ships in the Sea-by Grossett, Harry-Lippincott-Phil-1954-256p-Submarine rescue and salvage

Dragon In the Sea-by Herbert, Frank-Doubleday-1956-190p-Alt. title: 21st Century Sub

Dreadnought to Nuclear Subs-by Preston, Anthony-Pendragon House-1980-60p

Dreadnought to Polaris-by Hyatt, AM-USNIP-1973-125p

Drie-Cylinders Duiken Dieper-by Gerretse, KHL & Wijn, JJA-Van Soeren & Co, Amsterdam-1993-ISBN 9068810278-The Dutch "Dolphin" class submarine

Drill Book for the Use of Sub-marine Mining Engineer Volunteers-by Black, Adam E-Clowes, London-1887-54 plates

DTNSRDC Revised Standard Submarine Equations of Motion-by Feldman, J-David Taylor Research Center, Bethesda-1979-29p

DU Nautilus au Redoutable-by Le Masson, Henry-Presses de la Cite, Paris-1969-455p-History of French submariners from the Nautilus of 1800 to the Redoutable of 1969

Duell vor Australien-by Winter, Barbara-Mittler & Sohn Verlag-1994-359p-ISBN 3813204413-Caught in the Net

Duello nell' Atlantico-by Rayner, DA-Baldini & Castoldi, Milano-1958-Duel in the Atlantic

Duikboot en Volkenrecht-by Francois, Jean Pierre-Nijhoff-1919-375p-Considerations of submarine warfare and international law

Dynamite for Hire-CO of U-234-by Sellwood, AV-Werner Laurie-1956-264p

Dynamic America-by Niven, Canby, Welsh-Doubleday 1958-426p-A History of General Dynamics Corp

E

E-Boat Alert-by Tent, James Foster-USNIP-1996-286 pages-ISBN 1557508054-Contains newly released top-secret Admiralty reports, rare photographs and interviews with eyewitnesses from three countries about a little known campaign to defend the Normandy Invasion Fleet from the torpedoes of Germany's E-boats.

Eagle Against the Sun-by Spector, Ronald H-The Free Press-1985

Earth, Sea, and Sky-by Piccard, Auguste-Oxford, NY-1956

Eastern Sea Frontier War Diary-by Freeman, Robert H, ed-Shellback Press-1987

Eastward the Convoys-by Schofield, William G-Rand McNally & Co-1965

Eclipse of American Sea Power, The-by Knox, Dudley-American Army and Navy Journal-1922

Effects of the USS Thresher Disaster upon Submarine Safety-Callaghan, Phillip M-1987 85p-Thesis

Eight Spies Against America-by Dasch, George-Robert McBride Co-1959-241p-Eight Spies from a submarine invade the US (Author was one)

Einzelkaempher auf See-by Bekker, Cajus (pseud)-Stalling, Hamburg-1968-210p-German midget submarines and frogmen

Eisiger Atlantik-by Werner, Herbert & Hirschfeld, Wolfgang-Heyne Verlag, Munchen-1998-796p-ISBN 3453131711-**Icy Atlantic**-Contains two books: Die Eisernen Sarge and Feindfahrten

El Arma Submarina Espanola-by Ramirez, Gabarrus-EN Bazan, Madrid-1983-A history of the Spanish Submarine Force

El Primer Viajedel Submarino Mercante Deutschland-by Koenig, Paul-Schneider, Buenos Aires 1918-142p

El Submarino Peral-by Madariaga, Juan de-Madrid-1889-

El Submarino Torpedero en el Ataque-by Carrero, Guillermo-by Escelicer, Madrid-1941-104p

Electric Boat Diversification Efforts 1920 to 1972-by Browning, Samuel P-1994 163p

Electric Boat: Hearings before the United States Select Committee concerning Lilley and Lake submarine charges-GPO-1908-1659p-17 parts

Electric Boat: Report of the above entry-3 Volumes-1908

Electricity as Applied to Submarines: for instruction of the submarine personnel-by Gray AH & Arendt MF-USGPO-1918-318p

Electron, The and Sea Power-by Hezlet, A-Peter Davies-1975

Electronic Warfare-by de Arcangelis, Mario-Blanford Press, Poole-Dorset-1985-

Electronic Warfare-by Gordon, Don E-Pergamon Press-1981

Electronics and Sea Power-by Hezlet, Arthur-Stein & Day, NY-1975

ELF-An Essential Communication System-by Boyle, Dan-International Defense Review-1978

Eminent American Namesakes of the Polaris Submarine Fleet-Rickover, Hyman G-GPO-1972 316p-11 biographical sketches of Polaris missile submarine namesakes

Embleme, Wappen, Mailings Deutscher U-boote 1939-1945-by Hogel, Georg-Koehlers Velagsgesellschaft, Hereford-1987-228p-ISBN 3782204077-**Emblems and Insignia of German Submarines**

Emperors Codes, The-by Smith, M-Bantam Press-Describes the cracking of Japanese codes

Empires in the Balance-by Willmott, H-1982-478p-Details Japanese and Allied political, military and naval strategies in the Pacific during WW II

Encounter: Combat History of the Tinosa-by Watrous, Allen E-Rare

Encounter At Sea-by VanWylen, Gordon J & Inchiro Masstsunaga-Momentum Books-1994-264p-Former antagonists come together 50 years later to recount the battle between the USS Hardhead and the Japanese cruiser Natori. The authors served on those ships

Encyclopedia of British Submarines 1901-1955-by Paul Akermann-Maritime Books-1989 522p-ISBN 0907771424

Encyclopedia of Military History-by Dupuy, R Ernest & Dupuy, Trevor-Harper & Row-1986

End of the Imperial Japanese Navy-by Ito, Masanori & Pinean, Roger-WW Norton & Co-1956

Enemies Fighting Ships, The-by Launer, Jay-Sheridan House-1944-222p-The Naval Strength of the Axis

Enemy in Sight!-by Rogers-1943

Enemy on our Doorstep, The-by Neary, Steve-Jesperson Press-1994-German Attacks at Bell Is. Newfoundland in 1942

Enemy Sighted-by Hudson, Alec (pseud)-Macmillan-1940-61p

Enemy Submarine-U47 and Gunther Prien-by Frank, Wolfgang-William Kimber-1954-200p

Enemy Submarine, The-by the Naval Consulting Board and War Committee of Technical Societies, from information already published and other recently released-New York: Naval Consulting Board of the United States, Office of the Secretary-1918-47p

Engage the Enemy More Closely-Royal Navy in the Second World War-Barnett &Correlli-W.W. Norton, NY-1991-1052p-ISBN 0393029182

Enigma-by Kozaczuk, Wladyslaw-University Pubs. of America-1984 translation

Enigma Avant Ultra-by Block, Gilbert-1988

Enigma War, The-by Garlinski, Jozef-Charles Scribner's Sons-1979-Environmental Effects on Consciousness-by Schaeffer, Karl-Macmillan, NY-1962-146p

Entertaining on the Isle-by Officers' Wives' Club, Mare Island-1989-A Cookbook

Entscheidung im Atlantik-by Ambrosius, Hans Heinrich-1943-71p-**Decision in the Atlantic**

Ensayo Sobre El Arte De Navegar Por Debajo Del Agua-by Monturial, Narciso-Barcelona-1891 One of the earliest submarines invented-Very rare book

Epic of the USS Euryale AS-22-Cruise Book-1946

Epics of Salvage-by Masters, David-Little, Brown, Boston-1954-234-Wartime feats of the Marine Salvage men in WW II

Eroismo Italiano Sotto I Mari 1940-1943-by Nelli RB-G de Vecchi, Milano-1968

Escape-by Messimer, Dwight-USNIP-1992

Escape from Crete-by Lind, LJ-Australasian Publishing-100p-The author, a New Zealander, escaped from Crete in a submarine and reached Alexandria and safety.

Escort Commander-by Robertson, Terence-Bantam-1979-202p

Evolution of Maritime Strategy-1977-1987-by Hattendorf, John B-Naval War College-1988

Evolution of Naval Radio-Electronics and contributions of the Naval Research Laboratory-Gebhard, Louis A.-USGPO-1979

Evolution of Sea Power-by Domville-Fife, Charles W-Rich & Cowan-1939-258p

Evolution of the Submarine-by Skerret, Robert G-1904

Evolution of the Submarine Boat, Mine and Torpedo from the Sixteenth Century to the Present Time, The-by Sueter, Murray F-UK-1907-384p-200 illus

Explorations-Autobiography-by Ballard, Robert

Exploring Under the Sea-by Cook, J Gordon-Abelard-Schuman, NY-1965-159p

Exploring Under the Sea-by Neurath, Marie-Lee & Sheppard Co, NY-1959-36p

Explorers of the Deep-by Cox, Donald W-1968-93p-For the young reader

Eyes and Ears of the Convoy, The: development of the helicopter as an anti-submarine weapon-by Robert M. Browning Jr.-Washington, DC: Coast Guard Historian's office, 1993-16p

F

Facher loos-by Plottke, Herbert-Podzun-Pallas Wofersheim-1994-153p-ISBN 3790905100-**Torpedoes Away**

Fabrik fur die Ewigkeit-by Aschenbeck, Nils et al-Junius Verlag-1995-148p-ISBN 3885062380-**Factory for Eternity-**About the U-boat Bunker in Bremen

Fackeln uber dem Atlantik-by Topp, Erich-Mittler & Sohn Verlag, Berlin-1996-287p-ISBN 35448239854-**Torches over the Atlantic-**Autobiography of this famous U-boat commander both during and after the war

Facts About The Submarine Service-Department of the Navy-NavPers NRB-44205-12 Sept. 1944

Falklands War, The: a review of the sea-based airpower, submarine and anti-submarine warfare operations-by Craig J. Lokkins-Maxwell Air Force Base, Ala: Air War College, Air University-1988-27p

Family of Spies-by Earley, Peter-Bantam-1988

Famous American Admirals-by Reynolds, Clark G-Van Norstrand Reinhold-1978

Famous Sea Battles-by Howarth, David-Little, Brown, Boston-1981-185p

Famous Ships of World War 2-by Ellis, Chris-Arco Publishing Co, NY-1977

Famous Underwater Adventures-by Wagner, Frederick-Dodd, NY-1962

Far and the Deep, The-Stafford, Edward P-GP Putnam's Sons-1967-384p-History of the Development of the Submarine through-out the world

Far Distant Ships-RCN in WW II-by Schull, Joseph-Queens Printer-Ottawa-1952

Fast Attack Submarine: The Seawolf Class-by Payan, Gregory-Children's Press-2000-48p-ISBN 0516235389-Youth oriented

Fatal Decisions, The-by Freiden, Seymour & Richardson, William-Berkley Publishing Corp-1958

Fatal Submarine Accidents-Romig, Mary F-Rand, CA-1966-22p

Fatal Voyage-Sinking of the USS Indianapolis in WW II-by Kurzman, Dan-Antheneum-1990 331p-ISBN 0689120079

Fateful Seagull, The-by Mill, Thomas-Bradley & Son-1919-225p

Father of the Submarine-The Life of Reverend G Pasha-by Murphy WS-Maritime Books-1986

Favorite Recipes-by Navy Officer's Wives Club, Pascaguola, MS-1980

FDR's Undeclared War 1939-1941-by Fehrenbach, TR-David Mckay Co-1967

Feind im Fadendreuz, U-Boot auf Jagdim Atlantik-Enemy in my Sights: U-Boat at War in the Atlantic-by Hartmann, Werner-die Heimbrucherei-1942-232p

Feidhahrt-by Higgins, Jack-Neue Schweizer Bibliothek, Zurich-1979-316p-**War Patrol**

Feindfahrten: Das Logbuch eines U-Boot-Funkers-by Hirschfeld, Wolfgang-**War Patrol**: The Diary of U-Boat Radio Operators-Neff & USNIP-1982-Pub. also as Hirschfeld: The story of a U-Boat NCO who was a radioman on U-109 and on U-234

Few Survived-by Gray, Edwyn-Futura, London-1987-274p-ISBN 0850524997-A Comprehensive Study of Submarine accidents & disasters-31 photos

Fiercest Battle, The-Story of Convoy ONS5-by Seth, Ronald-WW Norton & Co-1961

Fifty Ships That Saved the World-by Goodhart-Anti-Submarine Warfare

Fifty Year War, The-by Friedman, Norman-USNIP-2000-597p-ISBN1557502641

Fifty Years: New York Shipbuilding Corporation-by same-1949

Fight for the Sea-The Past, Present and Future of Submarine Warfare in the Atlantic-by Lewis, David-Cleveland World Publications-1961-350p-Also Collier edition 1961 286p

Fighting Admirals, The British Admirals of the Second World War- by Stephen, M-Leo Cooper 1991

Fighting Fleets, The-by Paine, Ralph D-Houghton-Boston-1918-392p

Fighting Liberty Ship, The-by Huehling, Adolph A-Kent State U. Press-1990

Fighting Ships and Seamen-by Macintyre, Donald-Evans Bros, London-1963-192p

Fighting Ships of Australia and New Zealand-by Andrews, Graeme-Regency House-1973-64p-Originally published at Australasian Navies in 1971

Fighting Ships of the Imperial Japanese Navy-by Fukui, Shizuo-Tokyo-1970-327p

Fighting Ships of World War II-by Westwood, JN-Sidgwick & Jackson, London-1975

Fighting Tenth, The-The Tenth Submarine Flotilla-by Wingate, John-1991-ISBN 0850522005-The Battle for the Med by the RN's Tenth Flotilla

Fighting the U-Boats-by Chatterton, Edward K-Hurst & Blackette, London-1942-216p

Fighting Under the Sea-by Macintyre, Donald-Norton, NY-1965-174p-A tribute and insight into the achievements of British and US Submariners during the war

Fightn' Oil-by Ickes, Harold L-Alfred A. Knopf-1943

Filament Wound Composites for Submarine Hulls-R&D in the USSR-by Tunik, Alfred Delphic Assoc.-1989-131p

Films and the Second World War-by Manvell, Roger-AS Barnes & Co, NJ & NY-1974

Final Assault on the Empire-by Foster, S-London-1994

Find and Destroy: Antisubmarine Warfare in WWI-by Messimer, Dwight-USNIP-2001-312p-25 photos-ISBN 1557504474

Fino a Scapa Flow-by Prien, G-GC Sansoni, Firenze-1943-Up to Scapa Flow

Fire in Anger-by Mars, Alistar-Mill, NY-1958-222p-Also same as Atomic Submarines: A story of Tomorrow

Fire on the Beaches-by Taylor, Theodore-Norton, NY-1958-248p

First Book of Submarines, The-by Icenhower, Joseph B-Watts, NY-1957-60p-Young

First In, Last Out-by Frame, TR & Swinden, GJ-Kangaroo Press-Australia-208p-ISBN 0864172893-The Australian submarine A2 and the Australian naval bridging train at Gallipoli in 1915

First Submarines, The-by Preston, Anthony & Batchelor, John-Phoebus Pub Co, UK-1974

First Under the North Pole-The USS Nautilus-by Anderson, William-World, Cleveland-1959-64p

First World War, The by Gilbert, Martin-Owl-615p-1996-50 maps

Fleet Admiral King-by King, Ernest J & Whitehill, Walter M-WW Norton & Co-1952-465p

Fleet Submarine in the US Navy, The-A Design and Construction History-by Alden, John D-USNIP-1979-290p-ISBN 0870211870-The definitive history of the fleet-type submarine from its inception in World War I, through its heyday in the Pacific, to the last representatives of the 1970s. Text discusses in detail the design of the submarines and their technological development, especially the reasons why the boats were built as they were, what they were intended to accomplish, and how the designers achieved their ends. Hundreds of photographs and plans, including several foldouts, extensive appendix material on the technical aspects of the submarines. Reissued by USNIP in 2001

Fleet Submarines of WW II-History of Gato, Balao, Tench Class Submarines-Walkowiak, Tom Picture Histories Pub. Co.-1988-ISBN 0933126727-49p,84 photos-Author was founder of Floating Drydock

Fleet Type Submarine-NAVPERS-1946-204p-Prepared by ComSubLant

Fleets In, The-by Beigel, Harvey-1995-120p-101 photographs-A complete survey of the comedies and musicals, dramas, carrier movies, submarine movies, classic sea stories, and epic battle recreations produced in Hollywood between 1939 and 1964.

Includes material on the actors, directors, scripts, filming, and a critical evaluation of nearly 50 major films from Mr. Roberts to The Caine Mutiny

Flight of the Avenger-George Bush at War-1991-178p

Flying Sub, The-by Snell-1925

Flying, Submarining and Mine Sweeping-by Anderson, Jane-Causton, London-1916-36p

Flot Nashei Rodiny-by Kornienko, Daniil I.-Moscow-1957-Our Homeland's Fleet

Flot v Pervoi Mirovoi Voine-by Pavlovich, NB-Moscow-1964-The Navy in the First World War

Flot v Sud'be Rossii-by Chernavin, Vladimir N (Adm)-Russian-**The Fleet and the Destiny of Russia**

Flugzeuge jagen U-Boote-by Price, Alfred-Stuttgart-1976-372p, 73 photos + maps-Traces the development of anti-submarine warfare aircraft. **Aircraft hunting U-boats**

For the Common Defense-A military history of the United States of America-by Millett, AR & Maslowski, P-NY-1984

Forces Adrift-by Charlton, Chuck-On-Line Book

Foreign Systems of Torpedoes as Compared With Our Own-by Craighill, William E-1888

Forged In War-The Naval-Industrial Complex and American submarine construction. 1940-61- by Weir, Gary E-US Gov-1993-314p-ISBN 0160382580

Forging the Military-Industrial Complex: World War II's Battle of the Potomac-by Hooks, Gregory-U. of Illinois Press-1991

Forgotten Fleet-by Madsen, Daniel-USNIP-1999-236p-The Mothball Navy

Forlorn Hope 1915-by Brodie, C-1956-91p-British Submarine Operations in the Dardanelles

Four Thousand Years Under the Sea-by Diole, Philippe-Messner, NY-1954

Fourth Service: Merchantmen at War 1939-1945-by Slader, J-New Era 1995

Foxvog Saga, The-by Foxvog, Donald R-Chevy Chase Press-1959

Fran Hajen 1904 til Hajen 1954-Anonymous-1954-Swedish

Freedom of the Seas-by Kenworthy, JM & Young, George-H Liverright, NY-1928?-283p

Fremantle's Secret Fleets-by Cairns, Lynne-Western Australia Maritime Museum-1995 96p-ISBN 0730964329

French Navy in World War II-by Auphan, Paul & Mordal, Jacques-USNIP-1959-413p

Fresh Water Submarines-The Manitowoc Story-by Nelson, William T-Hoeffner Printing-1986

Fringes of the Fleet-by Kipling, Rudyard-Doubleday, Page & Co, NY-1916-122p

Frogman Commander Crabb's Story-by Pugh, Marshall-C Scribner's Sons-1956-208p

Frogmen VC-Midget Sub in the RN-by Fraser, Ian-Angus & Robertson-1957 216p

From 1900 Onward-by Bacon, Reginald Hugh-Hutchinson, UK-1934

From Churchill's Secret Circle to the BBC-Biography of LtGen. Sir Ian Jacob-by Richardson, C Brassey's-1991

From Palau to Paramushiru-by Garon, Allen J-Self published, New Orleans-1976-450p-A documented study of eight World War II Submarine patrols related by former Lieutenant Allen J. Garon / ed. by Henry A. Garon, with excerpts from Patrol Reports Submitted by four submarine commanders.

From Polaris to Trident-by Spinardi, Graham-1994

From Pulpit to Prison-by Niemoeller, Martin-Hodge, UK-1937

From Sails to Atoms-by Portsmouth Naval Shipyard-1963-36p

From Submarines To Satellites-by Hyde, Margaret-Whiltlesey House-1958

From the Dreadnought to Scapa Flow-by Marder, Arthur J-Oxford U. Press, London-1961

From the Sea-by Alexander, John and Photography by Wolff, Brian-Osprey Publishing-256 pages-300 images-A book relating the telling images of sailors and marines, their families and their ships.

From the Turtle to the Nautilus-by Hoyt, Edwin P-Boston, Little, Brown-1963-134p

From U-Boat to Concentration Camp-by Niemoeller, Martin-Hodge, UK-1939-281p

From U-Boat to Prison-by Niemoeller, Martini-1937-This is an a version of U-Boat to Pulpit with an appendix

From U-Boat to Pulpit-by Niemoeller, Martin-Hodge, London-1936-217p

Fuhrer Conferences on Naval Affairs-by Raeder and Doenitz-Brassey's Naval Annual 1948, William Clowes & Sons, London-Notes by Erich Raeder and Karl Doenitz on meetings held with Hitler with some bias toward the Navy's view and not Hitler's.

Fuhrer Let, But We Overtook Him, The-by Durham, Phil-Pentland Press, Australia-1996-ISBN 1858213657

Full Committee Consideration to stop the sale of one submarine to Peru-USGPO-1976-54p

Full Crash Dive-by Bosworth, Allan R-Regnery-Chicago-1942-27p

Full Fathom Five-by Syme, Ronald-Peter Lunn, London-1946-243p

Fulton Bow Plane-3 Anniversary-by DeBlanc, AC-1944-34p

Fundamental Knowledge of Submarines-by Zhong, S-Beijing, China-1985

Fundamentals of Acoustics-3rd Edition-by Kinsler, Lawrence & Austin Frey-John Wiley & Sons 1982

Fundamentals of Submarine Theory-by Yefim'yev, NN-Russian

Funkpeilung als alliierte Waffe gegen deutsche U-Boote 1939-1945-by Bauer, Arthur O-Self published-1997-323p-ISBN 3000021426 -Communications direction-finding as an Allied weapon against the U-boats-Covers hf/df, enigma, metox and other encryption and detection technologies.

Future of the Sea-Based Deterrent-by Tsipis, Kosta-MIT Press-1973-266p-ISBN 0262560127

G

Gallant Gentlemen-by Chatterton, Edward K-Hurst, UK-1931

Galley Gourmet Cookbook-by Officer's Wives Club-Portsmouth Naval Shipyard-1975

Game of Foxes-by Farago, Ladislas-David McKay, NY-1971

GCHG-by West, Nigel-George Weidenfeld & Nicolson-1986

Geheim. Deutsche U-Boote zum Schwarzen Meer-by Enders, Gerd-Mittler & Sohn, Verlag, Berlin 1997-130p, 185photos+maps-ISBN 3813205207-**Secret, German U-boats to the Black Sea**-Describes the overland movement of 6 U-boats type IIB to the Black Sea

Geheimnis um U-977-by Schaeffer, Heinz-Buenos Aires-1950-299p

Geleitzug PQ 17-by Karweina-Mosaik-Verlag, Hamburg-1964-254p-**Convoy PQ-17**-Some rare photos included

Geleitzugschlachten-by Schofield, Paul-Herford-1980

Geleitzugschlachten im Marz 1943-by Rohwer, Jurgen-Motorbuch Verlag, Stuttgart-356p-ISBN 3879433836-**Convoy Battles March 1943**

General Board Minutes-US Navy-1930-38-Unpublished-US Navy Yard-Wash. DC

German, Japanese, and Italian submarine losses. World War II-by Chief of Naval Operations, Navy Department-1946-28p

German Military Dictionary-by US War Department-1944-446p-Translates German military words and terms into English, and English into German

German Naval History-The U-Boat War-1989

German Naval Strategy Across Two Wars-by Ruge, Vice Admiral Fredrich-USNIP

German Naval Vessels of the World War Two US Naval Intelligence-1943 176p-ISBN 1557503044-1200 illustrations. Re-issued in 1993 by USNIP

German Navy 1939-1945-The Picture Book-by Stalling G, Translator-Dial, NY-1974

German Navy at War-1935-45 The U-Boat Vol 2-by Breyer, Siegfried-Westchester, Schiffer-1989

German Navy at War-Vol II U-Boats-by Breyer, Siegfried & Koop, Gerhard-Schiffer Publications Ltd-1989-188p-270 photos

German Navy in Nazi Era-by Thomas, Charles S-USNIP-1990-266p-ISBN 0870217917

German Navy in World War II-An Illus. Reference Guide to the Kriegsmarine 1935-45-by Showell,-JPM-USNIP-1979-224p-ISBN 0870219332-300 illustrations

German Navy in World War II, The-by Von der Porten, Edward-by Thomas Crowell-1969-274p-Also 1972, London, 286p-An account of a vital phase of WW II which is more than an analysis of grand strategy, and includes descriptions of dominant naval personalities behind the scenes and their relationships with other military services and with Hitler himself

German Navy, The-1939-1945 Picture Book-by Bekker, Cajus D-Dial-1974

German Navy of World War II, The-The U-Boat-by Breyer, Siegfried & Koop, Gerhard-Schiffer1997-188p-270 photos

German Pirate, The-Ajax (pseud)-Pearson, London-1918-120p

German Submarine Activities on the Atlantic Coast-by USN-Washington-1920-163p

German Submarine Mail of World War I-by Hennig, Bernard-1991

German Submarine War, The-1914-1918-by Gibson, RH & Prendergast, M-Smith, NY-1931 438p

German Submarine Warfare-by Frost, Wesley-Appleton, NY-1918-243p

German Submarine Warfare-by Spindler, Arno-Oberursel, Germany-1945-35 leaves

German Submarines-2 volumes-by Lenton, HT-MacDonald & Co-1965-Navies of the Second World War. Volume I deals with conventional submarines designed before the war, and volume II with war time designs which were not put into production

German Submarines in the Far East-by Saville, Allison W-USNIP-1961

German Subs in Yankee Waters-James, Henry J-Gotham, NY-1940-208p-WW I

German U-Boat Bunkers Yesterday and Today-by Schmeelke, K.H. & Schmeelke, M.-1999

German U-Boat Losses During World War II-by Niestle' Axel-USNIP-1998-302p-ISBN 1557506418-Details and locations of losses

German U-Boat Crews 1914-1945-by Williamson, Gordon-64p

German War Artists, The-by Weber, John Paul-151p

German Warships of the Second World War-by Lenton HT-MacDonald & Janes-1975   ISBN 0356046613-Details of the entire German wartime fleet as well as the many experimental types, few of which were ever built

German Warships of WW I-by Friedman, Norman-USNIP-1992-ISBN 1557503036

German Warships of WW II-by Ian Allen-1973-168p-A detailed description of Fighting Ships of the German Navy including those ships taken over from other countries and which served as an integral part of the German Navy

German Warships of WW II-Taylor, J.C.-Doubleday & Co-1966

German Warships, 1815-1945-Vol II: U-Boats & Mine Warfare Vessels-by Groner, Erich-1991 256p-ISBN 155750301X-450 Drawings

German, Italian, Japanese U-Boat Casualties-by Great Britain Admiralty-HMSO-1946-35p

Germany's High Sea Fleet in the World War-by Scheer, Reinhardt-Cassell, London-1920-375p

Germany's Last Mission to Japan: The Failed Voyage of U-234-by Scalia, J.M.-USNIP-2000

Geschichte des deutschen U-bootbaus-by Rossler, Eberhard-Lehmann, Munich-1974-448p-88 pictures, 200 tables, 200 plans. ISBN 3763758003-Covers WW I, WW II and present-**History of German Submarine Construction**

Geschichte des U-Boot-krieges 1939-1945-by Pellard, Leonce-Heyne Verlag & Neff, Vienna (1970) 1980-472p-ISBN 3453003810-**The History of the U-Boat War**

Gesunken und Verschollen-by Muller, Wolfgang & Kramer, Reinhard-Menschen & Schiffsschicksale, Ostsee-1945-**Sunken and Missing**-1996 edition, ISBN 3782206657

Ghost Fleet of Truk Lagoon-by Stewart, William H-Montana Pictorial Histories Pub Co-1986

Ghost of the Chimera and the Stowaway-by McLeod-1988

Ghost of War-by Dingman, Roger-USNIP-1997-ISBN 1557501599-The sinking of the Awa Maru and American-Japanese relations 1945-1995

Gli Angeli Senza Ali-by Crepas, A-CB Paravia & C, Torino-1939-The Angels Without Wings

Gli Arditi del Mare Sottomarini Mas Maiali 1940-1943-by Silvani, L-G. de Vecchi, Milano-1972-The Daring Men of the Submarine Sea Torpedo Boat Maiali 1940-1943

Gli Squali del Terzo Reich-by Martinelli, F-G. de Vecchi, Milano-1966-The Sharks of the Third Reich

Global Logistics and Strategy 1940-1943-by Leighton, Richard M & Coakley, Robert W-OCMH 1955

Global Mission-by Arnold, Henry H-Harper & Bros-1949

Glossary of submarine terms (German to English)-by U.S. Portsmouth Naval Shipyard, New Hampshire-1945?-506 leaves

Glow in the Dark-Under the Sea-by Jean Lewis, Eugenie

Go Deep!-Wingate-1985

Go In and Sink-RN captures a U-Boat-Reeman

Golden Horseshoe or Night Raider of the Atlantic-Life of Otto Kretschmer-by Robertson, Terrence-Evan Bros-1955-210p

Good Hunting-by Carr-Hutchinson, London-1940

Grand Scuttle, The-by van der Vat, Dan-USNIP-1986

Graue Wolf-Wilde See-Gray Wolf-Wild Sea-by British Admiralty-Erich Pabel-1973-Aboard the U-124 in WW II plus history of the U-64

Graue Wolfe auf allen Meeren U-VII-by Nowarra, Heinz-Podzun-Pallas-Verlag, Friedbert-1977 48p-ISBN 3790900648-**Grey Wolves to Every See, U-VII**

Graue Wolfe in blauer See-by Alman, Karl-Heyne Verlag, Munchen-1977-316p, 67 photos-ISBN 3453011937-**Grey Wolves in the Blue Sea**-Data on U-Boat ops in the Med

Graveyard of the Atlantic-Shipwrecks of the N. Carolina Coast-by Stick, D-U. of NC Press-1952

Gray Steel and Blue Water Navy-by Cooling, Benjamin F-Archon Books, 1979

Gray Thunder-Confederate Navy-1997-168p

Gray Wolf-Wild Sea-Rastatt/Baden-1973

Great Admirals-by Sweetman, Jack (Ed)-USNIP-1997-576p-ISBN 087021229X-Command at sea, 1587-1945

Great Adventure, The-by Fredericks, Pierce G-EP Dutton, NY-1960

Great Book of Submarines, The-by White, D-1988

Great Crusade, The-A New Complete History of the Second World War-Willmott, HP-The Free Press-1989

Great Lakes First Submarine-by Harris, Patricia AG-Hubbard Co-1982-85p

Great Naval Race, The-by Padfield, Peter-Hart Davies

Great Sea Battles of World War II-Sweetman, Jack-48

Great Sea War, The-by Nimitz, Chester & Potter, EB-Prentice-Hall-1960

Great War At Sea, The-by Hoehling, AA-Galahad Books, NY-1965-336p

Great Weapons of World War II-by Kirk, John G-Bonanza Books, NY-1961-347p

Greatest Anti-Submarine Action of All Wars, The-by Hillyer, RB-1993-283p

Greatest Depths, Probing the Seas to 20,000 feet and below, The-by Soule, Gardner-Macrae Smith Co, Phila-1970-194p

Greenpeace Book of the Nuclear Age-by May, John-Pantheon, NY-1989-378p-ISBN 0679729631-Contains listing of submarine accidents

Grey Seas Under, The-by Mowat, F-Little, Brown & Co.-1958

Grey Wolf, Grey Sea-by Gasaway, E-Ballantine-1970-345p-ISBN 0345338170-U-124 was a very successful U-Boat, sinking 226,946 tons before she was trapped and sunk in April 1943

Grey Wolves of the Sea-by Schiffer-Schiffer Pubs Ltd-1992-ISBN 0887404014

Grosadmiral Karl Donitz-by Busch, Fritz-Otto-Pabel Verlag, Rastatt-1963-80p

Grosse U-Boat Buch, Das-by Francis, Timothy L-Heel Verlag, Konigswinter-1998-94p, 175 photos-ISBN 3893656456-**The Big U-Boat Book**-A history from 1620 to the present

Growler & Grayback: Two of a Kind-by Stumpf, David D-Graphic Enterprises of Marblehead, MA-1996-49p in 5 ½ X 8 ½" format

Guardians of the Sea-by Johnson, Robert E-USNIP-1983

Guerra Negli Abissi-by Nassigh, R-U. Mursia & C, Milano-1971-War in the Depths

Guerrilla Submarines-by Dissette, Edward-Ballantine (Bantam in 1980)-1972-238p-Story of US submarine missions to the Philippines from Feb 43 to Jan 45

Guida ai Sommergibili dalle Origini ad Oggi-by Galuppini, G-A Mondadori, Milano-1985-Guide to Submarines from Origins to Today

Guidance and Control of Ocean Vehicles-by Fossen, Thor I-John Wiley & Sons-1994

Guide for the Classification of Manned Submersibles-American Bureau of Shipping-1968-47p

Guide to the Soviet Navy-by Polmar, Norman & Breyer, Siegfried-USNIP-1977-353p-ISBN 0870212370

Guide to U.S. Naval Vessels-by Shirlaw, David-Self Published-1995-Lexington Media, 1226 E Sunset Dr. #510, Bellingham, WA, 98226

Guides to the Microfilmed Records of the German Navy-1850-1945
#2 by Mulligan, Timothy   National Archives and Records
Administration, Washington D.C.

Gunboat Diplomacy, 1919-1979-by Cable, James-St. Martin's Press-
1981-2nd Ed-204p-Political Applications of Limited Naval
Force

H

H.M. Submarines-by Kemp, Peter K-H. Jenkens-1952-224p

H.M. Submarines in Camera, 1901-1996-by Tall & Kemp-Submarine
design in general or British subs in particular.

H.M. U-Boat-by Drummond, John Dorman-Allen, UK-1958

Haie im Pardies: Der Deutsche U-Boat Krieg im Asiens 43-45-Sharks
in Paradise; The German U-boat war in Asian Waters-
Brennecke, Hans Jochen-Herford, W. Germany-1967

Half Mile Down-by Beebe, Charles W-Sloan & Pearce, NY-1934

Handbook of Ocean and Underwater Engineering-by Myers, John J
and others-McGraw Hill, NY 1969-1070p

Handbook of Sea Floor Sonar Imagery-by Blondel, Philippe &
Murton, Bramley-John Wiley & Sons-1997-ISBN 0471962171

Handbook on Japanese Military Forces: Official Technical Manual-
Compiled by US War Dept-440p

Handbuch fur U-Boot-Kommandanten-by Breyer, Siegfried-Podzun-
Pallas-Verlag, Friedberg-1996-160p-ISBN 379090581X-Reprint
of the original Handbook for Submarine commanders

Handleskrieg mit U-Booten, Der-by Spindler, Arno-Mittler & Sohn Verlag,
Berlin-1932-**The Trade Warfare with U-boats**-5 volumes/rare
Vol 1-Vorgeschichte (Prehistory) 1932
Vol 2-Februar bis September 1915 1933
Vol 3-Oktober 1915 bis January 1917 1934
Vol 4-Februar bis Dezember 1917 1941/1966
Vol 5-Januar bis November 1918 1966

Handels-U-Boot Deutschland-by Kunstmann, Emil-1916?-64p

Handels-U-Boot Deutschland Fahrt Nach Amerike-by Lassen, Ernst-Montanus, Siegen-1916-111p

Hard Lessons Vol 1-by Harms, Harmon E.-ISBN 0944539009

Hearings before the Committee on Naval Affairs...on Submarine Boats-by US Congress-1902-314p

Hearings on H.R. 3980, to allow the obsolete submarine United States Ship Albacore (AGSS-569) to be transferred to the Portsmouth Submarine Memorial Association-USGPO-1983-321p

He's in Submarines Now-by Felson, Henry G-McBride, NY-1942-175p-Sub School/New London

He's in the Sub-busters Now-by Rathbone, Alfred D-McBride, A-1943-224p

Heisenberg's War-by Powers, Thomas-Alred A. Knopf, NY-1993

Heldenkampf unserer U-Boote-by Sanders-Bremen, Friedrich-Askanischer Verlag, Berlin-1918 192p-**The Heroic Struggle of our U-Boats**

Hell At 50 Fathoms-by Lockwood, Charles & Hans Christian Adamson-Chilton-1962-299p

Hell's Angels of the Deep-by Carr, William G-Hutchinson, London-1932-288p-WWI action

Hellcats of the Sea-by Lockwood, Charles & Hans Christian Adamson-Greenberg, NY-1955 335p-The entry into the Sea of Japan.

Hellions of the Deep-by Gannon, Robert-Penn State Press-1996-276p-Development of American Torpedoes in WW II

Her Majesty's Secret Service-by Andrew, Christopher-Viking, NY-1986

Here's To Good Eating-Idaho Falls-1965

Hero in a Bottle-by Walker, Norman H-Rainbow Books, Highland City, FL-1998-The author who served on the 426, 344, 419, 424, 214 tells of his personal war with the bottle.

Hero of the Upholder-by Allaway, Jim-Airlife-UK-1991-191p-Biography
of Britain's best sub driver in WW II

Heroes of Annapolis-by Hatch, Alden-Julian Messner, 1943

Heroes of the Atlantic-by Halstead, Ivor-EP Dutton & Co, NY-1942

High Seas, Naval Passage to an Unchartered World, The-by Owens,
William A (Adm)-USNIP-1995-188p-ISBN 1557506612-The making of the Cold War Naval Policy

Hirschfeld: Story of a U-Boat NCO 1940-1946-by Hirschfeld,
Wolfgang-USNIP-1996 296p-ISBN 1557503729-16 photos-3 maps

His Majesty's Submarines-by Great Britain Admiralty-HM Stationary
Office-1945-64p

Histore Maritime de la Premiere Guerre Mondiale-by Chack, Paul &
Antier-Paris-1969

Histoire Generale de la Guerre Sous-marine 1939-1945-by Peillard,
Leonce-Laffont, Paris-1970

Histoire Mondiale du Sous-Marin-by Antier, Jean-Jacques-Laffont,
Paris-1968-389p

Histoire Sous-Marine de Hommes-by Foex, GA-Laffont, Paris-1964

Historic Naval Ships: Visitors Guide-Historic Naval Ships Association
/printed by USNIP-1995-81p-Lists all ships under care of this
Association including all the Submarines as museum boats

Historic Submarines-by Lipscomb, Frank W-Praeger, NY-1970-35p-
Finely executed color plates begins with the 1898-99 French
Naval, includes submarines of various nations, and ends with
USN atomic Polaris missile submarine USS George Washington

Historical Atlas of the U.S. Navy-by Symonds, Craig-USNIP-2001-
264p, 64 photos, 143 maps-ISBN 1557509840

Historical Bibliography of Sea Mine Warfare-by Patterson, A &
Winters R-National Academy of Sciences-1977-137p

Historical Manuscripts in the Navy Department Library: A Catalog-
by Emery, George-GPO

Historical Review: Boston Naval Shipyard-by Mansfield, George-
Dept. of the Navy-1957

History and Development of Submarine Signals-by Fay, Harold, J-Boston-1912-17p

History of a Fighting Ship-by Kinsella, Adm-USS Ray

History of Canopus-by Sackett, EL-Office of Chief of Naval Operations, Washington-1947

History of Communications-Howeth, Linwood S-GPO-1963-Electronics in the U.S. Navy

History of German submarine warfare, 1914/1918-by Spindler, Arno-History of German submarine warfare, 1914/1918-35leaves

History of Naval Administration-by Paullin, Charles O-USNIP-1968

History of Naval Tactical Thought-by Fioravanzo, Giuseppe-USNIP-1978-251p

History of Rocket Technology-by Miles, Wyundham D-Wayne State U-1964

History of Ships-by Kemp, Peter-Galahad-1979-288p

History of Submarine Medicine in World War II-by Shilling, CW & Kohl JW-New London, Conn.: U.S. Naval Medical Research Laboratory, U.S. Naval Submarine Base-1947-328p

History of Submarine Mining and Torpedoes-by Ehrenkrook, Fraiedrich V-Berlin-1879?

History of the Boston Naval Shipyard 1800-1937-by Hamlin, Paul W-Boston 1948

History of the Confederate States Navy-by Scharf, J. Thomas-Fairfax Press, Baltimore-1887

History of the Bureau of Engineering-by Navy Department-GPO 1922

History of the German General Staff-1657-1945-by Gorlitz, Walter-Praeger-1953

History of the Great War-Naval Operations-by Corbett, Sir Julian-Longmans, UK-1920

History of the Joint Chiefs of Staff in World War II: The War Against Japan-by Hayes, Grace P-USNIP-1982

History of the Norfolk Naval Yard in World War II-by Barksdale, Arthur S-Unpublished-Held by Navy Department Library, Washington, D.C.

History of the Petroleum Administration for War 1941-1945-by Frey, John W-Ide, HC-USGPO-1946

History of the Royal Navy-by Kemp, PK, ed-New York-1969

History of the Second World War-by Liddell Hart, BH-Paragon Books-1979

History of the Second World War-The War Against Japan-by Kirby, SW-London-1957-1969 5Vols

History of the Sulzer Low-Speed Marine Diesel Engine-Sulzer Brothers, Ltd-Winterhur, Switzerland-1984

History of the U.S. Navy-1775-1941-Vol 1-by Love, Robert W-Stackpole Books-1992

History of the U.S. Navy-1942-1991-Vol 2-by Love, Robert W-Stackpole Books-1992

History of the United States Navy-by Knox, Dudley-Putnam-1948-revised ed.

History of the World War-by March, Francis A-Leslie-Judge Co, NY-1921-7 Volumes

History of Torpedo Warfare-by Bradford, Royal-USN Torpedo Station-Newport RI-1882-90p

History of U.S. Submarine Veterans of WW II-Compiled by Bastura, Bernard-Submarine Library & Museum-1981-353p-History of the Organization, letters, memorials, subs on display, poems, books, plank owners, charter members, C&Bylaws, officers and more.

History of United States Naval Operations in World War II-by Morison, Samuel Eliot-Atlantic Little Brown-Boston-1950+
Vol 1-The Battle of the Atlantic Sep 39-May 43
Vol 2-Operations in North African Waters Oct 42-Jun43
Vol 3-The rising Sun in the Pacific 31-Apr 42
Vol 4-Coral Sea, Midway and Submarine Actions May 42-Aug 42
Vol 5-The Struggle for Guadalcanal Aug 42-Feb 43

Vol 6-Breaking the Bismarck's Barrier Jul 42-May44
Vol 7-Aleutians, Gilberts and Marshals Jun42-Apr44
Vol 8-New Guinea and the Marianas Mar 44-Aug 44
Vol 9-Sicily-Salerno-Anzio Jan 43-Jun 44
Vol 10-The Atlantic Battle Won May 43-May 45
Vol 11-The Invasion of France and Germany 44-45
Vol 12-Leyte Jun 44-Jan 45
Vol 13-The Liberation of Philippines, Luzon, Mindanao, the Visayas 44-Aug 45
Vol 14-Victory in the Pacific 45
Vol 15-General Index and Supplement

History of United States Naval Operations: Korea-USGPO-1962

History of US Submarine Operations During WW II-by Roscoe, Theodore-USNIP-1950

History of Warships-by George, James L-USNIP-1997-312p-ISBN 1557503125-From ancient times to the twenty-first century

History of World War II-by Miller, FT-1945-966p

History Under the Sea-by McKee, Alexander-Hutchinson, London, 1968-Dutton, NY-1968 342p

History Under the Sea-by Peterson, Mendel L-Smithsonian, Washington-1965-108p-A handbook for underwater exploration-Also 1969-208p

Hitler and His Admirals-by Martiensen, Anthony-Secker & Warburg, UK-1948-Also: Dutton, NY-1949

Hitler and the Middle Sea-by Ansel, Walter-Duke U Press-1972-514p-German Med. Sea Strategy

Hitler vs. Roosevelt-by Bailey, Thomas A & Ryan, Paul B-Free Press, NY-1979-303p-The undeclared naval war

Hitler in History-by Jackel, Eberhard-Brandeis U. Press-1984

Hitler's Spies-by Kahn, David-Macmillan-1978˙

Hitler's Spies and Saboteurs-by Wighton, Charles and Peis-Henry Hold & Co-1958

Hitler's Naval War-by Bekker, Cajus-Doubleday-1974-400p-The story of Germany's underrated, undermanned naval force that almost won the war. Based on previously held secret documents and photos

Hitler's U-Boat War The Hunters 1939-1942-by Blair, Clay-Random House-1996-809p-ISBN 0394588398-18 Appendixes-Vol 1 of 2- The book was issued in trade paperback in 2000 and in German in 1997. This is the monumental work by Blair who wrote the massive volume Silent Victory.

Hitler's U-Boat War The Hunted 1942-1945-by Blair, Clay-Random House-1998-909p-ISBN 0679457429-Vol 2 of 2. 20 Appendixes and the Bibliography for both volumes is in this book. The book was issued in Trade paperback in 2000. Also in German as Der U-Book-Krieg by Heyne Verlag, Munchen in 1999

Hitting the Enemy A Hard Naval Blow (Dave Darrin After the Mine Layers)-by Hancock, Harrie Irving-Saalfield, Akron-1919-251p

HM Submarines in Camera-Tall, JJ & Kemp, Paul-USNIP-1997-256p- ISBN 155750380X A fascinating collection of 350 photographs, all fully captioned, from the archives of the Royal Navy Submarine Museum, the Imperial War Museum, the Storico Navale in Venice, and private collections gives a graphic view of life in British submarines from the tiny Holland class of Queen Victoria's time to the Vanguard class of the nuclear age

HM U-Boat-by Drummond, John D-WH Allen, London-1958-228p-U- 570 was captured, and operated as H.M.S. Graph

HMS Thule Intercepts-by Mars, Alastair-Elek Books-1956-256p

Holland submarine boats: hearings before the Committee on Naval Affairs, House of Representatives: statements of Mr. Charles E. Creecy-USGPO-77p

Holland submarine torpedo boat: Mr. Daniel presented the following papers on the military value of the Holland submarine boat and the need of additional boats of the Holland type-32p

Hollenmaschine im U-Boot, Die-by Sauer, Herbert-A. Scherl G.m.b.H., Berlin-1928-145p-**The Infernal machine in the U-boat**

Hollywood Goes to War-by Koppes, Clayton & Black, Gregory-The Free Press, NY-1987

Hostile Waters-by Huchthausen, Peter & Kurdin, Igor & White, Robin A-St. Martin's Press-1997-303p-ISBN 0312169280-16 p photos-The explosion and sinking of the Soviet Yankee K-219 off Bermuda in 1986-Movie was made from the book

How Atomic Submarines are Made-by Cooke, David C-Dodd, Mead, NY-1956 (revised 1967)-64p

How Do Submarines Dive?-Random House Value-1991

How the Laconia Sank-by Gibbons, Floyd-Daughaday, Chicago-1917

How They Won the War in the Pacific: Nimitz and His Admirals-by Hoyt, Edwyn-Weybright and Talley, 1970

How To Locate Anyone Who is or has been in the Military-by Johnson, Richard-Reference Books Annual-1990-170 pp.

HR.MS 0 21 & de kat met negen levens-by Claes, Wijnand-Van Soeren & Co, Amsterdam-1997 ISBN 9068810766-Dutch-World War II diary of a crewmember of the Dutch submarine O 21

HR. MS.O-22-by Ort, H.M.-Van Soeren & Co, Amsterdam-1995-ISBN 9068810561-Report about the Dutch submarine "O-22", which was lost in 1940 and found in 1993

HR.MS. K XVII en Hr.MS O 16-by van Royen, Dr. P.C.-Van soeren & Co, Amsterdam-1997-ISBN 9068810758-Dutch-The loss of two Dutch submarines K XVII and O 16 in the South China Sea 1941

Human Factors in Undersea Warfare-National Research Council-1949

Human Mechanism and the Submarine, The-USNIP-1940

Hunter-Killer US Jeep Carries vs U-Boats-by Y'Blood, William T-USNIP-1983

Hunter-Killer Submarines-by Rawlinson, J. Hunter-Rourke Corp-48p

Hunters and the Hunted-by Brennecke, Hans Joachim-Norton, NY-1957-320p-A dramatic account of the U-Boats of WW II by a former German naval officer. This book reports many very unusual situations and circumstances encountered during the U-Boat war

Hunters and the Hunted, The Italian Navy-by Cocchia, Aldo-USNIP-1958-179p-The author was Chief of Staff at the Italian submarine base at Bordeaux. He was much involved in the sea war in the Mediterranean

Hunters of the Deep-The New Faces of War-Time-Life-1992-ISBN 0809486385

Hunting Submarine, The-by Trenowden, Ian-Kimber, London-1974-224p-The fighting life of HMS Tally-Ho, a T-class submarine that took a heavy toll on enemy shipping in the Malacca Straight between 1943-45, which is an area considered, at the time, to be too shallow for effective submarine action.

Hunting the German Shark-by Whitaker, Herman-Century, NY-1918-310p

Hut Six Story, The-Breaking the Enigma Codes-by Welchman, Gordon-McGraw-Hill-1982

I

I Corari degli Abissi-by Thomas, L-A. Salani, Firenze-1932-The Corsairs of the Abysses

I Found Israel's Atom Bomb Factory-by Kittredge, George W-Schooner Bay Printing, Rockport, ME-2000-320p-A unique book with very little to do with the title. The author commanded 3 submarines and after retirement started building one-man midget subs.

I Lupi e L'Ammiraglio-by Franck, W-Baldini & Castoldi, Milano-1959-The Wolves and the Admirals

I Mezzi d'Assalto-by USSM-USSM, Rome-1972/1992-The Means of Assault

I Mezzi d'Assalto della marina Italiana-by Brauzzi, A-Rivista Marittima, Rome-1991-The Means of Assault of the Italian Navy

I Nostri Sommergibili Durante la Guerra 1915-1918-by Ministero Marina, Italy-1933-331p-Launchings during the war 1915-1918

I Sank the Royal Oak-by Prien, Gunther-Grays Inn Press, UK-1954-196p

I Sank the Yorktown at Midway-by Tanabe, Yabachi-USNIP-1963
I Seek My Prey in the Waters-by Dudley-Gordon, Tom-Doubleday-1943
I Sommergibili dell' Asse-by U. Degli Uberti-K Kiel-La Verita, Rome-1941-Axis Submarines
I Sommergibili della II Guerra Mondiale-by Bagnasco, Erminio-E Albertelli, Parma-1973-Submarines of the Second World War
I Sommergibili della Seconda Guerra Mondiale-by Bagnasco, Ermino-Albertelli, Parma-1973 310p-Submarines of all nations in WW II
I sommergibili in Mediterraneo-by USMM-USMM, Rome-1972-Submarines in the Mediterranean

I Sommergibili Italiani 1895-1962-by Pollina, Paolo-Rome-1963-300p-Revised by Cocchia, Aldo
I Sommergibili Negli Oceani-by USMM-USSM, Rome-1976-Submarines in the Ocean
I Was There-by Leahy, William D-McGraw-Hill-1950
I'm Alone-by Randell, Capt. Jack-Bobbs-Merrill-1930 317p
I-Boat Captain-by Orita, Zenji & Joseph D Harrington-Major Books-1976-317p-The author, a Japanese submarine Captain tells of the exploits of his colleagues during four years of war
I.D. New Tales of Submarine War-by Masters, David-Eyre & Spottiswoode, NY-1935-296p Research into Lloyd's of London records and interviews with survivors
Ideas and Weapons-by Holley, IB-Archon Books-1971
Ik Nader Ongezien-by Jalhay, P.C.-De Bataafsche Leeuw, Amsterdam-1997-ISBN 9067074470-The submarines of the Royal Netherlands Navy, 1906-1966
Il Battello Sottomarino-by Giorli, Ezio-Tipografia Sociale, Rome-1893-24p
Il Battello Subacqueo, La sua evoluz. attrav. gli scritti della rivista marittima-by Turrini, A-Rivista Marittima, Rome-1992-The

Underwater Boat, Its Evolution through the Writings in the Maritime Review

Il Caso Laconia-by Brennecke, J-Baldini & Castoldi, Milano-1961-The Laconia Case

Il Caso del Laconia-by Peillard, L-Garzanti, Milano-1963-The Case of the Laconia

Il Comandante Salvatore Todaro-by Boscolo, A-G. Volpe, Rome-1970-Commander Salvatore Todaro

Il Delfino Dorato-by Scardaccione, A-Schena, Fasano-1988-The Gilded Dolphin

Il Dolore sul Mare-by Darkling, L-Italianissima, Genoa-1922-The Anguish on the Sea

Il Lupo del Mediterraneo-by Von Moraht-O. Marangoni, Milano-1939-The Wolf of the Mediterranean

Il Mistero dei Sottomarini Atomici-by Solmi, A-A Mondadori, Milano-1981-The Mystery of Atomic Submarines

Il Mistero di Scapa Flow-by Korganoff, A-U. Mursia & C, Milano-1972-The Mystery of Scapa

Il Pericolo Sottomarino-by Jellicoe, E-Ist Polig. dello Stato, Rome-1936-The Submarine Danger

Il Ritorno dello Scire-by Vanni, P-Progresso, Firenze-1985-The Return of the Scire

Il Sommergibile-by Vainigli, L-Moderna, La Spezia-1954-The Submarine

Il Sommergibile Atropo-by Maraghini, G-Ardita, Rome-1934-The Submarine Atropo

Il Sommergibile F.7-by Falangola, Amm-Ardita, Rome-1933-The Submarine F-7

Il Sommergibile Spiegato al Popolo-by Guglielmotti, L-Libreria del Littorio, Rome-1928-The Submarine explained to the people

Il Sottomarino el la Guerra Navale-Giorli, E-L. Olivia, Milano-1915-Located in Italian Sub School-The Submarine and Naval Warfare

Il Sottomarino U.C. 55-by Sauer, H-O Marangoni, Milano-1939-The Submarine UC 55

Il Terrore sui Mari-by Valentiner, M-Fratelli Treves, Milno-1936-The Terror on the Seas

Il Toro di Scapa Flow-by Franck, W-Baldini & Castoldi, Milano-1960-The Bull of Scapa Flow

Illustrated Guide Modern Submarines-by Miller-1983

Illustrated History of the Submarine, The-by Horton, Edward-Doubleday-1974-160p

Im Kleinst-U-Boot-by Schulz, Werner-Brandenburgisches Verlagshaus, Berlin-1995-215p-ISBN 3894880856-Aboard midget submarines

Im Kustenvorfeld-by Ruge, Friedrich-Lehmann Verlag, Munchen-1974-143p-Coastal Battlefield

Im U-boot durch die Weltmeere-by Schulz, Paul-Velhagen & Glasing, Blielefeld, Leipzig-1931 192p-By U-boat through the world's oceans

Imperial and Royal Austro-Hungarian Navy-by Sokol, AE-USNIP-1968-172p

Imperial Japanese Navy-by Dull, Paul-USNIP-1978-402p-A Battle History 1941-1945 The story of the war at sea from the viewpoint of the Japanese

Impiego del SMG nella Guerra al Traffico oceanico-by Sez, Tattica-1942-Employment of the Submarine in the War Against Ocean Traffic

In Den Tiefen der Meere-Taillez, Philippe-Ullstein, Wien-1956-213p

In der Alarmkoje von U35-by Fechter, Hans-Ullstein, Berlin-1918-151p

In Fondo al Mare Impresa del C.3-by Turati, N-G. Biancardi, Lodi-1948-In the Depth of the Sea Exploits of the C#

In Full Flight-by Spooner, Anthony-Macdonald-1965

In Harm's Way: American Seapower and the 21st Century-by Ullman, Harlan K-Barteby Press, Silver Spring, MD-271p

In Memoria dello S.M. ed Equipaggio del SMG S Veniero-by Darkling, L-Rovv. Gen. dello Stato, Rome-1925-In memory of the Captain and Crew of the submarine San Veniero

In Peril on the Sea-by Bell, Robert W & Lockerbie, Bruce-Doubleday-1984-284p-ISBN 038518378X-20 Days Adrift after a U-Boat Strike

In Pursuit of Freedom-by Bishop, Jack-Leo Cooper-1977-126p-The author escaped from a sinking submarine and was imprisoned in Italy. He escaped, was recaptured and sent to Germany

In the Wake of Submarine Catastrophes-by Bukan, SP-Guild of Masters, Moscow-1992-ISBN 5851820012-In Russian

Increase in the Enemy Submarine Threat to U.S. Submarines During, The-by U.S. Fleet, Submarine Operations Research Group-1944-24p

Incredible Victory-by Lord, Walter-Hamish Hamilton-1968

Index to All Japanese Naval Vessels ONI41-42-Office of Naval Intelligence, Dept of Navy-Reprinted USNIP-1987

Index to World War II submarines, their patrols, commanders, records and final disposition: a statistical record of World War II commanders and submarines, includes dates, tonnage sunk and disposition of submarine-by Hertig, Norman K-1996-98p

Industrial America in the World War: The Strategy Behind the Line, 1917-1918-Houghton Mifflin Co, Boston-1923

Industrial Mobilization for War: History of the War Production Board and Predecessor Agencies-by Fesler, James W-Civilian Production Administration-1947

Infernal Machines-Confederate Subs and Mine Warfare-by Perry, Milton F-LSU U. Press-1965-231p-A concise but comprehensive account of the design, manufacture and use of mines, torpedoes, and sabotage weapons

Influence Of Sea Power in World War II-by Puleston, WD-Yale U. Press, New Haven-1947-310p

Influence of Sea Power on History, The-by Mahn, Alfred T-Little, Brown & Co-1890

of the German U-Boat battles of WW II-First published by Holt in 1969

Iron Cross-by Williamson, Gordon-Blandford Press-1984-176p-164 photos

Isaac Peral: La Tragedia del Submarino Peral-by Perez, Dionisio-Madrid-1935-186p

Istoriia Russkoi Armii I Flota-by Grishinsky, AS & Nkiolsky, VP-Moscow-1911-15 vol

Italian Navy in World War II-by Bragadin, Marc A-USNIP-1957-380p

Italian Sea-Power and the Great War-by Hurd, Archibald, Spicer-Constable, London-1918-124p

Italian Warships of World War II-by Fraccaroli, Aldo-1969-204p

J

Ja Het Moest-by Froma, Tonny-Bonneville, Bergen-1997-ISBN 9073304547 -Dutch-Personnel loses of the Dutch submarine service during World War II

Jack Speak-Pussers Rum Guide to Naval Slang-by Jolly, Rick-Palamando Press, UK-1995

Jagd auf de Woelfe-by Robertson, Terence-1960-224p, 25 photos-British ASW activity-**Hunt for the Wolves**-The story of Captain Walker, RN a U-Boat hunter

Jagd im Atlantik-by Busch, Harald-Gutersloh, 1943-**Hunting in the Atlantic**

Jager der sieben Meere-by Kurowski, Franz-Motorbuch Verlag, Stuttgart-1994-508p, 150 photos-ISBN 3613016338-Biographies of 22 Commanders. **Hunters of the seven seas**

Jager Gejagte Deutsche U-Boote, 1939-1945-by Brennecke, Jochen-Koehlers, Herford Germany-1956-434p

Jager im Weltmeer-by Buchheim, Lothar-Gunther-Berlin-1996-ISBN 3455111726-**Hunter at Sea**-Originally published in 1943

Jager im Weltmeer-Hunters on the World's Oceans-by Suhrkamp, Berlin-1943

Jager und Gejagte-by Brennecke, Jochen-Ullstein-Verlag, Berlin-1999-672p-42 photos-ISBN 354824534X-The Hunters and the Hunted in English version-

Jaken pa U-Batar-by Noyes, Alfred-Lundberg & Olzon, Stockholm-1916-79p

Janes Combat Simulations: 688(I) Hunter/Killer-Electronic Arts-1997-234p-Instruction Book for the computer game

Janes Fighting Ships-Janes Information Group-Began 1898 and produces annually since 1901

Janes Fighting Ships of WW II-Military Press-1989-320p-Statistical information about tonnage, ordnance, flags, dimensions, of more than 6000 ships. Over 100 photographs and drawings.

Janes Fighting Ships Recognition Manual-by Faulkner, Keith-1994-633p-Complete basic data, dimensions, weapons, systems, and aircraft. Includes detailed line diagrams and full page photographs of each class

Janes Pocket Book of Naval Armament-by Archer, Denis, ed-Macdonald & Janes, London, 1976

Janes Pocket Book of Submarine Development-by Moore, John E-Collier Books-1976-240

Janes Special Report, Maritime communications Electronic Warfare Systems-by Janes Information Group

Janes Underwater Warfare Systems-Published yearly

Janes Underwater Warfare Systems-1992-1993-318p-600 items from 168 manufacturers of torpedoes, mines, depth charges, remote operating vehicles, with full technical details, diagrams and close-up photographs

Janes Underwater Warfare Systems-by Watts, Anthony-Janes-1994

Janes Warship Recognition Guide-by Falkner, Keith-Harper Collins, Glasgow-1996-541p-ISBN 0004709810-5"x7" Handbook showing all Classes of ships worldwide and 1 picture from each class. 63 submarine pages

Japan At War: An Oral History-by Cook, Haruko Taya-New Press, NY-1992

Japan's Economy in War & Reconstruction-by Cohen, Jerome B-U. of Minn. Press-1949

Japan's First Submarines-by Barnes, Robert H-USNIP-1943

✓ **Japan's Imperial Conspiracy**-by Bergamini, D-Wm. Morrow, NY-1971

Japan's Undersea Carriers-by Long, John E-USNIP-1950

Japan's War-by Hoyt, Edwin P-McGraw Hill-1986-

Japanese Merchant Ship Recognition Manual-ONI 208-J-Office of Naval Intelligence, Dept. of Navy-1942

✗ **Japanese Naval Vessels at the End of War (II)**-by Fukui, Shizuo-WE, Greenwich-1970 edition reprint of 1947 version-225p-Author was an officer in the IJN during WW II and later an officer in the Japanese Self Defense Force

Japanese Naval Vessels of WW II-by Baker, AD-Arms & Armour-1987

Japanese Navy at the End of World War 2-by Fukui, Shizuo-We-New Greenwich, Ct-1970

✓ **Japanese Navy in World War II In the Words of Former Japanese Naval Officers**-by Evans, DC-USNIP-1969, 1986

✓ **Japanese Navy in World War Two**-by O'Connor, Raymond-USNIP-1969-192p

✓ **Japanese Submarine Force and WW II**-by Boyd, Carl & Akihiko Yoshida-USNIP-1996-272p-An appraisal of the shortcoming of Japanese submarines in World War II which draws on research in recently declassified materials as well as secret Japanese radio messages during the war. the authors discuss the technical development of the Japanese submarine, its weapons, equipment, personnel, and share support and analyze various successes and failures of these submarines. Includes lists of Japanese submarine losses, biographies of key officers, specially commissioned maps and rare illustrations

✓ **Japanese Submarine Losses to Allied Submarines in WWII**-by Miller, Vernon J-Merrian Press-1999-36p-ISBN 1576381617

Japanese Submarine Tactics-by Torisu, Kennosuke-USNIP-1961

Japanese Warships of WW II-by Watts, Anthony-Doubleday-1970

Japanese WWII Naval Records, Microfile of-At U.S. Naval Historical Center, Washington D.C.

Jennifer Project-Glomar Explorer, Russia, Intelligence-by Burleson, Clyde-Texas A&M-1997 179p-ISBN 0890967644

Jesse James of the Java Sea, The-USS Seawolf SS197 in WW II-by Carmer, Carl-Farrar & Rinhard-1945-119p

Jimmy Carter: American Moralist-by Morris, Kenneth-U. of GA Press-1996-321p-A biography of the President with references to his selection to the Naval Academy and his selection to the Nuclear Power program and interaction with Rickover

John P. Holland-by Morris, Richard-Arno Press-1980-also USNIP 1966

John P. Holland 1841-1914-by Morris, Richard K-USNIP-1966-211p

Journal of Submarine Commander Von Forstner-by Forstner, George G-Houghton Mifflin-1917-135p

Justice At Nuremberg-by Conot, Robert E-Harper & Row-1983-ISBN 006015117X

K

K. und K. Korvettenkapitan George Ritter von Trapp-by Schomaekers, Gunter-H. Ruhl-1964 84p-

K Boats, The-by Everitt, Don-Harrap, UK & Holt, Rinehart-1963-206p-Story of British WW I submarines and their curse

K-Men-German Frogmen and Midget Subs-by Bekker, Cajus (pseud)-William Kimber, London-1955-202p-Also G. Mann, London 1973

Kaigun: Strategy, Tactics, and Technology in the Imperial Japanese Navy, 1887-1941-by Evans, David C-USNIP-1997

Kaigun Suiraishi-by Oyabi, Shizuo-Tokyo,-1979-Torpedoes of the Imperial Japanese Navy--in Japanese

Kaiten Weapon, The-Yokoto, Yutaka & Harrington, Joseph-Ballantine Books-1962-256p

Kameraden auf See, Sqischen Minen und Torpedoes -by Lohman, Walter-1943-**Shipmates at Sea, Between Mines and Torpedoes**

Kameraden zur See-by Pfefferle, Ernst-1966-13 volumes-Author served on a minesweeper-Every volume contains U-boat info

Kampf um die Nordsee, Der-by Bathe, Rolf-G. Stalling, Oldenburg-1941-310p-**The Battle of the North Sea**

Kampf und Untergang der Deutschen U-Boot-Waffe-by Koop, Gerhard-Bernard & Graefe Verlag, Berlin-1998-250p-ISBN 3763759808-**Struggle and Downfall of the German U-boat Arm**

Kampf und Untergang der Kriegsmarine-by Bekker, Cajus (pseud)--A Sponholtz, Hannover-1953-278p, 172 photos-**Defeat at Sea**

Kapmffeld Mittelmeer-by Kurowski, Franz-Ullstein-Verlag, Berlin-1999-394p-ISBN 3548244807-**Battlefield Mediterranean**

Kangaroo Express-by Flanagan, Richard-RJL Express Publications-1997-174p-ISBN 0965999505-The epic story of the submarine USS Growler SS 215 with input from the XO who took the boat after Cdr. Gilmore's "Take her Deep" command and lost his life. Also recollections by skipper Arnold Schade

Kapitanleutnant Otto Steinbrinck-by Herzog, Bodo-Ruhl, Krefeld-1963-233p

Kapitanleutnant Otto Weddigen und Seine Waffe-Weddigen, Otto E-Marine-dank-Verlage, Berlin-1915

Kapitanleutnant Schepke erzahlt-Schepke Narrates-by Fuhren, Franz & Wilhelm Kohler-1943

Kapn Kolschbach-by Kolschbach, Otto-Koehler Verlag, Hamburg-1958-223p-**Captain Kolschbach**

Karl Doenitz: Der Grossadmiral-by Gorlitz, Walter-Musterschmidt-1972-94p-ISBN 3788100699

Keepers of the Sea-A Look at the Whole Navy-by Maroon, Fred & Beach, Edward-USNIP-1983-256p-ISBN 0870212818-218 Photos

Key to Victory-British Sea Power in WW II-by Kemp, Lt Cmdr PK-Little, Brown-1957-383p

Killer Subs-by Hirsch, Phil-Pyramid, NY-1965-9 stories

Killing Time, The-The U-Boat War 1914-1918-by Gray, Edwyn-Schribner, NY-1972-280p This book pays particular attention to the moral aspect of German submarine warfare as well as the strategic value of the underwater arm and the attitudes of different U-boat commanders.

Kincaid of the Seventh Fleet-by Wheeler, Gerald E.-USNIP-1996-ISBN 1557509360

Klaar voor onderwater-by Wytema, M.S.-Andires Blitz, Amsterdam-1936-The voyage around the world of the Dutch submarine K XVIII

Klein U-Boote im Ensatz 1939-1945-by Kemp, Paul-Motorbuch Verlag, Stuttgart-1999-279p ISBN 36113019361-Manned torpedoes and midget U-Boats in action 1939-1945

Knight's Cross Holders of the Wehrmacht/U-Boat Service-by Kurowski, Franz-Schiffer-1995-280p-150 photos-Capsule biographies including dates of birth, awarding of the various Knight's Cross grades, and other particulars to rank and career. Photo of each included.

Kola Run, The-Arctic Convoys 41-45-by Campbell, Ian & MacIntyre, Donald-Frederick Muller

Konstruktsiia Podvodnykh Lodok-by Pravdin, AA-Moscow-1947-282p-Construction of submarine boats

Konvoi-by Middlebrook, Martin-Ullstein-Verlag, Berlin-1995-296p-ISBN 3548235344-About the attacks on Convoys SC-122 and HX-229 in March 1943

Korabli Morskikh Glubin-by Sherr, SA-Voennoe Izdatelstvo, Moscow-1955-302p

Krieg der "Grauen Wolfe"-by Busch, Fritz-Otto-Pabel Verlag, Rastatt-1994-108p-ISBN 3811860798-**War of the Grey Wolves**, about the patrols of U-110

Krieg Unter Wasser-by Jung, HAK-Stalling, Oldenburg-1939-222p

Krieg Unter Wasser-by Kurowski, Franz-Econ Verlag, Dusseldorf-1979-400p-ISBN 3704340626-**War under water**

Krieg zur See 1939-1945, Der-by Rohwer, Jurgen-Urbes, Grafelfing von Munchen-1992-192p ISBN 3924896283-**The War at Sea 1939-1945**

Konvoi 1943-by Forester, C.S.-by Hase, Georg Oskar-v. Hase & Hoehler, Leipzig-1941-416p

Kriegsmarine erobert Norwegens fjorde-by Hase, Georg Oskar-v. Hase & Koehler, Leipzig-1941-416p-**The Kriegsmarine conquers the Norwegian fiords**

Kriegsmarine, Die-by Busch, Fritz Otto-Raumbild-Verlag O. Schonstein K.-G., Munchen-1942-83p-**The German Navy**

Kriegstagebuch der Seekriegsleitung-by German Naval Staff Diaries of the Operations Division-Also known as KTB-1/sk1-See War Diary of the Operations Division of the German Naval Staff

Kreigstagebuch des Oberkommandos der Wehrmacht-by Schramm, Percy E-Frankfurt-1963-3 Vol

Kriegswende Dezember 1941-by Rohwer, J & Jackel, T-Bernard & Graefe-1984

KTB U 1-U 50-by Ritschel, Herbert-Herbert Ritschel, Korntal-1996-426p-Edited patrol reports of these boats

KTB U 51-U 99-by Ritschel, Herbert-Herbert, Ritschel-2000-536p-War Diaries of U-51-U-99-Second volume of Ritschel's edition of the war diaries.

Kurs Amerika-by Rink, Hermann-Berlin-1943-**Course America**

Kurs Atlantik-by Moller, Eberhard-Motorbuch Verlag, Stuttgart-1995-286p, 140 photos-**Course Atlantic: U-Boat development to 1945**

Kurs Murmansk-by Blond, Georges-Stalling Verlag, Hamburg-200p-**Course Murmansk**

Kurs West-by Tarrant, V.E.-Motorbuch Verlag, Stuttgart-1993-276p-**Course West**-U-boat activity in both wars

L

L'Aventure Sous-Maraine-by Diole', Philippe-Michel, Paris-1951-267p

L'Angoisse des Veilles sousmarines-by Guierre, Maurice CL-Floury, Paris-1919 22p

L' Avventurosa Crociera Altantica del SMG. A Barbarigo-by Vingiana, G-A. Mondadori, Verona-1942-The Adventurous Atlantic Cruise of the Submarine A. Barbaigo

L'Enigme des sous-Marins Sovietiques-by Huan, Claude-France-Empire, Paris-1959-297p

L'Epopee Kamikaze-by Millot, Bernard-Robert Laffont-Paris-1970

L'Impegno Navale Italiano durante La Guerra Civile Sagnola 1936-1939-by Bargoni, Franco-Officio Storico Della Marina Militare, Rome, 1992-Italian

L'Inferno new Sommergibioli-by Spiegel, V-O. Marqngoni, Milano-1939-The Inferno in Submarines

L'Insidia Sottomarino-by Bravetta, E-U. Hoepli, Milano-1931-The Insidious Submarine

L'Organizzazione della Marina Durante il Conflitto-by USMM-USSM Rome-1972-1978-The Organization of the Navy During the War

L'Ultima Missione del sommergibile "Da Vinci"-by Mattisini, F-USMM, Rome-1989-The Final Mission of the submarine Da Vinci

La Affaire du Laconia-by Peillard, Leonce-Laffont, Paris-1988-ISBN 2221034392

La Base navale du havre et la Guerre Sous-Marine Secrete en Manche-by Chatelle, Albert-Editions-Medicis, Paris-1949-261p

La Bataille de L'Atlantique-by Peillard, Leonce-Laffont, Paris-1975-2 volumes

La Battaglia dell' Atlantico-by Peillard, L-Mondadori, Verona-1976-The Battle of the Atlantic

La Chasse aux Mines-by Great Britain Admiralty-HMSO-1943-62p

La Decouverte Sous-Marine-by Houot, Georges-Paris-1958

La Dratique Histoire des Sous-marins Nucleaires Sovietiques-by Giltsov, Lev-Robert Laffont-Paris-1992

La Ferre Bara degli Eroi-by Vicoli, F-Toscana, Firenze-1929-The Iron Bier of the Heroes

La Flotta Sovietica Oggi, Sottomarini e Sommergibili-by Martino, E-Intyrama, Genova-1967-The Soviet Fleet today, Submarines and Submersibles-

La Guerre de Mines-by Brasseur, Pierre-Nizet, Paris-1939-155p

La Guerre Moderne Sur Terre Dans Les Airs et Sous Les eaux-by Barzini, Luigi-Payot, Paris-1917-263p

La Guerra negli Abissi-by Michelsen, Amm-Milano-1933-The War in the Abysses

La Guerra Sottomarina-by Spiess, J-O Marangoni, Milano-1932-Undersea Warfare

La Guerra Subacquea il Sottomarino e il Potere Marittimo-by Hezlet, AR-Sansoni, Firenze-1969-The Undersea War, the Submarine and Maritime Power

La Guerre Sur Mare 191401918 al Commercio con I Smg-by Spindler, A-3 volumes-Polig. del Stato, Rome-1934-36-The War on the Sea 1914-1918 Against Commerce by Submarine

La Guerre Sur Mer, Strategie et Tactique-by Darrieus, Gabriel-Paris-1907-Pub. by USNIP in 1908 as War on the Sea: Strategy and Tactics

La Guerre Sous-Marine et les Torpedoes-by Daudenart, LG-Muquardt, Brussels-1872-93p

La Guerre Sous les Mers-by Delage, Edmond-Grasset, Paris-1934-253p

La Marina dall 8/9/1943 alla Fine del Conflitto-by USSM-USSM, Rome-1971-The Navy from 9/8/1943 to the end of the War

La Marina Italiana il 10 Giugno 1940-by Brauzzi, A-Rivista Marittima, Rome-1980-The Italian Navy on June 10, 1940

La marina Italiana nella Grande Guerra-by Vallecchi Editore, Firenze-8 volumes

La Marine Modern, ancienne histoire et questions neuves-by Bertin, LE-Flammarion, Paris-1914

La Nave Sommergibili-by Guglielmotti, Leandro-Milan-1931-297p

La Nave Subacquea-by Campagna, Enzo-Hoepli, Milan-1915-346p-Located in Italian Sub School-The Undersea Ship

La Navigation Sous-marine, geralites et historique-by Gaget, Maurice-Cberanger, Paris-1901-472p

La Navigation Sous-Marine-by Pesce, GL-Paris-1906

La Navigation Sous-marine-Pre WW I-by Radiguer, Charles-O. Doin et Fils-Paris-1911-361p-A technical overview of the art of submarining in the pre-World War I era, including a French-English bibliography

La Navigation Sous-marine a Travers les Siecles-by Delpeuch, Maurice-Juven, Paris-1902-450p

La Premmiere Attaque De Sous-Marin-by Protopapas, P-1933

La Storia del Siluro 1860-1936-by Whitehead-Whitehead, Fiume-1936-The Story of the Torpedo

La Tradedia dei Sommergibile-by Hashagen, E-Fratelli Treves, Milano-1935-The Tragedy of the Submarines

La Voce del Fondo-by Milanesi, G-Alfieri & Lacroix, Milano-1942-The Voice of the Deep

Laconia Affair, The-U-156-Peillard, Leonce-Putnam, NY-1963-270p-Also Bantam Books-1983-232p-ISBN 0553230700

Lagevortrage des Oberbehehlshabers der Kriegsmarine-1939-1945-by Wagner, Gerhard-University Press of New England-1981

Largest Event: A Library of Congress Resource Guide for the Study of World War II-GPO-1994-151p-ISBN 0160431336-Provides a narrative of World War II and its antecedents. Includes Library of Congress Resources Notes which describe where materials relating to various phases of World War II can be located in the Library of Congress' collections

Last Command-by Gray, Edwyn-1977-Fiction

Last Cruise, The-USS Cochino-by Lederer, William J-Sloane-1950-110p-includes sailing lists of the Cochino and the Tusk

Last Days of the German Fleet-by Fiewald, Ludwig-Constable, UK-1932-318p

Last Patrol, The-WW II Fleet Submarines-by Holmes, Harry-Airlife Pub. Ltd, UK-1994-212p-Distributed in US by USNIP-124 B&W photos-Republished by USNIP 2001

Last Voyage of the Luisitania-by Hoehling, Adolph-Holt, NY-1956-& Madison Books-1996 255p

Last Year of the Kriegsmarine, The-May 1944-May 1945-by Tarrant, VE-USNIP-1994-256p-ISBN 1557505101-59 b/w photos-Summarizes the final 12 months of the German Navy, as it was forced to rely on small battle units—E-boats, U-Boats and a bizarre assortment of semi-suicide weapons—to attack the vast invasion of shipping off Normandy

Laughing Cow, The-by Metzler, Jost-Kimber, UK-1955-217p-A U-Boat Captain's Story

Law and Custom of the Sea, The-Smith, HA-Praeger, NY-1950 (2nd edition)

Le Adventure di un Marinaio di Betasom-by Frandi, M-Erga, Genova-1992-The Adventures of a Sailor of Betasom

Le Blocus et la Guerre Sous-Marins 1914-1918-by Laurens, Adolphe-Colin, Paris-1924-215p

Le Cuirasse et Ses Ennemis Sous-marins-by Blanchon, Georges-Berger-Levrault, Paris-1913-299p

Le Goubet devant L'opinion publique-by Gautier, Emile-L. Vanier-Paris-1891

Le Mystere de Scapa Flow-by Korganoff, Alexandre-Arthaund, Paris-1969-271p

Le Navi-by Marulli J-Lega Navale Italiana-1928-Location in Italian Submarine School-

Leaders and personalities of the Third Reich Vol 1-by Hamilton, Charles-480p-876 photos

Leaders and Personalities of the Third Reich Vol 2-by Hamilton, Charles-480p-724 photos

Leadership and Indecision:American War Planning and Policy Process, 1937-1942-by Lowenthal, Mark M-Garland Pub., NY-1988

Lecture on Drifting and Automatic Movable Torpedoes, Submarine Guns and Rockets-by Barber, Francis M-USN Torpedo Station-Newport-1875-40p

Lecture on Submarine Boats-by Barber, Francis M-USN Torpedo Station-Newport-1874-39p

Legends of the Outer Banks-Whedbee, John F-John F Blair, Winston-Salem-1966

Les Bateaux Noirs-by Louzeau, Bernard-Chourg noz Paris-1992-French-A collection of nice photographs of recent French submarines with little text

Les Bateaux Sous-Marins-by Forest, Fernand-Dunod, Paris-1900-Two Vols

Les Bateaux Sous-Marins et les Submersibles-by Equevilley, Raymond-Gauthier-Villars, Paris-1902-164p

Les Decouvertes Sous-Marines Modernes-by Doukan, Gilbert-Payot, Paris-1954-329p

Les Loups de L'Amiral-by Noli, Jean-Fayard, Paris-1970-A story of German submarines in WWII

Les sous-marin, roi del la mar-by Toudouze, Georges G-Paris-1949

Les Sous-Marine-by Beckmann, A-Payot, Paris-1931-175p

Les Sous-Marine a Travers les Siecles-by Delpeuch, Maurice-Paris-1907-A complete history of submarines from the beginnings to 1907

Les sous-Mariniers-by Antier, Jean-Jacques-J. Grancher-Paris-1976-A story of the submarine crews from various nations over two world wars

Les Sous-Marins-Memoirs of Adm. Daveluy-by Clerc-Rampal, G-Hachette-Paris-1919-Historical and technical overview of submarines

Les Sous-Marins-by Darrieus, Gabriel-Academie de Marine, Paris-1927-143p-An overview on submarines, their past and future, by French experts of the time

Les Sous-Marins-by Korganoff, A-Hachette, Paris-1963

Les Sous-Marins-by La Revue Maritime-Paris-1955

Les Sous-Marins-by Roquebert-Toulon-1924-A secret report commissioned by the French Navy Department with a view to deriving lessons from WWI submarine activity. Good descriptions of French, British, American, Italian and German submarines

Les Sous-Marins Allemands-by Laubeuf, Alfred, M-Delagrave, Paris-1920-40p

Les Sous-Marins et la Prochaine Guerre Navale-by Noalhat, H-Berger-Levrault & Co, Paris-1903-246p

Les Sous-Marins et Submersibles-by Laubeuf, Max-Delagrave, Paris-1917-112p

Les Sous-Marins Francais 1945-1972-by Le Tallec, Jean-GL Valles, Paris-1992-Characteristics and photographs with little text

Les Sous-Marins Francais des Origines-by Masson, Henri-Editions de la Cite', Parris-1981-This is a new version of the 1959, Du Nautilus (1800) au Redoutable

Les Sous-Marins de la France Libre-Story of 5 "Free" French subs-by Dasquelot, Maurice-Presses de La Cite'-1981-A story of the five really Free French submarines and their crews, namely Narval, Rubis, Minerve, Surcouf, Junon

Les Sous-Marins et la Guerre Actuelle-by Blanchon, Georges-Bloud, Paris-1973-51p

Les Sous-Marins Francais 1945-1972-by LeTallec, Jean-GL Valles-Paris 1992-French

Les Sous-Marin, roi de la mar-by Toudouze, Georges G-A Lemerre, Paris-1949-An overview of the submarine from its beginnings

Les Sous-Marins, sa Situation dan le Droit des Gens-by Regnault, J-Domat-1934-Consideration of submarine warfare in international law

Les Sous-Marins WW I & WW II-by Chambard, Claude-Ed. France Empire-Paris-1967

Les Submersibles-by Rabeau, A-Colin, Paris-1925-214p

Les Torpilles-by Hennebert, Lt. Colonel-Hachette-Paris-1888-A broad history of torpedoes and mines as they were know in this era

Les Torpilles et les Mines Sous-Marines-by Noalhat, Henry-Berger-Levrault, Paris-1905-432p

Lets go Aboard a Nuclear Submarine-by Hamilton, Lee D-Putnam-1965-48p-Young

Letzte Boot, Das-by Hirschfeld, Wolfgang-Universitas Verlag, Munchen-1089-332p-ISBN 380041192X-**The Last Boat**-The authors second book about the last days on the U-234 and his time as a POW

Letzte Mann von der Doggerbank-by Herlin, Hans-Heyne Verlag, Munchen-1979-191p-ISBN 3453009827-**Las t Man on the Doggerbank**-About U-43 and the sinking of the Doggerbank in March 43

Letzter Befehl: Versenken-by Arendt, Rudolp-Mittler & Sohn Verlag, Hamburg-1998-236p-ISBN 3813205436-Story of U-23 written by her last commander

Leverage of Sea Power, The-by Gray, Colin S-The Free Press, NY-1992

Libro Bianco 1985 (La Difesa)-by Minister of Defense-Ministero Difesa, Rome-1985-White Book 1985 of Defense

Life Aboard a Soviet Destroyer and a Soviet Submarine-by Stoecker, Sally W-Rand Corp, Santa Monica-1983-25p

Life In A Submarine-by Ackworth, Bernard-Tuck, London-1941-48p

Life of Robert Fulton-by Colden, Cadwallader D-Kirk & Mercein, NY-1817-371p

Life of Robert Fulton, The-by Reigart, J. Franklin-CG Henderson, Phila-1856

List of Books Concerning the Great War-by Prothero, Sir George-1923

Life in a Submarine-by Acworth, Bernard-R Tuck & Sons Ltd, London-1941-46p

Life Line-by Graves, Charles-W. Heinemann, Toronto, London-1941-238p

Life on a Submarine-by Jones, HA-Dutton, NY-1920

Liga Maritima Brasileira, Submersiveis-by Costa, Thedim-Fiat-San Giorgio, Spezia-47p

List of Logbooks of U.S. Navy Ships, Stations and Miscellaneous Units, 1801-1947-National Archives and Records Service, 1978

List of Officers of the Navy of the United States and the Marine Corps, 1775-1900-by Callahan, Edward-Haskell House Publishers-1969

Little David, The-Soloman, Robert-SC-1970-44p-Concerns Confederate submarines

Little Known Facts About the Submarine-Electric Boat Submarine Library

Lloyd's Register of Shipping 1942-43-Society's Printing House-1942

Lloyd's War Losses: The Second World War-Lloyds of London Press-1989-Includes US, Allied and neutral merchant vessel losses

Lo Schnorchel Italiano-USMM-USSM, Rome-1986-The Italian Snorkel

Lockwood Papers-1925-1945 Personal Papers donated to Lib. of Congress-by-Lockwood, Adm-Located at Lib. of Congress

Log of a U-Boat Commander-by Hashagen, Ernst-Putnam, UK-1931

Logbook of the Second War Patrol of the USS Seahorse SS304-Beachcomber Books-140p

Lone Wolf-by Mulligan, Timothy-Praeger-Werner Henke was the U-Boat commandeer of U-515. This tells the story of that boat-Reprinted by U. of Okla. Press, 1995

Lonely Ships, The-by Hoyt, Edwin P.-David McKay-1976

Longest Battle, The-The War at Sea 1939-1945-by Hough, Richard-Morrow-1987

Longest War, The-by Allen, L-London-1984-1941-45

Look at Submarines-by Young, Edward P-Hamilton, London-1964-95p-Young readers

Lord Northcliffe's War Book-by Northcliffe, AH-George H. Doran Co, NY-1917-Largely comprised of telegrams written during the war

Lord of the Seas-by Strang, Herbert (pseud)-Hodder, UK-1933-238p

Lorient-by Fahrmbacher, F-Weissenburg, Hamburg-1956-135p-The history of this base from 1940 to 1945

Los Modernos Barcos Submarinos al Alcance de Todos-by Montery y de Torres, Enrique de-P Orrier, Madrid-1920-441p

Loss of the USS Thresher-Gov Printing Office-1965-192p

Lost Men of American History-by Holbrook, Stewart-Hall-Macmillan, London-1946-370p-Includes story of Ezra Lee and the Turtle

Lost With All Hands-by Gray, Edwyn-Chas. Scribner's-1970

Lure of Neptune-Germ-Sov Naval Collaboration and Ambitions 1919-1941-Philbin, Tobias R. III U Of SC Press-1994-192p

Lusitania-by Simpson, Colin-Little, Brown, Boston-1973

Lusitania Case, The-Droste, CL & Tantum, WH-7C's Press-1973-Compilation of new articles, editorials, court records, etc.

Lusitania's Last Voyage-by Lauriat, Charles E-Houghton Mifflin-Boston-1915-158p-being a narrative of the torpedoing and sinking of the R. M. S. Lusitania by a German submarine off the Irish coast May 7, 1915, by Charles E. Lauriat, jr., one of the survivors

M

MacArthur's Ultra-by Drea, Edward U of Kansas Press-1992-Code Breaking and War Against Japan 1942-1945

Macchine Infernali-by Bravetta, Ettore-Fratelli Treves, Milan-1917-240p

Maggie of the Suicide Fleet-by Buranelli, Prosper-Doubleday, NY-1930-278p-From the log of a USNR Lt.-Tales of a WW I Submarine Chaser

Mahon on Sea Power-by Livezey, William E-Okla. U Press-1980-427p

Makers of Modern Strategy-by Paret, Peter-Princeton U Press-1986-ISBN 0691027641

Makers of Naval Policy 1798-1947-by Albion, Robert-USNIP-1980

Malta Convoys-by Woodman, R-John Murray-1994-

Man and the Underwater World-by Latil, Pierre de-Jarrolds, UK-1956

Man Beneath the Sea-by Penzias, Walter & Goodman, MW-Wiley-Interscience, NY-1973-831p-Comprehensive review of underwater engineering

Man Under the Sea-by Dugan, James-Harper & Brothers, NY-1956

Man Under Water-by Billings, Henry-Viking Press, NY-1954-189p

Man Who Broke Purple, The-by Clark, Ronald-Little, Brown & Co-1977-A biography of William and Elizabeth Friedman

Maneuvering as a Defense Against Attack by Submarines-by Bates, Lindell, T-Mail and Express Job Press-1918-35p

Manitowoc Submarines: Manitowoc, Wis.: Published under the sponsorship of the Manitowoc County Historical Society-1968-31p

Manned Submersibles-by Busby, R. Frank-Office Of Oceanography of Navy-1976-764p

Manned Undersea Activities of Federal Agencies-USGPO-1974-51p

Manner von U 96, Die-by Wiebicke, Karl-Koehler an Amelang, Leipzig-1934-208p-**The Men of U-96**

Manual of Instructions for Submarine Periscopes-by Bureau of construction and repair, Navy department-1927-115p

Mar Sanguigno-by Milansi, G-A. Stock, Rome-1927-Bloody Sea

Marine Engineering-by Harrington, Roy L, ed-Society of Naval Architects and Marine Engineers-1971

Marine Nachrichten und Ortungsdienst, Der-by Giessler, Helmuth-Lehmann, Munich-1971-156p-The German wireless and detection service and ASW during WW II

Marinekleinkampfmittel-by Fock, Harald-Lehmans-1968-156p, 148 drawings-**Naval midget forces**

Marinens fartyer og Deres Skjebne-by Abelsen, Frank-Sem & Stenersen, Oslo-1986-304p-**Norwegian Naval Ships 1939-1945**

Maritime History of Russia-by Mitchell, Mairin-Macmillan, UK-1949-544p

Maritime Power in the China Sea: Capabilities and Rationale-by Sherwood, Dick-Australian Defense Force Academy-1994

Martial Justice: The Last Mass Execution in the United States-by Whittingham, R-USNIP-1997 A German submariner POW Werner Drechsler was willing to sacrifice the bond of comradeship to save his homeland. Seven fellow submariners saw him as a traitor.

Martin Niemoller-1892-1984-by Bently, James-Free Press-1984-WW I U-Boat Commander who defied Hitler

Maru Killer, The USS Seahorse War Patrols-by Bouslog, Dave-Self Sarasota, Florida-1990-224p-ISBN0965172007-History of one of America's most effective WW II undersea raiders as told by the men who lived the events. Seahorse wreaked havoc on her enemy's navy and merchant marine, sending 24 ships to the bottom. Her legendary skipper, Slade Cutter, ranked 2nd among all U.S. sub commanders in numbers of ships sunk

Marvel Book of American Ships-by Jackson, Orton P & Evans, Frank E-Frederick Stokes, NY-1917-407p

Master of Seapower-by Buell, Thomas-Little Brown-1980-A Bibliography of Adm Ernest King

Master Plan of SUBASE NLON-CNO Office-GPO-1988

Masters of Battle-by Wilcox, J-Sterling/Cassell-1998-Includes a study of U-boat commanders

Mathematical Magick: or the Wonders That May Be Performed by mechanical Geometry-by Wilkins, John-1648-This author offered a prescription for Drebbels early submarine design

Maverick Navy-by Moffat, Alexander W.-Wesleyan U. Press-1976-157p

Max Horton and the Western Approaches-by Chalmers, William S-Hodder & Staughton-1954 302p-also Musson, Toronto

Mechanics of Underwater Noise-by Ross, Donald-Peninsula Publishing -1987

Med, The-by Langmaid, Rowland-Batchworth-1948-130p-The Royal Navy in the Med. 1939-45

Medal of Honor Recipients, 1863-1963-by Subcommittee on Veterans' Affairs-GPO-1964-1057p

Medal of Honor Recipients 1863-1994-by Lang, George-1995

Mediterranean, The-by Whipple, ABC and editors of Time-Life-Time-Life, Chicago-1981-208p-WW II

Mediterranean Submarines-by Wilson, Michael & Kemp Paul-1997-219p-ISBN 0947554572

Meeting the Submarine Challenge: a short history of the Naval Underwater Systems Center-Merrill, John & Wyld, Lionel D.-US Dept of Navy/Washington D.C.-1997-372p

Mein Solatisches Leben-by Donitz, Karl-A new edition of the book Zehn Jahre, Zwanzig Tage-1998

Mein wechselvolles Leben-by Doenitz, Karl-Musterschmidt-Germany-1975-227p-ISBN 3926584483 (1998 edition) The Life and career of former Commander-in-Chief of the German Submarine Force up until 1934. Very little during the war period.

Mein Weg nach Scapa Flow-by Prien, Gunther-Deutscher Verlag, Berlin-1941-190p

Memoire sur la Navigation Sous-Marine-by Bougois, Simeon-Paris-83p

Memoirs-10 Years and 20 Days-by Doenitz, Karl-USNIP (Greenhill in 1959)-1990-520p ISBN 0870217801-Da Capo Press edition in 1991 ISBN 0306807645

Memoirs of Ships and Men-by Diamond, Walker D-Vantage Press, NY-1964

Memoria Sobre o Submarino Fontes-by de Mello, Pereira & Fontes, Joao A-Typographia, Lisbon-1902-70p

Memories and Memorials-by Ewing, Steve-Pictorial Histories Pub. Co., Missoula, Mt-1986

Men in the Sea-Briggs, Peter-Simon & Schuster-1968-128p

Men, Machines, and Modern Times-by Morison, Elting E-MIT Press-1966

Men of War-by Howarth, Stephen-St Martin's Press, NY-1993-ISBN 0312088442-Great Naval Captains of WW II-Essays by Lockwood, Kretschmer, Prien, Doenitz, Horton and Walker

Men Under the Sea-by Larsen-1955

Men Under the Sea-by Ellsberg, Edward-Dodd & Mead, NY-1939-365p-Hard hat diving and stories of the salvage of the USS S-4, S-51 and Squalus SS-192

Menace, the Life and Death of the Tirpitz-by Kennedy, Ludovic, HC-Little Brown, Boston-1979 176p

Menschlichkeit im Seekrieg-by Schmoeckel, Helmut-Koehler Verlag, Hamburg-1988-256p, 50+photos-**Humanity in the War at Sea**-Former CO of U-802 describes many acts of humanity by U-boats toward enemies

Merchant Seaman's War, The-by Lane, T-Manchester U. Press-1990

Merchant Shipping and the Demands of War-by Behrens, Catherine-HMSO, UK-1955

Merchant Shipping Losses-by Great Britain Admiralty-1919-HMSO-164p-Aug 1914 to Nov 1918

Merchant Tonnage and the Submarine-by Great Britain Admiralty-1918-HMSO-8p

Merchant U-Boat-by Messimer, Dwight R-USNIP-1988-234p-ISBN 0870217712-Adventures of the Deutschland 1916-1918

Mes Navires Mysterieux-by Campbell, Gordon-Payot, Paris-1929-260p

Met Hr. Ms. K.XIII naar Nederlandsch-Indie-by Linden, C & Wytema, M-Scheltens & Giltay-1927-252p-Voyage of 20,000 miles by a Dutch Submarine

Messenger Gods of Battle-by Devereux, Tony-Brasseys-1991-ISBN 0080358292-The story of electronics in war; radar, radio and sonar

Met de Hr. Ms. Onderzeeboot K XVIII de wereld rond-1934-35-1997-ISBN 9056792334-Dutch-The famous voyage around the world of the K XVIII

Me Hr. Ms. K XIII naar Nederlands-Indie-by van der Linden, C & Wytema, M.S.-Scheltens &-Giltay, Amsterdam-1927-The voyage of the Dutch submarine K XIII to the Dutch East Indies

Meutes Sous-Marines-by Busch, Harald-Paris-1953

Mezzi d'Assalto X Flottiglia Mas 1940-1945-by Spertini, ME-E. Albertelli, Parmi-1991-means of Assault of the Tenth PT Flotilla

Midget Raiders, The-by Warren, Charles E. Thornton-W. Sloan Assoc, NY-1954-318p-The wartime story of human torpedoes and X-craft midget submarines of the RN

Midget Submarine-by Waldron, T & Gleeson, J-Ballantine Book, NY-1975-159p

Midget Submarine Attack on Sydney, The-by Lind-1990

Midget Submarines-by Kemp, Paul J-Sterling Publishing-1990-125p-ISBN 1861760426

Midway-by Fuchida, Mitsuo & Okumiya, Masatake-USNIP-1955

Mikado's Guests-by Bancroft, A & Roberts, RG-Australia-An account of two survivors of the sinking of the HMAS Perry and their ordeals in a POW camp.

Milag: Captives of the Kriegsmarine-by Thomas, G-Milag POW Assoc-1995-Merchant Navy POW's

Military Industrial Complex, The A Historical Perspective-by Koistinen, Paul-Praeger, NY-1980

Military Industrial Complex and U.S. Foreign Policy, The-by Carey, Omer L-Washington State U. Press-1969

Military Medals, Decorations & Orders of the U.S. & Europe-by Ball, Robert & Peters, Paul-184p-500 photos

Military Misfortunes-by Cohen, Eliot A. & Gooch, John-The Free Press-1990-The Anatomy of Failure in War

Mines Against Japan-by Johnson, Ellis A & Katcher, David A-Naval Ordnance Laboratory-1973

Mine and Countermine-by Low, Archibald-Sheridan House-1940-224p

Mines et Torpilles-by Stroh, Henri C-Colin, Paris-1924-183p

Mines, Minelayers and Minelaying-by Cowie, JS-Oxford U. Press-1949-216p

Miracle of Midway-by Prange, GW-McGraw Hill-1982

Missile Base Beneath the Sea-by DiCerto, JJ-St. Martins, NY and Macmillan, Toronto-1967165p-Describes the Polaris nuclear submarine program and surveys the history, development and operation and also examines the selection and training of their crews

Missile Systems-by Birtles, Philip & Beaver, Paul-Runnymede, UK-1985

Missing Dimension, The-by Andrew, Christopher-U of Ill. Press-1984-Governments and Intelligence Communities

Missione Segreta Mar Nero-by Cepparo, R-Ist Europa-1970-Black Sea Secret Mission

Mit Dem Einhorn Gegen Engelland-by Frowis, Franz J-Published by author in Austria-1999-With the Unicorn Against England-This book deals with U-763 and U-1195

Mit Schwertern und Brillanten-by Fraschka, Gunter-E. Pabel, Rastatt in Baden-1958-237p-Covers the 27 men who were awarded the Knights Cross with Oak Leaves, Swords and Diamonds. **With swords and diamonds.**

MIT Professional Summer-by Jackson, Henry-Submarine Design Notes

Mk 14 Submarine-launched Torpedo-Newport, R.I.: Naval Undersea Warfare Center Division-1994-26p

Model Submarines for Beginners-by Gilmore, Horace H-Harper, NY-1962-122p-87 pictures

Model Yachts, Sailing Boats and Submarines-by Haydon, AL-Boys' Own Paper, London-191070 pages on submarine models

Modern History of Warships-Conway Maritime-1920

Modern Maritime Salvage-by Milwee, William I-Cornell Maritime Press-1996-790p-The "bible" of maritime salvage

Modern Submarine Hunters-by Miller, David-Smithmark-1992

Modern Submarine Warfare-by Miller, David MO & John Jordan-Crown-1987-208p ISBN 08610133174-Hundreds of color photos

Modern Submarines-by Miller, David-Prentiss Hall-1989-77p-ISBN 0135890127

Modern U.S. Submarines-by Genat, Robert & Robin-1997-96p-ISBN 0760302766-70 color photos. A very good book for understanding the modern subs and what life is like aboard one

Modern Weapons of War-by Hall, Cyril-Blackie, London-1915-192p

Moderne Kusten U-Boote-by Nohse, Lutz & Roessler, Eberhard-Lehmann, Munich-1972-140p

Month of the Lost U-Boats, The-May 41-43 Boats-by Jones, Geoffrey-William Kimber-1977

More Power from Submarine Batteries-by Smith, David-1995

Most Dangerous Sea-by Lott, LtCdr Arnold-USNIP-1959-322p

Most Formidable Thing, The-by Jameson, William-Hart Davis-1965-280p-The Submarine from it's earliest days to the end of WW I

Most Unsordid Act, The-by Kimball, Warren-Johns Hopkins Press-1969-Lend Lease, 1939-1941

Mr. Roosevelt's Navy-by Abbazia, Patrick-USNIP-1975-The Private War of the US Atlantic Fleet 1939-1942

Mud, Muscle, and Miracles-Marine Salvage in the U.S. Navy-by Bartholomew, CA-GPO 1990-ISBN 0945274033

Munitions Industry, Special Committee on Investigation of-U.S. Congress-1936

Murder at Sea-The Luisitania-by Hurd, Archibald Spicer-Unwin, UK-1916-38p

Murder of Captain Fryalt-by Anon-Hodder & Stoughton, NY-1916-47p

My Family is a Military Family-Navy Family Services Center-1991-34p

My Life-by Raeder, Erich-USNIP-1960

My Love Affair With the Navy-by Bosworth, Allan-Norton, NY-1969-288p-ISBN 393074498

My Memoirs-2 Vol-by Tirpitz, Alfred-Dodd, Mead & Co-1919

My Mystery Ships-by Campbell, Radm-Doubleday-Doran-1929-318p-British "Q" ships and WW I anti-submarine operations-Reissue 1936 Hodder, London

My objects are to take the sting out of the submarine, relieve the mine of its punch, yet be economical and practical-by Bassford, Thomas S-Bassford, NY-1917-231p

My War At Sea-by Scott, Ian-Jenkins, UK-1943

My War In the Boats-by Ruhe, Capt, William J-Brassey's-303p

Mystery Ships: Trapping the U-Boats-by Noyes, Alfred-Hodder, London-1916-181p

N

Na Podmorske Lodi Odvazne Vypravy Kapitana Jana Siria-Czechoslovakia-1915-45p

Nach Kompas-by Merten, Karl-Friedrich-Mittler & Sohn Verlag, Berlin-1994-511p, 50 photos ISBN 3813204146-**By Compass**-An autobiography of the CO of U-68 and later Flotilla 24 CO

Nacht der U-Boote, Die-by Lund, Paul & Ludlam, Harry-Heyne Verlag, Munchen-1982-189p ISBN 3453016521-**The Night of the U-boats**-About the attacks on convoy SC-7 in Oct, 1940, the first by a coordinated wolfpack

Narciso Monturiol y la Navegacion Submarina-by Estrany, Jeronimo-Gili, Barcelona-1915-152p

Narrative by Commander DH McClintock, March 9, 1945-Located in Office of Naval Records and Library, Navy Department

Nasses Eichenlaub Soaken Oak Leaves-by Brustat-Naval, Fritz & Suhren, Teddy Ullstein-Verlag, Berlin-1995-175p, 37 photos-ISBN 3548235379-Biography of CO of U-564, Ted Suhren

National Archives of Canada
    MG 26William Lyon Mackenzie King Papers
    MG 30Read Admiral L.W. Murray, RCN, Papers
    RG 2War Cabinet Committee Papers and Minutes
    RG 24NSHQ Central Registry Files
    Atlantic Command Files
    Captain (D), Halifax, Files

Senior Canadian Naval Officer (London) Files

Naval Member, Canadian Staff (Washington) Files

Flag Officer, Newfoundland, Files

Assession 83-84/167, Various Files

Nations at War, The-by Abbot, Willis J-Leslie-Judge Co-1917-338p-Many illustrations and paintings by various artists

NATO & Warsaw Pact Submarines Since 1955-by Kolesnik, Eugene M-Blandford-1987-128p

NATO Anti-submarine Warfare: Strategy requirements and the need for co-operation-North Atlantic Assembly-1982-51p

NATO Major Warships-Grove, Eric J-Tri-Service Press-1990-208p, 100 photos-ISBN 1854000063

Nautilus, The-by Nautilus crewmembers-Albert Love, Atlanta-1957-223p-Pictorial and Historical Events of the World's First Nuclear Vessel

Nautilus-The Story of the Man Under the Sea-by Davies, Roy-USNIP-1995-239p-ISBN 1557506159

Nautilus 90 North-by Anderson, William & Clay Blair-World Publishing Co-Cleveland-1959-The account of the first atomic submarine's voyage from the Pacific to the Atlantic beneath the Arctic ice pack written by the skipper to did it

Naval Accidents 1945-1988-by Arkin, William & Handler, Joshua-Greenpeace-1989-88p-Covers some 1300 accidents

Naval Annual, 1913, The-by Hythe, Viscount, ed-Arco Publishing, NY-1970-520p

Naval Annual, 1914, The-by Hythe, Viscount, ed & Leyland, John, ed-William Clowes and Sons, Ltd, London-1970-456p

Naval Armament-by Richardson, Doug-Janes, NY-1981, 2-144p

Naval Architecture Aspects of Submarine Design-by Arentzen, ES & Mandel P-1961

Naval Battles of the Russo-Japanese War-by Togo, Kichitaro-Tokyo-1970

Naval Battles of World War I-by Bennett, Geoffrey-Batsford-1968

Naval Command Control-by DiGirolamo, Vinny-AFCEA Inter. Press, Fairfax, VA-1992-Policy, Programs, People and Issues

Naval Documents of the American Revolution 1775-1783-by Office of Naval History-1964-10 volumes-Abundant descriptions of Bushnell's Turtle and other devices of that nature

Naval Engineering and American Seapower-by King, Randolph-Nautical & Aviation Publishing Co-1989

Naval Front, The-by Maxwell-1920

Naval History Magazine 1992-USNIP-Various-USNIP-1993-352p-ISBN 155750606X

Naval History of the World War, The-3 Vol-by Frothingham, Thomas G-Harvard U. Press-1927

Naval Institute Guide to Combat Fleets of the World-by Baker, AD-USNIP-1995

Naval Institute Guide to Maritime Museums of North America-by Smith, Robert-USNIP-256p

Naval Institute Guide to the Ships and Aircraft of the U.S. Fleet, 17th Edition, The-by Polmar, Norman-USNIP-672p-ISBN 1557506566-For decades this comprehensive and authoritative guide has served the needs of naval officers, military analysts, congressional staffs, journalists, defense contractors, and others with an interest in the current capabilities of the U.S. Navy. The author, internationally respected naval analyst Norman Polmar, shares expertise gained from years of service as a consultant to members of Congress, secretaries of the navy, and senior naval officers. With this updated edition he reinforces a reputation of reliable excellence by accurately cataloging and updating the assets of the U.S. Navy as they exist today and by assessing the various trends that portend the navy of tomorrow

Naval Institute Guide to the Soviet Navy-by Polmar, Norman-USNIP-1991-ISBN 0870212419

Naval Institute Guide to World Naval Weapons Systems-1991-1992-by Friedman, Norman-USNIP-1991-Also 16th Edition 1997

Naval Innovators 1776-1900-by Christman, Albert B-Naval Surface Warfare Center, Dahlgren, VA-1989

Naval Inventions-by Smith-1917

Naval Lessons of the Great War-by Kittredge, Tracy B-Double, Page & Co, NY, Toronto-1921 - 472p

Naval Memoirs-by Keyes, Roger-Thornton Butterworth, UK-1934

Naval Mining and Degaussing-1939-1945-by London Science Museum-HMSO, London-194627p

Naval Officers' Wives of Washington Entertain-by Officers' Wives Club-Washington, D.C.-1982

Naval Operations-by Corbelt, J & Newbolt, H-Longman-1920

Naval Operations Analysis-by Wagner, Daniel H, ed, Mylander, Charles W, ed-USNIP-3rd ed, 1999-372p-ISBN 1557509565

Naval Operations in the '80s USN-by Skinner, Michael-Presidio Press-1986-142p-ISBN 0891412093

Naval Policy and Operations in the Mediterranean-by Lumby, EWR-Navy Records Society-1970-481p-For 1912-1914

Naval Policy Between the Wars-by Roskill, SW-Collins-1968

Naval Proceedings-US Naval Institute-This is the magazine published monthly by the Naval Institute

Naval Radar-by Friedman, Norman-USNIP-1981

Naval Reactor Program and Polaris Missile System-by AEC-Hearing 86th Congress-1960-39p-: Hearing before the Joint Committee on Atomic Energy, Congress of the United States, Eighty-sixth Congress, second session on review of progress in the Naval reactor program and developments in the Polaris missile submarine system. April 9, 1960

Naval Service of Canada, The-by Tucker, Gilbert N.-King's Printer-Ottawa-1952-It's Official History-2Vol

Naval Shipbuilders of the World-by Winklareth, Robert I-Chatham Publishing, London-2000-384p-ISBN 186176121X-

Naval Ships Technical Manual. Chapter 594, Salvage, submarine safety, escape and rescue devices-by Naval Sea Systems Command-21p

Naval Staff History Second World War, Submarines-Historical Section Admiralty, London-1956

Naval Strategy and National Security-by Miller, SE-Princeton U. Press-1988-408p

Naval Terms Dictionary-by Noel, John V & Beach, Edward-USNIP-5 editions since 1952-313p-The last edition has some revisions to make it current with popular usage.

Naval War Against Hitler, The-by Roskill-Scribner's, NY-1971

Naval War in the Med. 1914-1918-by Halpern, Paul G-USNIP-1987

Naval War in the West, The Wolf Packs-by Dupuy, Trevor Nevitt-Franklin Watts, NY-1963-60p

Naval Weapons of World War II-by Campbell, John-Conway, London-1985

Navie Bugie-by Lo Martire, NB-Schena, Fasano-Ships and Lies

Navies of World War III-by Preston, Anthony-Crown Publishes, NY-1984-192p

Navi Militare Perdute-by USMM-USSM, Rome-1975-Naval Ships Lost-Volume 2

Navies in the Nuclear Age-Ed: Gardiner, Albert & Friedman, N-USNIP-1993-224p-Warships Since 1945

Navies of the Second World War-Lenton, HT-Doubleday-1965-German Submarines

Navigation Aerienne et Navication Sous-Marine-by Noalhat, Henry-Geisler, Paris-1910-200p

Navy and Industrial Mobilization in World War II, The-by Connery, Robert H-Princeton U. Press-1951

Navy Bluebook, The-by Compere, Tom-Military Publishing Institute-1960-374p

Navy Book of Distinguished Service, The-by Stringer, Harry R-Fassett Publishing Co-1921

Navy Department Annual Reports 1940-1947

Navy Shipbuilding Problems at General Dynamics-US GOV Printing Office-1987

Navy Shipbuilding Programs: nuclear attack submarine issues/ statement by Richard Davis, Director, National Security Analysis, National Security and International Affairs Division, before the Subcommittee on Seapower, Committee on Armed Services, U.S. Senate-USGAO-1995

Navy Ships: Lessons of Prior Programs May Reduce New Attack Submarine Cost Increases and Delays: report to Congressional requesters-USGAO-1994-18p

Navy ships: Problems Continue to Plague the Seawolf Submarine Program: report to Congressional requesters-by United States General Accounting Office-1993-44p

Navy Times Book of Submarines: A Political, Social and Military History-by Harris, Brayton and Boyne, Walter (ED)-Berkley Pub Group-1997-400p-ISBN 0425157776

Navy Trivia-206p-What was the first enemy submarine sunk by the Navy? Name the Navy's only two reactor sub

Navy, The-It's Role, Prospects for Development & Employment-V'yunenko, NP Makayev, BN Voyenizdat-Moscow-1989-Russian

Navy's Submarine Launched Ballistic Missile Force is Highly Ready: report to the Congress/by the Comptroller General of the United States-GAO-1978-48p

Nazi Prisoners of War in America-by Krammer, Arnold-Scarborough House-1991

Nederlandse Onderzeedienst 75 jaar-by Jalhay, P.C.-Bussum-1982-151p-75 years of Dutch submarine service

Neptune Papers No. 3: Naval Accidents 1945-1988-by Arkin, William & Handler, Joshua-Greenpeace-1989

Neptunis Rex Records, Reserve Cruise of Sub-Div 1-34 in USS Sablefish SS 303-1963-43 p

Neutralitat, Blockade und U-Bootkrieg-by Buhler, Ottman-Berlin-1940

New Attack Submarine: hearing before the Military Procurement Subcommittee of the Committee on National Security, House of Representatives, One Hundred Fourth Congress, first session, hearing held September 7, 1995-USGPO-1996-127p

New Attack Submarine: more knowledge needed to understand impact of design changes: report to the Secretary of Defense-by USGPO-1998-18p

New Attack Submarine: program status: report to Congressional committees-by USGAO-1996-20p

New Illustrated Guide to Modern Warships-by Gibbons, Tony-Smithmark Press-1992-155p

New Perspectives On Anti-submarine Warfare and Oceanology-Washington, D. C., Data Publications-1967-155p

New Submersible Battle Cruiser with 16inch Guns-by Briggs, Raymonde-Briggs, NY-1940-28p

New Tales of the Submarine War-by Masters, David-1935-296p

New World 1939-1946- by Hewlett, Richard & Anderson, Oscar-Penn. State U-1962

Newport New Shipbuilding: The First Century-by Tazewell, William-1986-256p

Night of Terror-by Caulfield, Max-1958-See "Tomorrow Never Came" Story of the SS Athenia

Night of the U-Boats-by Lund, Paul & Harry Ludlam-W. Foulsham & Co LTT-1973-Convoy SC7 sailed from Nova Scotia. It sailed disastrously into a night assault by a wolf-pack of U-Boats

Night Raider of the Atlantic-by Robertson, Terence-Dutton, NY-1956-256p-Also Ballantine, 1974-192p-Also known as **Golden Horseshoe**

Nightmare at Scapa Flow-by Weaver, Harry J-Cressvelles, UK-1980

Nimitz-by Potter, EB-USNIP-1976

Ninety Feet to the Sun-by Collenette, Eric J-1984-Fiction

Ninth Time Lucky-by Toschi, Elias-Kimber, UK-1955-216p-Italian midget submarines, WW II

Noise Survey and Repair Procedures for Submarine Noise Reduction-by USN-Washington-1951-80p

None More Courageous-by Holbrook, Steward H-Macmillan, NY-1942-245p

Nor Death Dismay-McCoy, Samuel Duff-Macmillan Co, NY-1944

North Atlantic Run-by Milner, Marc-USNIP-1985-ISBN 0870214500-The Royal Canadian Navy and the battle for the convoys

Notes on aids to submarine hunting, March-April, 1918-Struthers, JG-1918-125p

Notes on Anti-submarine Defenses-by Navy Department, Office of Naval Intelligence-1917-70p

Notes on Explosives-Hill, Walter N-US Torpedo Station-1875-60p

Notes on Submarine Mining in England-by Abbott, Henry L-U.S. Engineer School-1883

Notes on Torpedoes, Offensive and Defensive-by Stotherd, Richard H-GPO, Washington-1872-318p-About mines

Nothing Friendly in the Vicinity: My patrol on the submarine USS Guardfish during WWII-Conner, Claude C-Savas Pub, Mason City, IA-1999-230p

Notre Marine Marchande Pendant la Guerre-by La Bruyere, Rene-Payot, Paris-1920-384p The French Merchant Marine during WW I and the submarine war

Now Hear This! Histories of US ships in WW II-by Motley, John J & Kelly Philip R-Zenger Pub. Co, Washington-1979-282p-ISBN 0892010576

Now it Can Be Told-by Groves

NS402 Submarines-USNA Staff-Kendall-Hunt-1993-160p-Available at USNA only

NSL Fact Book, The-Naval Submarine League-1987 (1st ed)-1993 edition includes Submarine Sea Stories and Such

NSL History Book, The-Turner Pub Co

Nuclear Flight-by Gantz, Kenneth F-Duell, Sloan & Pearce, NY-1960

Nuclear Navy-1946-1962-by Hewlett, Richard G & Duncan, Francis-U. of Chicago Press-1974 544p

Nuclear Power From Underseas to Outer Space-by Simpson, John W-American Nuclear Society 1995-480p-ISBN 0894485598

Nuclear Powered Submarines-by AEC-Oakridge, TN-1965-56p

Nuclear Powered Submarines-by Beaver, Paul-Arms & Armour Press NY-1986-72p

Nuclear Powered Submarines-by Bond, Guyla-self-1966-A Checklist of Periodical Articles

Nuclear Powered Submarines-by Duthie & Donald-1964

Nuclear Powered Submarines-by Noyes

Nuclear Powered Submarines-1950-1965-by Bond-1966

Nuclear Powered Subs-by Curren, Thomas-Lib. of Parliament/ Canada-1988-Potential Environmental Effects

Nuclear Ship Propulsion-by Crouch, Holmes F-Cornell Maritime Press-1960

Nuclear Ship Propulsion-by Pocock, Rowland-Ian Allen, London-1970

Nuclear Submarine-by Rossiter, Mike-Gloucester Press, NY-1983-37p-Youth-Introduces aspects of the atomic submarine and describes it's use as a weapon, including ways of retaliating against it

Nuclear Submarine Construction Cost Study: survey and analysis of differences between costs of constructing certain nuclear submarines at naval and private shipyards-Arthur Andersen & CO, Chicago-1964

Nuclear Submarine Decommissioning and Related Problems-by Lesage, LG-Kluwer Academic Publishers-1996-343p-ISBN 0792341899

Nuclear Submarine Skippers and What They Do-by Steele, George-Franklin Watts, NY-1962 140p-Young

Nuremberg Trial, The-by Tusa, Ann & John-Atheneum, NY-1984

Nuremberg Trial, The and Aggressive War-by Glueck, Sheldon-Doubleday-1965

Nuremberg: Infamy on Trial-by Persico, Joseph E-Viking Penquin, NY-1994

Nuremberg: The Last Battle-by Irving, David-400p

O

O Neslyshimykh Zvukakh-by Kudr, BB-Moscow-1958-143p-ISBN 0965517101

Observer's Directory of Royal Naval Submarines-by Cocker, MP-USNIP-1982

Of Nukes and Nosecones-by Bivens, Arthur Clark-Baltimore, MD: Gateway Press-1996-125p

Okrety Podvodnye-by Grabowski, Zygmunt-Warsaw-1962-125p-

Onde Insanguinate-by Sulliotti, I-Omen oni, Milano-1930-Bloody Waves

Onderzeeboten in beeld-by van der Veer, MHJ th.-1989-ISBN 9028847367-Photographs and picture postcards of submarines (about ½ are Dutch) in the period of the 1930's

One Hundred Days: The Memoirs of the Falklands Battle Group Commander-by Woodward, Adm Sir John & Robinson, Patrick-USNIP-1992-351p-ISBN 1557506515

One Hundred Years of Sea Power-by Baer, George W-Stanford U. Press-1994

Only Four Escaped-by Warren, CET & Benson, James-1959-219-The sinking of the submarine Thetis

O.N.I.208-by CNO-1942-Japanese Merchant Ship Recognition Manual

Operations of the Fremantle Submarine Base 1942-1945-by Creed, David-Naval Historical Society of Australia-64p-ISBN 0909153094

O.R. in World War II-by Waddington, CH-Elek, London-1973-253p-Operational research against the U-Boat

Observer's Directory of Royal Naval Submarines-1901-1982-by Cocker, Maurice-Warne, London-1982-128p

Ocean Engineering Studies-by Stachiw, Jerry D-Naval Ocean Systems Center-1990

Odyssey of a U-Boat Commander, The-by Topp, Erich & Eric C Rust-Praeger-1992-258p ISBN 0275939980-Recollections of Erich Topp via diaries and journals

Of Nukes and Nose Cones-by Bivens, Arthur Clark-Gateway Press, Baltimore-1996-125p-ISBN 0965517101-Author-direct-Fairfax, VA-The experiences of one of "Rickover's Boys" in the U.S. Navy in the fifties and sixties. The author took part in sea trials with Rickover and later went on to take part in the development of the first ballistic missile submarines, all of which he recounts here with special knowledge and humor

Official Chronology of the U.S. Navy in World War II-by Cressman, Robert J-USNIP-2000-367p-ISBN 1557501491-Author works in Naval Historical Center in Washington D.C.

Ohotnika Za Podvodnimi Lodkami Submarines and Submarine Warfare-by Schekotov, Evginy-Voenizdat, Moscow-1960-125p

Oil & War-by Goralski, Robert-& Freeburg, Russell W-William Morrow & Co-1987

Omega 9-by Pasetti, A-Bietti, Milano-1969

On Active Service in Peace and War-by Stimson, Henry L-Harper & Bros-1947

On Board a United States Submarine-by Theiss, Lewis F-Wilde-Boston-1940-308p

On the Bottom-by Ellsberg, Edward-Dodd, Mead-1929-324p-Raising of the USS S-51

Onder de bloedvlag van de O 21, 1940-1945-by van Dulm, Ltz J.F.-Scheltens & Giltay, Amsterdam-1947-War history (WWII) of the Dutch submarine O 21

One Hundred Days-by Woodward, Sandy & Robinson, Patrick-Harper Collins, UK-1992-The memoirs of the Falklands Battle Group Commander-Also by USNIP-Blue Jacket Books-1997-400p-ISBN 1557506523

One Hundred Years of Sea Power-by Baer, George W-Stanford U. Press-1994-553p-The US Navy, 1890-1990

One Man Band-by Bryant, Benjamin-Kimber, UK-1958-238p-World War II submarine ops with British subs Sealion and Safari

One of Our Submarines-by Young, Edward P-R. Hart-Davis, London-1953-316p-RN submarines, specifically the S-Class in the 40's

Only Four Escaped-by Warren & Bensen-Sloane-1959-219p-Sinking of
   the Submarine Thetis in 1939
Open Boats-by Noyes, Alfred-Stokes, NY-1917-91p
Open Fire!-by Hudson, Alec (pseud)-Macmillan-1942
Opening Pandora's Box-Desjardins, Marie-France-Can. Centre for
   Arms Control-1988-Nuclear Powered Subs and the Spread of
   Nuclear Weapons
Operation Drumbeat-Gannon, Michael-Harper & Row-1990-490p-
   ISBN 0060161558-Softback (512p)-Germany's U-Boat Attacks
   along the American Coast in WW II
Operation Paukenschlag-by Gannon, Michael-Ullstein-Verlag,
   Berline-1997-510p-ISBN 3860479059-Operation Drumbeat
Operation Unter Wasser-by Schutze, Hans G-Koehler Verlag,
   Herford-1985-252p, 42 photos ISBN 378220347X-**Operation
   Under Water**-The author was a doctor aboard U-382, U-221
   and U-358
Operation Vittles-by Officer's Wives' Club, Pearl Harbor-1946-A
   cookbook
Operational History-Submarines-by Voge, Richard-1500p
Operational History of Naval Communications (Japanese)-US
   Army/Army Library Wash DC
Operations of the Fremantle Submarine Base 1942-1945-by Creed,
   David-Naval Historical Soc. of Australia-1986-ISBN 0909153094
Ordeal by Sea-by Hurd, Archibald Spicer-Jarrolds, UK-1918-227p-The
   story of the British Seaman's Fight for Freedom
Ordeal By Sea-by Helm, Thomas-Dodd, Mead-1963-The Tragedy of
   the USS Indianapolis
Ordeal by Water-by Keeble, Peter-Doubleday, Garden City-1958-216p-
   British Hard Hat diving on the U-307
Orientation Information on Spatial Displays-by Yungkurth, Erika J.-
   Bruce G-Coury-1990 Periscope Operation
Origins of the Maritime Strategy-by Palmer, Michael-USNIP-1990-
   The Development of American Naval Strategy, 1945-1955

Orzel's Patrol-by Sopocko, Eryk-Methuen, London-1942-146p-Story of the Polish submarine

Os Submarinos-by Mariotte-Almeida, Miranda & Sousa-Lisbon-1916-132p

Os Submersiveis-by Ferreira, Vasco Taborda-Ottosgrafica, Lisbon-1929-251p

Ostsee-by Bekker, Cajus-G. Stalling, Oldenburg-1959

Otto Kretschmer-by Herzog, Bodo-Patzwall Verlag-2001-153p-ISBN 3931533441

Otto Weddigen: Ein Lebensbild-by Rishter, Heinrich-Leipzig-1915-149p

Otto Weddigen und Seine Waffe-by Weddigen, Otto-Marinedank, Berlin-1915-157p-Written by CO of U-9 who sank three cruisers in 135 minutes

Otus AS20-by VanAntwerp, EI-1946?-47p

Ouelli di Betasom SMGG Italiani in Atlantico-by Raiola, G-Volpe, Rome-1965-Those of Betasom, Italian Submarines in the Atlantic

Our Force's Finest-by Submarine Officer's Wives Club-Charleston, SC-1985-A cookbook

Our Little Submarine-by Mantegazza, G

Our Little Submarine-by Hale, Robert-USNIP

Our Navy at War-Daniels, Josephus-Navy Department, Pictorial Bureau-1922

Our Special Blend-by Officers' Wives' Club, Mare Island-1991-A cookbook

Our Valiant Few-by Mason, Francis-Little & Brown-Boston-1956-436p

Out of the Mists-by Carr, William G-Hutchinson, UK-1942-176p-Great deeds of the Navy

Overdue and Presumed Lost-USS Bullhead-by Sheridan, Martin-Marshall Jones Co-1947 & 1959-143p

Over-Sexed, Over-Paid and Over Here-by Moore, John-302p-Americans in Australia 1941-1945

Oxford Companion to Ships and the Sea-Kemp, Peter, ed-Oxford U. Press-1994-971p-This work contains over 3700 entries including concise biographies of famous seaman and naval heroes, descriptions of pivotal naval battles, naval architecture, engineering, navigation, ship handling are but some of the covered topics.

Oxford Companion to World War II-ed by Dear, ICB & Foot, MRD-Oxford U. Press-1368p-An international team of 140 experts cover every aspect of the conduct and experience of the war. 300 photos and 120 maps.

P

Pacific Campaign-by Van der Vat, Dan-Simon & Schuster-1991-ISBN 0671738992

Pacific Partners-by Frame, Thomas-Hodder & Stoughton-ISBN 034045585 X

Pacific War, The-by Costello, John-Quill, NY-1981-An overview of war in the Pacific

Pacific War, The-Ienaga, S.-Pantheon Books-1978-World War II and the Japanese 1931-1945

Pacific War Atlas, The-1941-45-by Smurthwaite, David-Mirabel Books Ltd, London-1995-144p-ISBN 0816032866-75 color maps-and 50 b&w photos

Pacific War Diary-by Fahey, James-Houghton Mifflin-1963 2nd ed-1942-1945

Panic at Fort Stevens-by Webber, Bert-Japanese Bomb Oregon in WW II

Passenger Carrying Submersibles-by Hathaway, William T-National Technical Info. Serv.1989

Patch Guide-US Navy Ships & Submarines-Roberts, Michael L-Turner Pub Co-1992-169p-ISBN 1563110830

Patrol-by Rose, Brittany-1937-The Story of the Suicide Fleet

Patrol Reports of World War II-USGovt-Archived Navy Yard-Wash. D.C.-All 1,682 reportsare declassified

Paukenschlag vor Kapstadt-by Mielke, Otto-Munchen-1954-**Drumbeat off Capetown**-The operations of wolfpack Eisbar (U-68, U-159, U-172, U-504 in 1942)

Peace Moves and U-Boat Warfare-1916-1917-by Birnbaum, Karl-Archon Books, Hamden-1970-388p-ISBN 208009086-A study of Imperial Germany's policy towards the United States, April 18, 1916-January 9, 1917

Peace or War-by US Congress 64th Session-1916-155p

Pearl Harbor: Final Judgment-by Clausen, Henry C. & Lee, Bruce-Crown Publishers-1992-485p-38 photos-ISBN 0306810352

Pearl Harbor: Verdict of History-by Prange, Gordon & Goldstein, Donald & Dillon, Katherine-by Viking Penquin-1991-699p-ISBN 0140159096

Pearl Harbor: Warning and Decision-by Wohlstetter, Roberta-Stanford U. Press-1962

Peleus Trial, The-by Cameron, John-W Hodge Co Ltd, UK-1948-War Crimes Trials, Vol 1

Penang Submarines, The-by Gunton, Dennis-City Council of Georgetown-1970

People's Navy, The-by Hagan, Kenneth-The Free Press-1991

Perceptions of organization and leadership behavior: a study of perceptions of organization structure and their social correlates in a submarine squadron of the United States Navy-by Scott, Ellis L-Columbus, Ohio: Ohio State University Research Foundation -1953-100p

Peril of the Sea-by Lockhart, J.G.-Allan, London-1924-294p

Perilous Sea, The-Yankee Books, Dublin, NH-1985-192p-ISBN 0899090656

Perils of the Port of New York-by Rattray, JE-Dodd, Mead-1973-Maritime Disasters

Periscope Depth-by Poolman, Kenneth-Kimber, London-1981-199p-A short history of submarines through the end of WWII-ISBN 0718301587

Periscope Op!-by van Beers, Ltz A.C.-The Netherlands Publishing Co, Ltd, London-1945-War history (WWII) of the Dutch submarine force

Periscope Patrol-by Turner, John F-GG Harrap, UK-1957-218p-The Saga of the Malta Submarines

Periscope Red-by Rohner-1980

Periscope View-by Simpson, GWG-Macmillan, UK-1972-315p-autobiography

Periscope Views: The picture story of Submarine Squadron 6, June 1953-June 1954-Atlanta, Ga.: Albert Love Enterprises, 1954-1 vol, unpaged

Periscopes, People, and Progress-by Walker, Bruce H-Excelsior Printing, 1984

Phantom of Scapa Flow, The-by Korganoff, Alexandre-I Allan, London-1974-235p

Phantom Submarine-by Brightfield, Richard

Phantom War in the Northwest-by Shrader, Grahame F-Self Published-1970-2nd printing-Includes an account of Japanese submarine operations on the west coast of the U.S. 1941-1942

Philadelphia Naval Shipyard-by Ahern, Joseph-James-1997

Pictorial History of the German Navy in WW II-by Porten, E-Thomas Crowell-1976

Picture World of Submarines, The-by Stephen, RJ-1990

Pigboat Thirty-Nine-by Gugliota, Bobette-Kentucky U. Press-1984-264p-ISBN 0813115248 An American Submarine Goes to War

Pigboats-by Roscoe, Theodore-Bantam-1949 449p ISBN 053130404-Originally US Submarine Operations in WW II-The True Story of the Fighting Submarines of WW II

Pipe Dream of Peace-by Wheeler-Bennett, John W-William Morrow Co-1935

Pirate's Progress, The-by Archer, William-Chatto & Windus, London-1918-96p-A Short History of the U-Boat

Plan Book-Gato and Balao Class Submarines-Floating Drydock-1994-150 scale drawings of exterior fixtures. Many photos of boats in that Class from the 40's showing various modifications

Planrolle-by Kohl, Fritz-Bernard & Graefe Verlag, Koblenz-ISBN 37673760008-Design plans: Type XXI U-boat

Planrolle-by Kohl, Fritz & Niestle, Axel-Bernard & Graefe Verlag, Koblenz-ISBN 3763760083-Design Plans: Type VIIC U-boat

Planrolle-by Kohl, Fritz & Niestle, Axel-Bernard & Graefe Verlag, Koblenz-ISBN 3763760083-Design Plans: Type XXIII U-boat

Podgotovka Rossii k Mirovoi Voine po More-by Petrov, MA-Moscow-1926-Russia's preparedness at sea for the World War

Podvodnye Lodki Imperialisticheskikh Gosudarstv-by Gerasimov, Vladimir N-Moscow-1962-301p

Podvodnye Lodki Protiv Podvodnykh Lodok-by Suzdalev, NI-Moscow-1968-163p-Anti-Submarine Warfare

Podvodnye Transportnye Suda-by Tokmakov, AA-Leningrad-1965-266p-Nuclear Subs

Podwodne Kwadrygi-Nowak, Jan-Gdynia-1960-85p

Pokorenie Glubin Pod nauch. red I s predisi. akad. L.A. Zenkevicha-Diomidov, Mikhail N-Leningrad-1069-382p

Polaris Missile Strike, The-by Kuenne, Robert E-Ohio State U. Press-1967-434-A General Economic Systems Analysis

Polaris System Development-by Sapolsky, Harvey M-Cambridge U. Press-1972

Polaris!-by Barr, James & Howard, William-Harcourt-1960-245p

Polaris Missile Strike, The-by Kuenne, Robert-Ohio State U. Press-1966

Politics of Frustration-Little Brown & Co.-1976-The US in German Naval Planning 1889-1941

Politische und Militärische Bedeutung des Unterseebootskrieges 1914-1918-by Grosse, Karl F-Druck Rosenheimer, Rosehneim-1937-163p

Porpoises Among the Whales: Small Navies in Asia and the Pacific-by Morgan, Joseph R-Hawaii:East-West Centre-1994

Portsmouth Built-by Winslow III, Richard E-Portsmouth, NH Marine Society-1985-211p Submarines of the Portsmouth Naval Shipyard

Portsmouth Navy Yard, The: some interesting facts about the Atlantic submarine repair and construction base-Portsmouth, NH: Portsmouth Chamber of Commerce-1922-17p

Post Mortems on Enemy Submarines-ONI-Washington-1942-45

Postwar Defense Policy and the U.S. Navy, 1943-1946-by Davis, Vincent-U. of NC Press-1962

Postwar Naval Revolution, The-by Friedman, Norman-Conway Maritime Press-1986-240p-ISBN 0851774148

Postwar Rearmament of Japanese Maritime Forces, The-1945-1971- by Auer, James E-Praeger, NY-1973-345p-ISBN 0275286339

Practical Construction of Warships-by Newton, RN-Longmans, London-1966-464p

Prepare to Dive!-by Coggins, Jack-Dodd, Mead-1971-128p

Preparing SubPac for War-by Withers, Thomas-USNIP-1950

Present Status of Chemical Research in Atmospheric Purification and Control on Nuclear Powered Submarines-by USN-ONR-Washington-1960-173p

Price of Admiralty, The-by Keegan, John-Viking, Penquin-1989-292p-ISBN 067081416-Four of the world major sea battles are analyzed

Prien gegen Scapa Flow-by Korganoff, Alexandre-Motorbuch Verlag, Stuttgart-1992-228p, 65 photos-ISBN 3879434972-**Prien against Scapa Flow**

Prien Greift an-by Frank, Wolfgang-Kohler Verlag, Hamburg-1942-279p, 77 photos-**Prien on Attack**

Prima di Andare a Malta-by Cappellini, A-Ed. Europa, Milano-1947-Before Going to Malta

Principles of Naval Architecture-by Comstock, John P-Soc of Nav. Arch & Mar., UK-1967

Principles of Naval Engineering-by US Navy-1970

Principles of Naval Weapons Systems-by Frieden, David R-USNIP-1985

Principles of Underwater Sound-by Urick, Robert J-1983-McGraw Hill-ISBN 0070660875

Prisoner of the U-90-by Isaacs, Edouard V-Houghton, Boston-1919-185p-1919

Prize, The-by Yergin, Daniel-Simon & Schuster-1991-History of Oil

Procedures for Evaluation of Fracture Toughness of Pressure-Vessel Material-by USN-ONR-1961-30p

Procurement of Naval Ships-by Cole, Brady M-Industrial College of the Armed Forces-1079

Progress of Torpedo Warfare-by Barber, Francis M-United Service-1880

Project Cold Feet-by Leary, William-LeSchack, Leonard-USNIP-1996-240p-ISBN 1557505144-40 photos-Secret Mission to a Soviet Ice Station

Proyektirovaniye Atomnykh Podvodnykh Lodok-See Atomic Powered Submarine Design-Russian

Psysiology and Medicine of Diving and Compressed Air Work-by Bennett, Peter & Hallen, David Bailliere, London-1969-Williams & Wilkins, Baltimore-1969-532p

Pull Together-by Bayly, Adm Lewis-Harrap, UK-300p

Pursuit of Power, The-by McNeill, William H-U. of Chicago Press-1982

Q

Q Boat Adventures-by Auten, Harold-Jenkins, London-1919-280p-"Q" ships battle the U-boats by a Q boat commander

Q-Ships and their Story-by Chatterton, Edward K-USNIP-1972-288p

Q-Ships Versus U-Boats-by Beyer, Kenneth M-USNIP-1999-236p-ISBN 1-557500444-Written by a man who served on one of the two Q-Ships used.

Quadratur der Mere, Die-by Reche, Reinhard-1948-The Quadrature of the oceans-for the conversion of the naval quadrants chart

Quarterdeck and Bridge-by Bradford, James C-USNIP-1996-512p-ISBN 1557500738-20 photos-Two Centuries of American Naval Leaders including H. Rickover, Adm King, Halsey, Dewey, John Paul Jones, Matthew Perry and others

Quota Periscopio-by Lo Martire, NB-Stato Magg. Marina, Rome-1990-Periscope Depth

QXP, im U-Boot auf Feindfahrt-by Kaiser, Ernst-Koehlers, Herford-1981-236p-ISBN 37882202570-QXP; In a U-Boat on patrol

R

R Sommergibile Scire-by ANMI-ANMI, Pistoia-1986-Return of the Submarine Scire

Rabochaya Gloobena (Working Deep)-by Mikhailovski, AP-St. Petersburg, Naooka-220p-ISBN 5020282723

Raccolta di Rapporti su Azioni Navali di SMGG nella 2 GM-by Uf Stato Maggiore R.M.-UF Stato Maggiore R.M., Rome-1978-Collection of Submarine Naval Action Reports during WWII

Radar At Sea-by Howse, H Derek-USNIP-1993-383p-ISBN 155750704X -64 photos-Royal Navy in World War 2

Radar in World War II-by Guerlac, Henry E-Tomash Publishers-

Radio Direction Finding-by Watson, DM & Wright, HE-Von Norstrand Reinhold-1971

Raiders of the Deep-by Thomas, Lowell-Garden City Books, NY-1928-363p-Also re-issued by Sun Dial in 1940, Award 1964

Ranglist der Deutschen Kriegsmarine-by Deutsches Kriegsmarine-E.S. Mittler & Sohn, Gmbh, Hamburg-1941-Rank and Seniority List of the German Navy

Rasskazy o Podvodnolodke-by Bolgarov, NP-Moscow-1960-230p

Ratsel der U-Bootswirkung-by Hochstetter, Franz-Politik, Berlin-1919-31p

RCN in Retrospect 1910-1968-by Boutilier, James A-U of BC Press-1982

RCN in Transition: 1910-1985-by Douglas, WAB-U. of Toronto Press-1986

Reactor Shielding Design Manual-by Rockwell, Theodore-NTIS-1956-ISBN 0870793381

Ready for Sea-by Oram, HPK-Seeley Service, London-1973-245p-Memoirs of a seaman, including wartime service in British submarines

Ready to Answer All Bells-by Bruhn, LtCdr David-USNIP-1997-216p-ISBN 1557502277 A blueprint for successful naval engineering

Real Book About Submarines, The-by Epstein, Samuel & Williams, Beryl-Garden City Books, NY 1954-222p-Youth oriented

Realm of the Submarine, The-by Cohen, Paul-MacMillan-1969-274p

Rebel Shore, The-by Merrill, James Mercer-Little & Brown-Boston-1957

Rebirth of a Submarine: A History of the USS Requin (SS-481/SSR-481)-by James L. MandelblattSelf Published-60p

Records Relating to U-Boat Warfare 1939-1945-by Mulligan, T-Guides to the microfilmed records of the German Navy, 1850-1945: No 2—National Archives-263p

Recueil des sous-marins anciens del la Marine Nationale-DGA/DCN-Paris-1988

Red Duster at War-by Simpson, GW-Macmillan-1972-British Merchant Marine and the Battle of the Atlantic, 1939-1941

Red Ensign-by Rutter, Owen-London-1942-A history of Convoy

Red Fleet in the Second World War-by Isakou, Ivan S-Hutchinson, UK-1947-124p

Red Navy at Sea-by Watson, Bruce W-Westview Press, Boulder, CO-1982

Red Scorpion-by Sasgen, Peter T.-USNIP-1995-448p ISBN 1557507600-The War Patrols of the USS Rasher-Written by crew members son-The submarine Rasher sank 18 enemy ships and destroyed nearly 100,000 tons of shipping, and is remembered for her involvement in a now legendary skirmish with a Japanese convoy in 1944 off the Philippines. This book discusses the building of the ship and its operations as well as the routines of submarine combat

Red Star Rising At Sea-by Gorshkov, Sergei-USNIP-1974

Regierung Doenitz-by Ludde-Neurath, W-Goettingen, 1951 & Musterschmidt, 1953-Doenitz's last days in power by a member of his staff

Register of Ships of the U.S. Navy 1775-1990-by Bauer, K Jack & Roberts, Stephen-Greenwood-1992-376p-ISBN 0313262020

Register of Type VII U-Boats-by Adams, Thomas & Lees, David-Kendal-1991-ISBN 0905617606

Regulus: The Forgotten Weapon-by Stumpf, David-Turner Publishers-1996-192p-ISBN 1563112779-A comprehensive history of Chance Vought's Regulus I and II guided missiles. Regulus was the first operational cruise missile in the U.S. Navy and was deployed on aircraft carriers, cruisers and submarine. The author covers the research and development, testing and deployment of Regulus I as well as the research and development of Regulus II. Over 100 photographs and drawings plus a complete list of patrol dates for the Regulus submarine strategic deterrent patrols.

Reiches und Kriegsmarine geheim 1919-1945-by Lakowski, Richard-Brandenburg Verlagshaus, Berlin-1997-205p-ISBN 3894880317-**German Naval Secrets 1919-1945**

Reichsleitung un V-Bootseinsatz 1914-1918-by Bauer, Hermann-Lippoldsberk-1956-111p

Reluctant Admiral, The-by Agawa, Hiroyuki-1979-397p-Adm Yamamoto

Reluctant Allies-by Krug, Hans-Joachin & Hirama, Yoichi & Sander-nagashima, Berthold & Niestle', Axel-by USNIP-2001-400p, 17 photos-ISBN 1557504652-German-Japanese naval relations in World War II

Reminiscences-by Daveluy, Admiral-Economica, Paris-1991-Memoirs of Admiral Daveluy, one of the first French early submariners.

Reminiscences of Adm. George W. Anderson, Jr-USNIP-1983-2 Volumes

Reminiscences of Captain Slade Cutter-by Slade Cutter-USNIP-1985-Oral History located at Nimitz Museum at Annapolis

Rendezvous-by Hudson, Alec (pseud)-Macmillan-1942-94p

Rendezvous by Submarine-by Ingham, Travis-Doubleday, Doran-1945-255p-The story of Charlie Parsons and the guerrillas in the Philippines

Report and Recommendations on Submarine Safety and Salvage-by the Submarine Board, appointed by the Secretary of the Navy, June 29, 1928-USGPO-1932-8p

Report of Undersea Warfare Advisory Panel-by A.E.C.-G.E.-1953

Report on Need of Additional Naval Bases to Defend the Coasts of the United States, Its Territories and possessions-USGPO-1939-39p-From the Secretary of the Navy transmitting report of the Board appointed to report upon the need, for purposes of national defense, of additional submarine, destroyer, mine, and naval air bases on the coasts of the United States, its territories and possessions

Report on Salvage Operations-by Ellsberg, Edward-USGPO-1927-Submarine S-51

Report on the Salvage of H.M. Submarine "Truculent" in the Thames Estuary, January 12 to March 23rd, 1950-by Boom defense & Marine Salvage Department, Admiralty, London-1950

Report on the Interrogation of Survivors of U-569-USGPO-1943

Report on United States Nuclear-powered Attack Submarine Program-/by the Seapower and Strategicand Critical Materials Committee on Armed Services, House of Representatives, Ninety-sixth Congress, first session

Report Upon Experiments and Investigations of Mining-by Abbott, Henry L-Washington, D.C. 1881-444p

Reprogramming action—Trident submarine: hearing before the Seapower and Strategic and Critical Materials Subcommittee of the Committee on Armed Services, House of Representatives, Ninety-sixth Congress, second session, September 23, 1980-USGPO-1980-48p

Rescue, The-by Smith, Steven Trent-John Wiley & Sons-2001-326p-ISBN 0471412910-A Story of 40 Americans trapped on Negros Island in the Philippines in WWII, a set of secret Japanese Battle Plans and the Submarine (Crevalle) that saved them.

Rescuer, The-by Maas, Peter-Harper & Row, NY-1967-239p-Squalus disaster and "Swede" Momsen's role

Rethinking the Trident Force-by Mosher, D.-USGPO-1993

Return From the Deep-by Trimble, Hugh-McNew, 1958-Author was co-founder of SubVets of WWII group

Return From the River Kwai-Blair, Clay & Joan-Simon & Schuster-1979-ISBN 0671242784

Review of Naval Reactor Program and Adm Rickover Award-by A.E.C.-G.E.-1959-81p

Rickover-by Polmar, Norman & Thomas Allen-Simon & Schuster-1982-774p-ISBN 0671246151-Controversy And Genius: A Biography-

Rickover and the Nuclear Navy-by Duncan, Francis-USNIP-1990-239p-ISBN 0870212362 The Discipline of Technology

Rickover Effect, The-by Rockwell, Theodore-USNIP-1992-411p-ISBN 1557507023 How One Man Made a Difference

Rickover: The Struggle for Excellence-by Duncan, Francis-USNIP-2001-408p-45photos ISBN 1557501777

Ricordi di un Sommergibilista del smg Barbarigo-by Risaia, A-A. Risaia, Cremona-1984-Memoirs of a Submariner of the submarine Barbarigo

Rise and Fall of British Naval Mastery-by Kennedy, PM-Allan Lane-1976

Rise and Fall of the Third Reich-by Shirer, William L-Simon & Schuster-1960

Rise of a Navy Admiral-by Galantin, Adm IJ-Illinois U. Press-345p

Rise of American Naval Power, The-by Sprout, H-Princeton U. Press-1939

Rising Sun, The-by Toland, John-Random House-1970

Ritter Der Sieben Meerr-by Alman, Karl-Pabel, Verlag-1965-339p 67 photos-Collection:-**Knights of the Seven Seas/Stories of 18 U-Boat Aces**

Ritter der Tiefe-by Thomas, Lowell-Deutscher Verlag, Berlin-1931-366p. First published in 1928

Ritter der Tiefe, Graue Wolfe-by Herzog, B & Schomaekers, G-Welsermuhl-Munich-1976-563p-Biographies of the most successful U-Boat and submarine commanders of both wars-Also known as "Knights of the Deep/Gray Wolves

Ritterkreuztrager der U-Boote-Waffe BD. 1 A-J-by Dorr, Manfred-Biblio-Verlag, Osnabruck-1988-320p, 200 photos-ISBN 3764811536-**Vol 1 of Knight's Cross recipients of the U-Boat Service**

Ritterkreuztrager der U-Boote-Waffe BD. 2 L-Z-by Dorr, Manfred-Biblio-Verlag, Osnabruck-1988-320p, 220 photos-ISBN 3764811536-**Vol 2 of Knight's Cross recipients of the U-Boat Service**

Road to Pearl Harbor, The-by Collier, Richard-Antheneum-1981

Robert Fulton-Dickinson, HW-John Lane, London & NY-1913

Robert Fulton, Naval Warfare Genius-by Hutcheon, Wallace S-USNIP-1981-191p-Pioneer of Undersea Warfare

Robert Fulton: A Bibliography-by Philip, Cynthia-Watts, NY-1985-371p

Robert Fulton And the Submarine-by Parsons, William-AMS Press-1922(1967)-154p-

Robert Fulton, Engineer and Artist, His Life and Works-by Dickinson, HW-John Lane, London-1923

Robert Fulton in France: he invents and designs the first Paris panorama and invents and demonstrates the first submarine torpedo-boat-by Alice Crary Sutcliffe-New York: Century Co-1908-931p

Robert Fulton: Pioneer of Undersea Warfare-by Hutcheon, Wallace-USNIP-1981-191p-ISBN 0870215477

Rochefort, Joseph J Oral History-Nimitz Library, Annapolis

Roger Keyes-by Aspinall, O-Cecil, UK-1951-478p-Biography of Admiral of the Fleet, Lord Keyes in WW II

Rokov'e Bermudi-Murmurs off Bermuda (Russian)-by Nikitin, Yevgeni-Unpublished manuscript account of the loss of Yankee Class SSBN K-219

Romance of Submarine Engineering, The-by Corbin, Thomas W-Lippincott-Phila-1913-315p

Romance of the Submarine, The-by Jackson, George G-Lippincott-1930-244p

Room 39 Naval Intelligence in Action 1939-1945-by McLachlan, Donald-1968

Room 40-British Naval Intelligence 1914-1918-by Beesley, Patrick-Haish House, UK-1982

Roosevelt and Churchill, Their Secret Wartime Correspondence-by Loewenheim, Francis L Langley & Jonas-Saturday Review Press /EP-Dutton-1975

Rough Notes on Seven Lectures on Submarine Mining-Chatam, England-1877-32p

Royal Australian Navy in World War II, The-by Stevens, David-Paul & Co-1996-240p

Royal Navy in the Mediterranean-by Halpern, Paul G-Temple Smith, UK-1987

Royal Navy in World War II: An Annotated Bibliography-by Law, Dereck G-Greenhill Books, London-1988

Royal Navy Submarine Service, The-by Preston, Anthony-USNIP-196p-80 illustrations-ISBN 0851778917

Royal Navy Submarines-by Cocker, MP-Frederick Warne, UK-1982-ISBN 0723229643

Royal Navy, The-by Watts, Anthony J-256p-An Illustrated History

Royal Netherlands Navy-by Lenton, H.T.-1967-Macdonald & Co, London-The Royal Netherlands Navy in WWII. Book contains technical data of all navy ships and submarines

Royal Oak Disaster-by Snyder, Gerald Presidio-1978-240p-Scapa Flow and Gunther Prien

Run Silent, Run Deep, Run to the Kitchen-by Officer's Wives Club, Norfolk-1980

Running Critical-by Tyler, Patrick-Harper & Row-1986-774p-The Silent War, Rickover, General Dynamics

Russia at War 1941-1945-by Werth, Alexander-Dutton, NY-1964-1100p

Russia's Arms Catalog-by Spassky, Nikolai, ed-Military Parade, Moscow-1996-1997-A series of seven catalogues

Russian Convoys, The-by Schofield, B-Ballantine Books-1964

Russian Fleet in the First World War, The-by Gregor, Rene-Liverpool-1972

Russian Sea Power-by Fairhall, David-Gambit, Boston-1971-286p

Russian Submarines in Arctic Waters-by Kolyshkin, I-David Skvirsky-Translator-Bantam-1985-246p-First published in Moscow in 1966

Russians at Sea-by Woodward, David-Praeger, NY-1966-254p-A History of the Russian Navy

Rustbucket 7-by Robers, Douglas L-Mill Pond Press-1995-170p-The author was a young officer on the USS PC 617, a subchaser in the Atlantic in WW II.

S

S-54: Stories of the Sea-by Ellsberg, Edward-Dodd & Mead-1932-278p

Sacred Warriors, The-by Warner, Dennis & Peggy & Seno, Cmdr Sadao-Van Nostrand, NY-1982-Japan's Suicide Legions

Safe Submarine Vessels and the Future of the Art-by Lake, Simon-Inst. of Naval Architects, London-1907-28p

Saga of the Submarine Scabby-by Christodoulou, Nicholas-Self Published, 1985-208p-USS Scabbardfish

Saga of the USS Pelias AS-14-Anon-Schwabacher-Frey Co-SF-1946-24p

Sailing on the Silver Screen-by Suid, Lawrence-USNIP-352p-ISBN 1557507872-Hollywood and the US Navy

Sailors, Subs and Senoritas-by Minarik, William H-Brandon Press, Boston-1968-349p-Memoirs of a Navy man

Salad Recipes-by SubDevRon12-1978

Sally's Submarine-by Anderson, Joan & George Ancona-USNIP

Salt and Steel-by Beach, Edward L-USNIP-1999-299p-ISBN 1557500541-Reflections on his Life as a Submariner

Salvage Man-by Alden, John D-USNIP-1997-384p-ISBN 1557500274-Edward Ellsberg and the U.S. Navy

Salvage! Rescued from the Deep-by Williams, David L-Ian Allen, London-1991-160p-ISBN 0711019360

Samuel Colt's Submarine Battery-by Lundeberg, Philip K-Smithsonian -1974-90p

San Diego's Navy-by Linder Bruce-USNIP-2001-272p, 150 photos-ISBN 1557505314

Sangokai, Middoueto, sensuikan kaku sakusen, 1942-nen 5-gatsu-1942-nen 8-gatsu-by Samyueru E. Morison cho; Nakano Goro yaku by Morrison. See Coral Sea, Midway and Submarine actions

Sanitatsdienst Bei der deutschen U-Boot-Waffe-by Noldeke, Hartmut & Harmann, Volker-Mittler & Sohn Verlag, Berlin-1996-280p-ISBN 3813205010-**The Medical Service of the U-boat Arm**

Sank Same-Mellor, William B-Howell, Soskin, NY-1944

Scapa Flow in War and Peace-by Hewison, WS-Kirkwall-1995

Schatten voraus!-by Reymann, Paul-Franz Schneider Verlag, Berlin-1944-187p-**Vessels Ahead**

Schepen van de dKoninklijke Marine in W.W. II-by Mark, Chris-De alk B.V., Alkmaar-1997-ISBN 9060135229-Technical data and brief history of the ships of the Royal Dutch Navy in WWII

Schicksal der deutschen U-boote 1938-1945-by Schurholz, Peter-Heidenheim-1950-118p-**The Fate of the German U-boats 1939-1945 Schiff 16**-by Rogge, Bernard-G. Stalling, Oldenburg-1955-A book about the raider Atlantis which sank 22 ships and in turn was sunk while refueling U-126 and U-68 Merten the day before **Ship 16**

Schiff Profile: U-Boot Type Vii C-by Richter, Werner-Flugzeug Publikations-Verlag-1996-42p, 90 photos-**Ship Profiles Type VIIC U-boat**

Schlacht im Atlantik, Die-by Ambrosious, Hans Heinrich-Hanseatische Verlag, Hamburg-68p-1941-**The Battle of the Atlantic**

Schlacht im Atlantik, Die-by Peillard, Leonce-Time-Life-1979-208p, 162 photos

Schlacht im Eismeer-by Irving David-Knaus-Verlag, Hamburg-1982-429p, 32 photos-A detailed view of PQ-17 Convoy from the Allied view-**Battle in the Arctic Sea**

Schlachtfeld Atlantik-by Van der Vat, Dan-Heyne Verlag, Munchen-1988-ISBN 345304230 The Atlantic Campaign

Schrecken der Meere, Der-by Valentiner, Max-Amalthea-Verlag, Zurich-1931-327p-The Terror of the Seas-

Schwarze Gesselen Torpedoboote und minen-sucher im grossen Kriege-by Neuerberg, Otto-Payne, Leipzig-1933-280 p

Schwarze Schiffe, weite See-by Brennecke, Jochen-W. Heyne, Munchen-1958-269p-**Black Ships, broad sea**

Schwarzer Mai-by Gannon Michael-ISBN 3550069871-See **Black May**

Science and the Navy: the History of the Office of Naval Research-by Sapolsky, Harvey M-Princeton U. Press-1990

Scientists Against Time-by Baxter, James P-Little, Brown & Co.-1950

Scientists and the Admiralty: conflict and collaboration in anti-submarine warfare, 1914-1921-by Wignall, Michael Brown-1987-456p

Scorpion operations phase II: mobile deep submergence / Apache, White Sands, Trieste II, [Submarine Development Group I-The Allen Co, Anaheim, CA-78p

Scraps of Paper-by Hyde, Harlow A-Medio Pub.-1988-ISBN 0939644460
-Disarmament treaties between the World Wars

Sea and its Story, The-by Shaw, FH & Robinson, EH-Cassell, London-
1910-From Viking ship to submarine, historical survey

Sea Battles in Close-up-by Slader, J-Kimber-1988

Sea Devils, The-by Borghese, JV-Chicago-1954-263p-Story of Italian
mini-subs in WW II

Sea Fox Story, The-by Smith, Daniel E-Self Published-800 pages-1944-
1970 History

Sea Hazard-Houlder Bros & Co, UK-1946

Sea Heritage-by Dreyer, Adm Sir Frederic C-Museum Press Limited-
1955

Sea Hunters, The-by Cussler, Clive & Dirgo, Craig-Simon & Schuster-
1996-364p-ISBN 0684830272-True Adventures with Famous
Shipwrecks

Sea Hunters, The-by Poolman, Kenneth-Arms and Armour, London-
1982

Sea in Soviet Strategy, The-by Rauft, Bryan & Till, Geoffery-USNIP-
1989

Sea Our Shield, The-by Fell, William Richmond-Cassell, London-
1966-232p

Sea Power 2000-by Ireland, Bernard-Arms & Armour-UK-1990-160p-
ISBN 0853689792-Current state and future trends in international sea power, naval aviation, submarine warfare, and mines

Sea Power A Modern Illustrated Military History-by Preston,
Anthony & Casey, Louis-Exeter-1979-392p

**Sea Power: A Story of Warships and navies from Dreadnaughts to
Nuclear Submarines**-by Hill-Norton, Lord & Dekker, John-
Faber & Faber-1982

Sea Power and Strategy-by Gray, Colin S & Barnett, Roger-Tri-Service,
Annapolis-1989-396p

Sea Power in the Machine Age-by Brodie, Bernard-Princeton U.
Press-1943

Sea Power in the Pacific, 1936-41-by Ellinger, Werner-Princeton U Press-1942&43-Saunders, Toronto-1944-462p-Oxford U Press edition with 255p

Sea Power of the State-by Gorshkov, Sergei G-Conway Maritime, UK-1979

Sea Power: A Naval History-Potter, EB & Nimitz, Chester-Prentice-Hall, NJ-1960

Sea Stories-by Mendenhall, Corwin-Dorrance Publishing Co-2000-331p-ISBN 080594804X An autobiographical account of RADM Mendenhall's submarine career and a sequel to his book Submarine Diary

Sea War-Reisenberg, Felix-Rinehart & Co-1956

Sea War in Korea, The-by Cagle & Manson-USNIP-1957-555p

Sea Warfare 1939-1945-by Cresswell, John-Longmans, UK-1950-344p

Sea Warfare 1939-1945-by Ruge, Friedrich-Cassell-1957

Sea Wolves, The-by Hoyt, Edwin J-Lancer Books, NY-1972-160p-ISBN 380752492

Sea Wolves, The-by Frank, Wolfgang-Rinehart-1955-340p-History of German U-Boats through WW II

Seaborne Trade-by Fayle, Charles Ernest-3 Vol-Longmans, NY-1920-24-Vol 1-Cruiser Period, Vol 2-The Opening of the Submarine Campaign, Vol 3-Unrestricted sub warfare

Seadragon-Northwest Under the Ice-by Steele, George-Dutton, NY-1962-255p

Search Find and Kill-by Franks, Norman-Aston-1990-168p-RAF VS Submarines in WW II

Seas and the Subs, The-by Rees, Ed-Duell, Sloan & Pearce-1961-253p-Nuclear Subs and the Polaris Revolutionize the U.S. Navy

Sechs Jahre U-Bootfahrten-by Spiess, Johannes-1925-212p, 33 photos-See **Six Years of Submarine Cruising**

Sechsiz Jahre Deutschen U-Boote-1906-1945-by Herzog, Bodo-Germany-1959

Second World War, The-by Churchill, Winston-Houghton Mifflin-1948+-6 vol

Second World War, The-by Keegan, John-Viking-1989

Second World War, The-by Buell, TB-Avery Publishing Group-1984-
  Europe and the Mediterranean

Second World War, The- by Cantwell, John D-HMSO-1993-A Guide to
  Documents in the Public-Records Office

Second World War-by Gness, Gwyn-G.P. Putnam's Sons-1967-Europe
  and the Mediterranean

Seconde Partie du journal du bord-Log of the "Goubet"-by Goubet,
  C-1901

Secret Capture, The-by Roskill, Stephen W-Collins, UK-1959-161p-
  Story of U-110

Secret Mission Submarine-by Jewell, Norman-Ziff-Davis, NY-1945-
  159p-Mission of HMS Seraph

Secret of the Sunken Sub-by Roddy, Lee

Secret Raiders, The-by Woodward, David-London-1955-288p-The
  story of the German Armed Merchant Raiders of the Second
  World War

Secret Service Submarine, The-by Thorne, Guy-Sully & Kleintech,
  NY-1915-190p

Secret War, The-by Russell, Francis and editors of Time-Life-Time-
  Life, Chicago-1981-208p-Spies, ciphers and sabotage in WW II

Secret War For the Ocean Depths, The-Burns, Thomas S-Rawson
  Assoc. Pub-1978-334p Soviet-American Rivalry for Mastery of
  the Seas-

Secret Weapon-by Williams, Kathleen B-USNIP-1996-312p-ISBN
  1557509352-22 photos-US HF Direction Finding in the Battle of
  the Atlantic

Secrets of the Sea-by Mallan, Lloyd-Arco, NY-1976-112p

Secrets of the Submarine-by Hay, MF-Dodd & Mead-1917-229p-
  Chapters on antecedents of the submarine; elements of design,
  safety devices, operation, antidotes, torpedoes and more

**Secret War for the Ocean Depths: Soviet-American Rivalry for
  Mastery of the Seas**-by Burns, Thomas-Rawson Assoc.-1978

Securing Command of the Sea-by Maloney, Sean M-USNIP-1995-276p-ISBN 1557505624 NATO Naval Planning, 1948-1954

See Inside a Submarine-by Rutland, Jonathan-Warwick Press, NY-1980-20p-ISBN 0531091724

Seehunde, Die-by Mattees, Klaus-Mittler & Sohn Verlag, Berlin-1995-224p-ISBN 3813204847-**The Seals**

Seek and Strike-by Hackmann, Willem-H.M. Printing Office-UK-1984-487p-Sonar, Anti-submarine Warfare 1914-1954

Seekrief im Ather-by Bonatz, Heinz-ES Mittler & Sohn-1981-376p-**Naval warfare in the either**

Seekrieg, Der 1939-1945-by Ruge, Friedrich-F.F. Koehler, Stuttgart-320p-**The war at sea 1939-1945**

Seekrieg, Schlachtschiffe und U-Boote, Der-Various authors-Moewig Verlag, Rastatt-1996-94p-ISBN 3811842218-**The Sea War, battleships and U-boats**

Sehrohr sudwarts-by Metzler, Jost-Wilhelm Limpert-Verlag, Berlin-1943-296p, 59photos-**Periscope southward-**Written by CO of U-69

Seizing the Enigma-by Kahn, David-Houghton Mifflin-1991-336p-ISBN 0760708630-The Race to Break the German U-boats Codes 1939-1943

Selected and Annotated Bibliography of American Naval History-by Colleta, Paolo E, ed University Press of American, Lanham, MD-1988

Selected Papers from the Citadel conference on War and Diplomacy-by Addington, Larry-Citadel Press-1978

Sensuikan I-124-by Lewis, Tom-131p-ISBN 0646322184-A history of the Japanese Fleet-This sub was sunk off Darwin 1-20-42 in 150′ of water by HMAS Deloraine

Serpent of the Seas-by Cope, Harley-Funk & Wagnall's-1942-252p-1942 Informative report on United States Fleet and S-type submarine operations during WW II as well as a historical perspective of the U.S. submarine service. Interviews with officers and crewmen

Servicing the Silent-by Bowers, Richard H-USNIP-1943

Servicing the Silent Service-Rodengen, Jeffrey L-1995-The Legend of Electric Boat

Seven Days to Disaster-by Hickey-Smith-1981-The Sinking of the Lusitania

Seven Miles Down-by Piccard, Jacque-NY-1961

Seventh Undersea Medical Society Workshop-by SubGru1-1974

Sharks In Paradise-See Haie in Paradies-Concerns German U-Boat War in Asian waters.

Sharks of Steel-by Stillwell, Paul-by Robert Y. Kaufman-USNIP-1993-152p-ISBN 1557504512-A photographic study of the Nuclear U.S. Navy

Shield of the Republic: The United States Navy in an Era of Cold War and Violent Peace 1945-1962 by Isenberg, Michael-St. Martins, NY-1993

Shinano-by Enright, Capt Joseph & Ryan, James W-St Martins, NY-1987-238p-ISBN 031200186X-USS Archerfish in WW II

Ship Dreadnought to Nuclear Submarine-by Preston, Anthony-Sheridan House-1980-ISBN 0112903193

Ship Steam Steel and Torpedoes-by Lyon, David-Sheridan House-1980-ISBN 0112903185

Ship With Two Captains, The-by Robertson, Terence-Evans-1957-192p-The story of HMS Seraph, the Secret Mission Submarine. One of her assignments was the landing of the American General, Mark Clark, on the shores of N. Africa in 1943

Shipbuilders, The-by Halacy, DS-Lippincott-1966-160p-From Clipper Ships to Submarines

Shipbuilding at Cramp & Sons-by Farr, Gail E-Philadelphia Maritime Museum-1991

Shipbuilding Business in the United States of America-by various-ed. by Fassett, Frederick G.,-Macdonald, London-1974-reprint of 1948 edition-2 vols

Shipbuilding Policies of the War Production Board, Jan 1942-Nov 1945-by Chaikin, William & Coleman, Charles-1947

Ships, aircraft, and weapons of the United States Navy-by the Office of Information and the Naval Material command, in coordination with the Deputy Chiefs of Naval Operations for Air, Surface and Submarine Warfare-USGPO-1980-51p

Ships and Aircraft of the United States Fleet, The-by Fahey, James C-Gemsco, NY-7 editions from 1941-1958-96p

Ships and Aircraft of the U.S. Fleet-16th Edition-by Polmar, Norman-USNIP-1996-656p ISBN 1557506868-830 photos

Ships and Sailors of the Red Navy-by Bishop, Reginald-London-1944

Ships and Submarines-by Grey, Michael-Watts, NY-1986-32p-Youth

Ships Beneath the Sea-by Burgess, Robert-McGraw Hill-1975-260p-ISBN 0070089582 A History of Subs & Submersibles-New edition by iUniverse in June 2000

Ships For Victory-by Lane, Frederic C-Johns Hopkins Press-1951

Ships of Canada's Naval Forces 1910-1981-by Macpherson, Ken & Burgess, J-Collins, Toronto-1981

Ships of the Esso Fleet in World War II-Standard Oil, NJ-1946

Ships of the German Fleets, The-1848-1945-by Hansen, Hans Jurgen-1988-192p-ISBN 0870216546-150 illustrations

Ships of the Royal Navy-Vol 1-1988-450p-ISBN 087021652X

Ships of the U.S. Navy-by Kirk, John & Klein, Aaron-New York-1988

Ships Under the Sea-by Ellacott, Samuel E-Hutchinson, UK-1961-142p

Ships, Machinery, and Mossbacks-by Bowen, Harold G-Princeton U. Press-1954

Ships, Submarines, and the Sea-by Gates, PJ & Lynn, NM-Royal Naval College, Greenwich-1990-178p-ISBN 0080347355

Shipwrecks in the Vicinity of Jupiter Inlet-by DuBois, Bessie Wilson-Privately printed-1975

Shock Design of Shipboard Equipment-USN-ONR-1960-60p

Shooting the War-by Giese, Otto-USNIP-1994-352p-ISBN 1557503079-104 photos-11 maps-Memoirs and Photos of a U-Boat Officer in WW II from the dawning of the war to his confinement in a British POW camp at war's end.

Sidewheelers to Nuclear Power-by Lemmon, Sue & Wichels, ED-Leeward Publications, Annapolis, MD-1977-A Pictorial Essay Covering 123 Years at the Mare Island Naval Shipyard

Sigint Secrets-by West, Nigel-Quill/William Morrow-1988-The Signals Intelligence War 1900 to Today

Signals, Noise, and Active Sensors: Radar, Sonar, Laser and Radio-by Minkoff, John-John Wiley & Sons-1992-249p-ISBN 0471545724

Silent Chase-by Kaufman, Yogi & Steve Kaufman-USNIP-1989-160p-ISBN 0934738386-Full color, all-photo survey of attack and missile submarines of modern US Navy

Silent Hunters-Savas, T.P. ed.-SPC Press-1997-224p-German U-Boat Commanders of WWII

Silent Marauders-by Cook-1976-British Subs in Two World Wars

Silent Running-by Calvert, James F-Wiley-282-Chronicles the wartime exploits of one of the Navy's most decorated World War II heroes and the men who served with him aboard the submarine Jack between 1943 and 1945. 15 Japanese vessels were sunk, many downed fighter pilots were rescued, and the ship unofficially visited Tokyo in September, 1945

Silent Service, The-by Lowder, Hughston E-Silent Service Books-1987-492p-ISBN 096191890X-US Submarines in WW II

Silent Service, The-by Chamblis, William C-New American Library-1959-reissue 1974-190p-Events are actual, dialogue is added for readability. Stories of the Seahorse, Thresher, Bergall, Harder, Perch and Sculpin

Silent Siege-by Webber, Bert-Ye Galleon Press, WA-1984-396p-Japanese Attacks against North America in WWII

Silent Victory-by Blair, Clay Jr-JB Lippincott-1975-1055p-ISBN 0397007531-1Vol HB (1975) Softback (1976) or 2-vol Book Club (1975) edition-USNIP Edition 2001 in Softback. The US Submarine War Against Japan. The Definitive Submarine History of WWII from the most diligent researcher of submarine books in the field. Every patrol is listed in the back 200 pages along with charts of sinkings by boat and skipper.

Silent War, The-By Craven, John Pina-Simon & Schuster-2001-304p-
ISBN 0684872137-The Cold War Battle Beneath the Sea. by
Form Chief Scientist, U.S. Navy Special Projects Office.
Silent War, The-by Deacon, Richard-Hippocrene Book, NY-1978-288p-
ISBN 0715375571 A History of Western Naval Intelligence
Silversides-by Trumbull, Robert-Henry Holt & Co-1945-217p-WW II
submarine SS 236-1990 edition by PW Knutson
Simsadus: London, The American Navy in Europe-by Leighton, John
L-Holt, NY-1920-169p WW I, USN subs in European theater of
operations\
Sing Along with Submariners-Pacific Fleet Submarine Memorial
Association-1981-157p-Located with Paine Collection at
Annapolis
Sink 'em All-by Lockwood, Charles A-1951-416p-Adm Lockwood's
arrival in Australia in 42 to war's end
Sinking of the Belgrano, The-by Rice-Gavshon-1984
Sinking of the Laconia-Grossmith, Frederick-Paul Watkins, UK-1994
Sinking of the Submarine S-4-by USGPO-1928-326-Hearings before
the subcommittee on naval affairs, United States Senate,
Seventeenth Congress, first session, pursuant to S. Res. 205, a
resolution directing the Committee on Naval Affairs to investi-
gate the sinking of the submarine "S-4". April 27 to May 26, 1928
Sinking of the USS Cairo, The-by Wideman, John C-Univ. Press of
Mississippi-1993-139p-ISBN 0878056173
Sinking of the USS Guitarro-Congress-USGPO-1969-254p-SSN665
**Sinuous Courses and the Automatic Course Indicator for
Naval Warfare-**by Bates, Lindell T-The Submarine Defense
Association, NY-1918-63p
Six Years of Submarine Cruising-by Spiess, Johannes-ONI-1926-130p
Sixth Quarter, The-by Graves, Philip-Hutchinson
Slaughter at Sea-by Coles-1986
**Slide Rules and Submarines American Scientists and Subsurface
Warfare in WW II-**by Meiogs, Montgomery C-US GPO-1990-
269p-Describes how the Allies learned to counter the U-Boat

threat during the first half of World War II. Using new technology and new tactics derived from scientific methods, they devised countermeasures to defeat the German submarine menace

So War der U-Boots-Krieg-by Busch, Harald-Deutscher Heimat, Bielefeld-1952-472p-1983 edition of 428p, 97 photos

Sole Survivor-by McCunn, Ruthanne L-Design Enterprise of San Francisco-1985

Sole Survivors of the Sea-by Wise, James E-Nautical & Aviation Pub. Co/Baltimore-1994-203p ISBN 1877853291-A compilation of first-person accounts of unusual seaman who lived, official records and interviews with family members. 21 stories in all

Sommergibila all' Attacco-by Cocchia, A-Rizzoli, Milano-1955-Attack Submarines

Sommergibile Italiani, cento anni di vita tra storia e leggenda-by Marcon, Flamign, Turrini-Rivista marittima, Rome-1990-Italian Submarines, 100 years of life between history and legend

Sommergibili Appoggio, Carenaggio, Trasporto, Recupero, Prova pressatura-by Bulwark-Marina Mercantile Italiana, Milano-1917-Submarines Support, drydocking, transport, recovery, pressure testing

Sommergibili Emersero all" Alba-by Donato, A-Baldini & Castoldi, Milano-1965-The Submarines Surfacing at Dawn

Sommergibili Il Monge, H,3 U.C 12 I Nostri-by Milanesi, Guido-Alfierei & Lacroix, Milano-1917-64lp-Located in Italian Sub School

Sommergibili in Guerra-by Bagnasco, E-E. Albertelli, Parma-1989-Submarines in War

Sommergibili in Guerra-by Marina Militare-1956-215p-WW II Italian subs in the Med

Sommergibili Italiani, fra le due guerre dondiali-by Turrini, A-Stato Magg. Marina, Rome-1989-Italian Submarines, between the two world wars

Sommergibili Italiani nell' Atlantico-by De Giacomo-L'Arnia, Rome-1950-Italian Submarines in the Atlantic

Sonar & Underwater Sound-by Cox, Albert W-Lexington Books-1974-144p

Sonar Engineering Handbook-by Loeser, Harrison T-Peninsula Pub-1993-ISBN 0932146597

Sonaranlagen der deutschen U-Boote, Die-by Rossler, Eberhard-Koehler Verlag, Herford-128p, 50photos, 60 drawings-**Sonar Equipment of the German U-boats**

Sopra di Noi L' Oceano-by Trizzino, A-Longanese & C, Milano-1962-Above us the Ocean

Sotto I Mari del Mondo, la Whitehead 1875-1990-by Casali & Cattaruzza-Laterza, Bari-1990-Under the Seas of the World, the Whitehead 1875-1990

Sottomarini, Sommergibili c Torpedini-by Bravetta, Eltora-Fratelli Treves, Milano-1915-230p-Located in Italian Sub School-Submarines, submersibles and Torpedoes

Source Book of Submarines and Submersibles, The-by Watts, Anthony J-Ward Lock, London 1976-127p

Sous-Mariners-by Guierre, Maurice CL-Flammarion, Paris-1948-306p

Sous-marins et submersibles-by Laubeuf, Maxime-Delagrave-Paris-1917-100p-WW1-A leading French submarine designer. Their development, role during WWI, and future role. Includes a survey of German submarines also

Sous-marins, Torpilles-by Tissier, M-Imprimene Nationale-1898

Sous-marins, Torpilles et Mines-by Laubeuf, Maxime-JB Bailliere-Paris-1923-810p-A reference work on submariners, torpedoes and mines at the end of WWI. Largely historical and extensive views of WWI German submarines. A lengthy bibliography of US, British, Italian and German sources

Soviet and Russian Nuclear Submarines-by Kopenhaven, Wilfried-40p-100+ illustrations

Soviet Fleet in Transition-by Friedman, Norman-USNIP-1983

Soviet Naval Operations in the Great Patriotic War 1941-1945-by Achkasov, VI & Pavlovich NB-USNIP-1981-393p

Soviet Naval Power-by Polmar, Norman-Nat. Strategic Info. Cntr.-Washington-1973

Soviet Naval Strategy-by Herrick, Robert W-USNIP-1968-197p

Soviet Naval Theory and Policy: Gorshkov's Inheritance-Naval War College Press-1988

Soviet Navy, The-by Saunders, Malcolm G-Praeger-1958-340p-5 pages on submarines

Soviet Russian Submarine Accidents 1956-1994-by Handler, Joshua-Greenpeace-1994

Soviet Sea Challenge, The-Eller, Ernest McNeill-Cowles, NY-1972-315p

Soviet Sea Power in the Caribbean-by Theberge, James-Praeger, NY-1972-175p

Soviet Submarine Design Philosophy-by Englehardt, John G-USNIP-1987

Soviet Submarine Fleet, The-by Berg, John-Jane's, UK-1985-ISBN 0710603614-A Photographic Survey

Soviet Submarine Operations in Swedish Waters 1980-1986-by Leitenberg, Milton-Praeger Pub 1987-199p

Soviet Submarine RECCE Guide: technical training naval intelligence officer intelligence specialist-Naval Intelligence Branch, Lowry AF Base, CO-1984-116p

Soviet Submarine Recognition Guide-Air Force Intelligence Center-1984

Soviet Submarine Vessels-by Dimetriev, VI-Military Publishing House, Moscow-1990-ISBN 5203002541-In Russian

Soviet Submarines-by Jordan, John-Sterling Publications-1989-192p-1945 to the Present

Soviet Submarines-by Breemer, Jan S-Jane's Info Group-1989-187p-ISBN 0710605269 Design, Development and Tactics

Soviet Submarines-by Miller, D-Rourke Publishing Group-1988-ISBN 086625336X

Soviet Submarines of Postwar Construction-by Shirokorad, AB-Arsenal Press, Moscow-1997-Sovetskiye Podvodnyee Lodki Poslevoyennov Postryki

Soviet Subs in Scandinavia-by Suggs, Robert S-USNIP-1930 to 1945

Soviet Union in Arctic Waters-by Ostreng, Willy-Sea Institute-1987-ISBN 0911189157

Soviet Warships 1945 to Present-by Jordan, John-London-1992

Soviet Warships of the Second World War-by Meister, Jurg-London-1977

Soviets as Naval Opponents, The-by Ruge, Friedrich-USNIP-1979-ISBN 0870216767-1941-1945

Sowjetflotte als Gegner im Seekrieg 1941-1945-by Ruge, Friedrich-Motorbuch Verlag, Stuttgart-1981-247p-ISBN 3879437793-**The Soviet fleet as enemy in the war at sea 1941-1945**

Special Specifications and Special Purchase Specifications for Propelling Machinery and Electric Plant for U.S. Submarine Rescue Vessels Chanticleer (ASR 7) Coucal (ASR 8) Florikan (ASR 9) Greenlet (ASR 10) Macaw (ASR 11)-by BuShips-1941-141p

Special and Purchase Specifications for Propelling Machinery and Electric Plant for U.S.

Submarine tenders Bushnell (AS15) Neptune (AS16) Nereus (AS17) Orion (AS18) Proteus (AS19)-BuShips-1941-282p

Spider Web, The-by P.I.X-Blackwood, London-1919-278p-Anti-Submarine Patrol in Flying boats

Splinter Fleet of the Ontario Barrage-by Millholland, Ray-Boobs, Merrill, 1936-307p-WW I mine warfare

Spy Book-by Polmar, Norman, Thomas, Allen-Random House-1996-ISBN 0679425144-The Encyclopedia of Espionage-A chapter on Ivy Bells

Spy Hunter: Inside the FBI Investigation of the Walker Espionage Case-by Hunter, Robert W-USNIP-250p-ISBN 1557503494

Spy Sub-USS Viperfish-by Dunham, Roger-USNIP-1996-ISBN 1557501785-Written by former crewmember of USS Halibut-Paperback edition by Onyx in 1997

Spying Beneath the Waves, Nuclear Submarine Intelligence Operations-by Kristensen, Hans M-Greenpeace-1994

Squali d' Acciao-by Maioli, G-Fratelli Melita, La Spezia-1988-Sharks of Steel

Squali d' Acciao-by Pegolotti, B-Racconti di Guerra, Rome-1959-Sharks of Steel

SSN-21 Seawolf-by Dille, Ed-Prima Pub-1994-ISBN 1559585277-Paperback-The Official Strategy Guide for the CDROM game

SSN-688-class Submarine Procurement-by USGPO-1981-67p-hearing before a subcommittee of the Committee on Appropriations, United States Senate, Ninety-seventh Congress, first session: special hearing, congressional and nondepartmental witness, Department of Defense—Navy

SSSR-Velikaia Morskaia Derzhava-by Kornienko, Daniil I-Moscow-1957-The USSR-A Great Sea Power

Stalag: U.S.A.-by Gansberg, Judith M-Thomas Crowell-1977

Stalin's Silver-by Beasant, John-216p-St. Martin's Press-ISBN 0312205902-U-859 sinks the SS John Barry carrying $380 million in silver and it's recovery 45 years later

Stalking the U-Boat-by Schoenfeld, Max-272p-ISBN 0156098403-35 b&w photos-USAAF Offensive Antisubmarine Operations in WW II

Stand by to Ram-by Lanyard, pseud-Lockwood & Son, London-1943-114p

Stand by to Surface-by Baxter, Richard-Cassel, London-1944-208p

Station X: The Codebreakers of Bletchley Park-by Smith, M-1998

Statistical Digest of the War-by Hancock, WK-HMSO, UK-1975

Statuis of Research in Underwater Physiology-by Nat. Academy of Science Comm. on Undersea Warfare-NAS, Washington-1956

Status of the Navy's New Seawolf-by Conahan, Frank-GAO-1990

Status of the Trident Submarine and Missile Programs-GAO-1977

Stealth At Sea-by van der Vat, Dan-Houghton Mifflin-1994-421p-ISBN 1857978671-The History of the Submarine

Steel Boats Iron Hearts-by Goebeler, Hans Jacob & Vanzo, John P-Wagnerian Publications, Holder, FL-1999-The Story of the U-505 and the man who pulled the plug on this captured U-Boat, just not quick enough. Their incarceration

Steel Boats Iron Men-by Rindskoph, RADM MH & Morris, Richard K-Turner Publishing Co-1994-208p-ISBN 1563110814-Compiled and sponsored by NSL-Many photos-History of NSL, Members biographies, early history, sea stories, corporate histories, roster, tenders, WWII fleet boat

Steel Ships and Iron Men-by Roberts, Bruce & Ray Jones-Globe Pequot-1991-145p-ISBN 0871062445-Details over thirty floating memorials to WW II battleships, cruisers, destroyers, PT boats and submarines that are open to the public, look down the barrel of [Alabama's] 18 inch guns, explore the confined quarters of the submarine Cavalla, and more

Steuermann durch Krieg und Frieden-by Schmid, Hans-Berg-Verlag-1994-ISBN 3861180324-**Helmsman through War and Peace**-A first person account of his duties on ships and U-boats

Stick and the Stars-RNT-class subs-by King, Cmdr William-WW Norton, NY-1958-192p-The author, commanded the submarine HMS Snapper in the North Sea at the beginning of the war, and at the end of the war he was the only commander who had been in action virtually throughout the six years

Stier von Scapa Flow, Der-by Frank, Wolfgang-Stalling Verlag Ordenburg-1958-292p-Written about Gunther Prien by a man who did one patrol on the U-47-**The Bull of Scapa Flow**

Stolen Submarine, The-by Griffith, G-FV White, NY-1945-320p

Storia del sottomarino Dai primi esper, di Fulton a quelli atomic-by Antier JJ-Sugar Editore, Milano-1969-History of the Submarine From the first experience of the Fulton to Atomic submarines

Storia Mondiale del Sommergibile-by Ghetti, W-G de Vecchi, Milano-1975-Global Story of the Submarine

Stories of Famous Submarines-by Ortzen, Len-A Barker, London-1973-170p

Struggle for the Mediterranean, The-by de Belot, Rear Adm Raymond-Princeton U. Press-1951-287p

Struggle for the Sea-by Raeder, Grand Adm-William Kimber-1959

Studies in the Law of Naval Warfare-by Mallison, William T-GPO-1968

Studies of War-by Blackett, PMS-Oliver & Boyd-1962-Nuclear & Conventional

Study of Leadership of Submarine Officers-by Donald T. Campbell-Columbus, Ohio: Ohio State University Research Foundation-1953-210p-: a study of perceptions of organization structure and their social correlates in a submarine squadron of the United States Navy

Stuifzeetjes over de P 322-by van Dapperen, Ltz J.-N.V. Nederlandse bedrijven der Koninkliijke Boekhandel-1964-The Dutch submarine "Zwaardvisch"

Sub Commander-by Sheffield, Richard G-Computer Publications-N. Car.-1988-A book written to teach people submarine tactics so that they can better control computer submarine games. Not technically correct

Sub Duty-by McLeod, Grover S-Southern U. Press-1986-581p

Sub vs Sub-by Compton-Hall, Sir Richard-Orion Books-1988-The Tactics and Techniques of Underwater Warfare

Sub-Chaser in the South Pacific-by Doscher-1994

Subchaser-by Stafford, Edward P-1988

Submarine-by Banning, Kendall-1942-51p-The story of Undersea Fighters

Submarine-by Bauer, Admiral, t by Rickover, HG-Newport, R.I.: Department of Intelligence, Naval War College, 1936-Its importance as part of a fleet, its position in international law, its employment in war, its future

Submarine-by Beach, Edward L-Signet-1946-312p-Wartime combat patrols of the USS Trigger, Seawolf, Tang, Harder, Archerfish, Wahoo & other famous U.S. subs during WW II Also published by Henry Holt in 1952

Submarine-by Clancy, Tom-Berkley-1993-328p-ISBN 0425138739-Paperback

Submarine-by Colby, Carroll B-Coward-McCann, NY-1953-48p-Youth oriented-Men and Ships of the U.S. Submarine Fleet

Submarine-by Crane, Jonathan-BBC, UK-1984-208p-ISBN 0563203269-Life in the British Sub Service

Submarine-by Hudson, Alec-Macmillan, NY-1940

Submarine-by Lake, Simon, Herbert, Corey, ed-Appleton, NY-1938-303p-The Autobiography of Simon Lake

Submarine-by Marriott-1986

Submarine-by Middleton, Drew-1976-Past, Present and Future-Playboy Press-1976-ISBN 087223472X

Submarine-by Thomas, Humble-F. Watts-1985

Submarine-Hunters, Killers & Boomers-Consumer Guide Edition-1990

Submarine-by Whitestone, Nicholas-Davis-Poynter, London-1973-ISBN 0706700791-The Ultimate Weapon-

Submarine-by Wingate, John-Spere Books-1982-212p **Submarine Admiral**-by Galantin, Adm IJ-Illinois U. Press-1995-345p-From Battlewagons to Ballistic Missiles

Submarine Advanced Reactor Gas Turbine Cycle Study-by A.E.C.-G.E.-1953-70p

Submarine Adventure of Little Jinks-by Jewett, HK-Wetzel-LA-1930

Submarine Against Rising Sun-*Dienesch, Robert M.*-1996-227-The impact of radar on the American submarine war in 1943 the year of change

Submarine Alliance, The-Anatomy of the Ship Series-by Lambert & Hill-Conway Maritime 1986-120p-ISBN 0870216880-360 Illustrations

Submarine Alone-by Hackforth-Jones, Frank G-1943-141p-A story of the HMS Steadfish

Submarine Alternatives Study: hearings before the Seapower and Strategic and Critical Materials Subcommittee of the Committee on Armed Services, House of Representatives, Ninety-sixth Congress, second session-by USGPO-1980-182p

Submarine and Anti-submarine-by Newbolt, Henry J-Doran, NY-1918-Longman, London - 312p

Submarine and Kindred Problems, The-US Naval Consulting Board-1917-15p

Submarine and Sea Power-by Domville-Fife, Charles W-G Bell, UK-1919

Submarine and Sea Power, The-by Hezlet, Arthur-Stein & Day-1967-278p

Submarine and U.S. National Security Strategy Into the Twenty-First Century, The-by Davis, Jacquelyn-Tufts University-1997-85p

Submarine at Bay-by Mars, Alistar-Elec, London-1956-164p

Submarine at War-by Hoyt, Edwin P.-Stein & Day, NY-1983-329p-The history of the American silent service

Submarine at War, The-by Low, Archibald M-Hutchinson & Co, London-1942-305p

Submarine at War-by Mori, K Stechert, NY-1931

Submarine Attacks on the West Coast-by *Reynolds, Clark G.*-1964-14 leaves

Submarine Badges and Insignia of the World-by Prichard, Pete-1997-136p-400 photographs This book is a complete compendium of the submarine badges of the world, dating from the Imperial Russian Naval Officer's Submarine School Graduation Badge of 1909 to the new South Korean Submariner's Badge issued in 1996. It covers all countries currently operating submarines as well as those no longer existing as political entities. It covers over 50 countries from the inception of their submarine forces to date. Privately published. 401-848-7252 to order

Submarine Boat, The-Merville-1902

Submarine Boat Argonaut, The-by Lake, Simon-NY-1900-16p

Submarine Boat and Its Future, The-Holland, John-1900-10 p

Submarine Boat, The-by Hutchinson, Miller Reese-NJ-1915-28p-Type of Edison Storage Battery

Submarine Boat Holland-USGPO-1898-11p

Submarine Boats-by Compton-Hall, Richard-Conway, London-1983-192p-The Beginning of Underwater Warfare

Submarine Boats-by Hovgaard, George W-Spon, London-1887-98p

Submarine Boats and Torpedo Operations-by Barber, FM-US Torpedo Station/Newport, RI-1875

Submarine Book, The-by Lawliss, Chuck-Thames & Hudson-1991-160p-A Portrait of Nuclear Submarines and the men who sail them

Submarine Casualties-USN-1915-1945

Submarine Combat System-SSN-21 AN/BSY-2 Development-by GAO-1989-14p

Submarine Command-by Longstaff, Reginald-Robert Hale, UK-1984-264p-A Pictorial History

Submarine Commander-by Schratz, Paul-USNIP-1988-322p-ISBN 00813116619-Pocket Books edition 1990-397p-Schratz was a US submarine Commander who tells the story of WWII from the Scorpion and continues the story into the Korean War era

Submarine Commander RN-by Bryant, Ben-William Kimber, UK-1958-258p-Titled "One Man Band" in the UK edition. Republished 1980 by Bantam. WW II memoirs of RADM Bryant ISBN 0553136658

Submarine Data-1965

Submarine Dead Ahead-by Goldberg, Kim-1959-ISBN 1550170538-Getting Nanoose Bay in Canada back from the US

Submarine Defense-by Bassford, Thomas-Bassford-1917-1919-231p-"My objects are to take the sting out of the submarine, relieve the mine of its punch, yet be economical and practical"

Submarine Design-by Gabler, Ulrich-Bernard & Graefe Verlag-1986-ISBN 3763701249

Submarine Design and Development-by Friedman, Norman-USNIP-1984-192p

Submarine Design for the Twenty First Century-by Zimmerman, Stan-Pasha Publications, Arlington, VA-1993-182p

Submarine Design Handbook-Rector Press-1994

Submarine Detection from Space-by Hung P. Nguyen-USNIP 1993-79p-ISBN 1557506396 A study of Russian Capabilities

Submarine Diary-by Mendenhall, RADM-Corwin/Bluejacket Books-1995-290p-ISBN 1557505829-Bluejacket Edition is softcover-The Silent Stalking of Japan

Submarine Disarmament-Douglas, Lawrence Henry-Unpublished On File Nimitz Library Annapolis-1970-276p-1919-1936

Submarine Engineering-by the Lake Co-1906-49p

Submarine Engineering-by Walker, Sydney-Pearson, UK-1914-126p

Submarine Engineering of Today-Domville-Fife, Charles W-G. Bell, UK-1914-323p

Submarine Escape History, Part G-1945-41leaves

Submarine Fighter of the American Revolution-by Wagner, Fredrick-Dodd, Mead-1963-145p The Story of David Bushnell

Submarine Fighters of World War II-by RADM Cope, H & Karig, Walter, CAPT-WW Norton & Co, NY-1951

Submarine Flotilla-by Hack forth-Jones, Gilbert-Hodder, London-1940-283p

Submarine Force Library & Museum Masters Thesis-by Williams-1971-192p

Submarine Grayback-by Rick Cline-RA Cline Publishing-1999-252p-ISBN 0966323513

Submarine Habitability-by Nall, Jane-Documentation Inc.-1959-31p-A literature survey

Submarine Hulls of Titanium-by Heggstad, Kare-Maritime Defense-1987

Submarine in Naval Warfare 1901-2001-by Lautenschlger, Karl-Princeton U. Press-1988

Submarine in Periodical Literature-by Hosmer, Helen R-Franklin Institute-Phila-1917

Submarine in the United States Navy, The-by Naval History Division-Washington-1960-32p 3rd edition of this book was published in 1949

Submarine in War, The-A study of relevant rules and problems-by Mori, K-Stechert, NY-1931-185p

Submarine in War and Peace, The-by Lake, Simon-Lippincott, Philadelphia-1918-302p

Submarine Insignia and Submarine Services of the World-by Thornton, WM-USNIP-1997-192p-200 color illustratio

Submarine Journal by Kiefer, Edwin Arnold-Kiefer Publications-This author publishes a quarterly journal in 8 ½ X 11" size. He also has written books in addition. He was a member of the USS Trout in WWII.

> **Submarine Journal March 1993**
>> Vote of a Lifetime-Being the Adventures of a land-roving sub
>> End of the Rainbow revisited by Edwin Kiefer-The USS Trout and the Gold Run
>> The Storm at Hunter's Point The Chaplain's Piece-Funeral Oration for a great submariner
>> Fate? or Murder at Midway?
>> The German and American Submarine Effort in WWII Compared

> **Submarine Journal Summer 1993**
>> Middleton on Torpedoes
>> The Wahoo and the Yellow Whale
>> Poem-A City in the Sea by Edgar Allen Poe
>> On Depth Charges
>> Robert Logue's Letter-A crewman off the Wahoo who was transferred to the Dolphin

> **Submarine Journal Fall 1993**
>> Defining Moments-George Bush and the Finback
>> Portfolio of Pictures and Documentation
>> Poem-Discipline
>> Roots of the German and American Submarine Experience Comparison
>> A Question of Mangoes

Submarine Journal Winter 1993/4
> German and American Submarine Effort in WWII
> compared Part II
> A Fifth of Tautog
> When Germans Invaded Holland, Dutch boats and
> Government were Gone
> War Diary of the USS Thresher

Submarine Journal Spring 1994
> A Frank Exchange with Eleanor Roosevelt
> The Spirit of "Pink Princess" Past
> International Submarine Association
> The Last Patrol
> Now the Lord Prepared a Great Fish

Submarine Journal Summer 1994
> John Denholm and the Nautilus
> The Nigger of the Trumpa or Pushing the Envelope
> Poem-Flight of the Penguins
> Diary of Sister M. Irene Alton
> Diary of Sister Helda Jaeger
> A Short History of the Sisters of the St. Joseph of
> Orange in the Island of Buka

Submarine Journal Fall 1994
> French Sub Surcouf Under a Microscope
> An Expressive French Gesture From a Former Crew
> Member of the Surcouf
> Facts and a Probable Reconstruction
> International Submarine Association Convention of
> Versailles, France

Submarine Journal Winter 1994-5
> The Story of the Failure of the German Submarine
> Policy in WWII and its Nemesis, the B-24
> A History of Seething, England—B-24 Air Base
> Lt. Col. Leroy Engdahl

Submarine Journal Spring 1995
> The Metamorphosing of Victory
> Lt. John Milton Buxton
> Two Fishes submitted by Michael Hourigan

Submarine Journal Summer 1995
> Photo Op
> Fate?...Or Murder at Midway

Submarine Journal Fall 1995
> Geck's Quartet of John J. Geck-USS Gurnard and USS
>   Besugo
> Sugar Boats without the Sugar-by Jack Brillowski of
>   S-30
> Typhoon

Submarine Journal Winter 1995/6
> Initial Indirection and Growing Will to Submarines
> Aborting an Army Shanghai
> Special Privilege for Presidential Candidate's Son
> Oops! Opening in the Fog shows a Sinking Hammer
>   and Sickle
> Harder's Dealey "Press-Gangs" a Name from the List
>   for want a little Salt
> The old "Sighted Sub sank Same" syndrome in the Air
>   Force
> Exotic Perfumes-Hidden Shores
> Savage Onlookers. One Lost, six saved
> Other Facets of Jewel: USS Sterlet crew comments
> German War Prisoners: The American Version of
>   Schlinder's List
> The Cat with the Wooden Leg

Submarine Journal Spring 1996
> The USS Aspro During WWII
> A Strafing Mission to Chofu Airfield (West Tokyo)
> A Moveable Feast

Submarine Journal Summer 1996
>The Two Faces of Penang
>Down Moon
>The University of Lockout
>Grenadier's Vital Signs Gone!
>Maximum Force Hits Everywhere Aft of the Engine
>>Room
>What Did the Navy Know and When Did They Know It?
>Grenadier Voiceless
>Engineering Officer and Electricians Regretfully
>>Despair
>Real Politic of Submarine Management
>More Trouble
>The Unwisdom of Following a Guitar Act with a
>>Guitar Act

Submarine Journal Fall 1997
>Historic Odyssey on U-188

Submarine Journal Spring 1998
>Survivor's Story of the USS Flier

Submarine Journal Summer 1998
>The U-188 Goes Asiatic and the Penang Connection

Submarine Journal Fall 1998
>The Base

Submarine Journal Winter 1998/9
>We Remember the Tambor SS 198
>Diary of Robert R. Hunt TM
>Shocking Record of U.S. Submarines
>Vote of a Lifetime
>A Portfolio of Wartime Crew of U-188

Submarine Journal Spring 1999
>Part one of Novel by Kiefer of the book Anatomy of Glory

Submarine Journal Summer 1999
>Part two of Novel-Anatomy of Glory

Submarine Journal Fall 1999
> Part three of Novel-Anatomy of Glory

Submarine Journal Winter 99/00
> Part four of Novel-Anatomy of Glory

Submarine Journal Spring 2000
> Contexts

Submarine Journal Books
Submarine Worlds-Book 1-Novel-The Anatomy of Glory
Submarine Worlds-Book 2-True Submarine Tales
Submarine Worlds-Book 3-Submarine History
Submarine Worlds-Book 4-The Rhyme and the Sea
> This volume contains 4 Appendices
>> A. Subpoena by Royal High Court of the Raging Main
>> B. Copy of Submarine Qualification Notebook
>> C. Notes on the Operation of the TDC
>> D. Sketches of Fleet Type Functional Subsystems

The Golden Belly of the 202 USS Trout
Pilgrim Fish
Asides Volume 1-1982-A Poetry booklet written by Kiefer
Asides Volume 2-1983-A Poetry booklet written by Kiefer
Submarine Maintenance Transition in the Mid-Atlantic Region- Peter F. Johnson-1999-62 leaves
Submarine Material Guide-by USN-Washington-1944-59p
Submarine Medical Practice-USN Bureau of Medicine and Surgery-1956 j-357p
Submarine Men and Ships of the U.S. Submarine Fleet-Colby, C.B.-New York, Coward-McCann 1953-48p
Submarine Mining-US Coast Artillery Office-GPO-1930-275p
Submarine Mines and Torpedoes, as Applied to Harbor Defenses-by Bucknill J. Townsend-New York, Wiley, 1889-255p

Submarine Navigation-Past and Present-by Burgoyne, Alan H-Dutton, NY-1903-2 Vol

Submarine Operation History WWII-by COMSUBPAC-US Navy-USGPO-1947-4 Volumes-World War II

Submarine Operations-Dec 1941-April 1942

Submarine or Phantom Target?: A search for the truth-by March, Allison E. & McElfresh-Silver Spring, Md.: Edisto Press-1998-384p

Submarine Peril, The-by Jellicoe, John R-Cassell, UK-1934-256p-The Admiralty Policy in 1917

Submarine Periscope, The-by Kollmorgen Corporation-1966

Submarine Pioneer-by John Philip Holland & Morriss, Frank-Bruce Pub. Co-1961-144p

Submarine Problems & Torpedo Defense-by Steinmetz, JA-Phila.-1915-96p

Submarine Recognition Manual-by NavPers-GPO, Washington-1965-38p

Submarine Recognition, Section no. 1. German submarines-by Office of Naval Intelligence-1942 21p

Submarine Registry and Bibliography-by Paine, Thomas-Submarine Warfare Library, CA-1992 828p-Lists 8000 submarines of 50 countries and a world wide bibliography

Submarine Research Apparatus-by Sasaki, Tadayoshi-Tokyo

Submarine Review, The-by Naval Submarine League-Quarterly Journal published since 1983-An index of all the articles and book reviews published since the Review's inception is included in Appendix IV

Submarine Safety, Respiration and Rescue Devices-by USN Bureau of Construction and Repair-1938-137p

Submarine Safety, Respiration and Rescue Devices-by USN-Washington-1946-29p

Submarine Sailor-by Perkins, J David-Seaboot Productions-Ca-1995-47p-ISBN 0969900201 The First World War Adventures of a Canadian Sub Captain

Submarine Secondary Batteries-Great Britain Admiralty-1920 (3rd)-
59p

Submarine Service Aptitude Test-by Cosgrove, Dana-1988-256

Submarine Sighting Guide-by USGPO-1958-17p

Submarine Signal Log-by *Fay, Harold J. W.*-Raytheon-1963-36p

Submarine Signaling-by Hayes, Hammond V-The Submarine Signal
Co, Boston-1920-27p

Submarine Signalling by Means of Sound-Millet, JB-London-1905-7p

Submarine Stories and Adventures-by Walters, EW-Kelly, London-
1917-256p

Submarine Structure-by Prasolov, SN & Amitin, MB-Russian-1973

Submarine Tankers-A feasibility Report-by General Dynamics-1959-
22p

Submarine Technology for the 21st Century-by Zimmerman, Stan-
Pasha Publications-1991-219 p-2nd edition-2000-ISBN 1552123308
-Chapters on Nuclear power plants, AIP propulsion, chemical
AIP systems, hulls, polymers, quieting, weapons, sensors and
tomorrows submariners

Submarine Tender USS Howard W. Gilmore AS 16-1966-44p-Cruise
book

Submarine, The-by Stirling, Yates-1917

Submarine The Capital Ship of Today-by Marriott, John-Ian Allen-
1986-128p-This book covers design, construction, roles,
weapons, sensors and communications and what life is like
onboard a modern submarine.

Submarine Torbay-by Chapman, Paul-Robert Hale Ltd, UK-1989-
ISBN 0709038216-Covers the first 11 patrols of the Torbay in
the Med 1941-1942 and it's sinking of 36 ships and earned it's
commander Tony Miers the Victorian Cross

Submarine Torpedo Boat, The-by Hoar, Allen-Van Nostrand, NY-
1916-211p-Illustrated-First Edition

Submarine Torpedo Boats, The-by Lake Torpedo Boat Company-NY-
1901-31p

Submarine Training Manuals-by NavPers

The Fleet Type Submarine NavPers 16160-B
Basic Enlisted Submarine Text-NavPers 10490-1963-Supercedes NavPers 16160-B
Submarine Main Propulsion Diesels NavPers 16161
Submarine Electrical Installations NavPers 16162
Submarine Refrigeration and A-C Systems NavPers 16163
Submarine Distilling Systems NavPers 16163A
Submarine Air Systems NavPers 16164
Submarine Periscope Manual NavPers 16165
Submarine Trim and Drain Systems NavPers 16166
Submarine Sonar Operators Manual NavPers 16167
Submarine Underwater Log NavPers 16168
Submarine Hydraulic Systems NavPers 16169
Torpedo Tubes, 21 Inch, Mk 32-39 NavPers 16164-A
Submarine U-93-by Gilson, Charles J-London-1916-295p-A Tale of the Great War
Submarine Upholder-by Hart, Sydney-Oldbourne-1960-This submarine was active in the Mediterranean, holding off supplies to Rommel's army. The Commander of Upholder won the VC and the DSO with two bars
Submarine Versus Submarine-by Compton-Hall, Richard & Mills, Don-Collins Publishers-Ca-1988-191p-ISBN 0002154331-Tactics and Technology of Underwater Confrontation
Submarine Versus the Submersible, The-by Lake, Simon-Washington, D.C.: Beresford Press-1906-116p
Submarine Versus U-Boat-Maritime Books-1986
Submarine Vessels, Including Mines, Torpedoes, Guns, Steering, Propelling and Navigating apparatus and with notes on Submarine Offensive and Defensive Tactics and Exploits in the Present War-by Dommet, W.E.-Whitaker, London-1915-106p
Submarine Veterans of World War II: a history of the veterans of the United States naval submarine fleet-Taylor Publishing-1991-4 volumes and separate Index volume

Submarine Victory-by Thomas, David A-William Kimber & Co, UK-1961-224p-The story of British Subs in WW II

Submarine Wahoo-by Davis, Gary-Crestwood House, NY-1994-48p-Youth oriented-ISBN 0382247531-One of nine in a series of "Those Daring Machines"

Submarine War, The-by Masters, David-Holt, NY-1935-296p

Submarine War on Commerce, The-by Catel, Fred, trans-Naval War College-1934

Submarine Warfare-by Abbott, Henry, L-UK-1966

Submarine Warfare-by Barnes, John S-Van Nostrand, NY-1869-233p

Submarine Warfare-by Colby-1967

Submarine Warfare-by Fitzgerald, Charles-London-1919

Submarine Warfare-by Fyfe, Herbert C-E. Grant Richards, UK-1907-302p-54 Illus

Submarine Warfare-by Gaget, Maurice-Liege-1901

Submarine Warfare-by Gardiner

Submarine Warfare-by Hall, Sidney S-London-1920

Submarine Warfare-USGPO-Monthly information bulletin. Supplement number 3-January 1926 170p

Submarine Warfare in the Arctic-Option or Illusion-by Sakitt, Mark-Stanford University-1988-93p-ISBN 0935371192

Submarine Warfare in the Strategy of American Defense and Diplomacy, 1915-1945-by Bemis, Samuel Unpublished in authors collection

Submarine Warfare-Monsters & Midgets-by Compton-Hall, Richard-Blandford Press-1985   160p-ISBN 0713713895-Features full descriptions, design, costruction and wartime history of these extraordinary submarines

Submarine Warfare of Today-by Domville-Fife, Charles W-Seeley, London-1920-304p-how the submarine menace was met and vanquished, with descriptions of the inventions and devices used, fast boats, mystery ships, nets, aircraft, &c., &c., also describing the selection and training of the enormous personnel used in this new branch of the navy. With 53 illustrations.

Submarine Warfare-Offensive and Defensive-by Barnes, John S-Van Nostrand-1869-233p offensive and defensive, including a discussion of the offensive torpedo system, its effects upon iron-clad ship systems, and influence upon future naval wars…with illustrations

Submarine Warfare-Today and Tomorrow-by Moore, Capt. John E-Adler & Adler-1986-308p

Submarine Warriors-by Gray, Edwin-Presidio-1988-275p-ISBN 0891413251-17 great submarine CO's from WW I and WW II

Submarine Wolfpack-by Hardy, William M-Dodd, Mead, NY-1961-175p

Submarine X7-by Pitman, Sir Isaac & Sons-Pitman, London-1917

Submarine!-by Beach, Edward-Henry Holt, NY-1946-301p-A Personal Account

Submarine!-by Banning, Kendall-Charles Rosner, NY-1942-52p-The Story of Undersea Fighter-For older children

Submarine!-by Hudson, Alec-Macmillan, NY-1943-160p

Submarine, Mines & Torpedoes-by Domville-File, Charles W-Hodder & Stoughton-1914

Submarine, The-by Bauer, Hermann-USN War College-1936 translation by Hyman Rickover It's importance as part of the fleet

Submarine-The Ultimate Naval Weapon-by Middleton, Drew-Playboy Press-1976

Submarine: A One Act Drama-by Lowther, George F-French, NY-1946

Submariner-by Anscombe, Charles-Kimber, London-1957-203p

Submariner-Coote, John-New York: Norton-1992-239p

Submariner!-by Degnan, James L-Dodd & Mead, NY-1959-96p

Submariner-by Lent, Henry-Macmillan, NY-1962-182p-The Story of Basic Training at the Navy's Submarine School-41 B&W photos of locations on Subase and classrooms

Submariner, The-by Stephens, Edward-Doubleday, NY-1973-215p-ISBN 0385088841

Submariner-The Ultimate Weapon-by Whitestone, Nicholas-Davy Poynter, UK-1973

Submariners-by Casing, James-Macmillan, London-1951

Submariners VC-by Jameson, William-Peter Davies-1962-207p-14 British submarine sailors who won the Victoria Cross

Submariners World, The-by Compton-Hall, PR-Redwood Burn Ltd-1983-144p-ISBN   0859373037

Submariners: The Story of Underwater Craft-by Stephen, Edward-Golden Press for Children-1959

Submarines-by Chant, Christopher-Cavendish, NY-1989-64p-Youth-Illustrated Guide series

Submarines-by Compton-Hall, Richard-Wayland Publishers, Hove, England-1982-64p-ISBN 0853409560

Submarines-by Dadin, Michael-Rand-McNally, Chicago and Allen, Toronto-1963-96p

Submarines-by Garrett, Richard-Little, Brown-1977-143p

Submarines-by Gibbons, Tony-1987-48p- ISBN 0583310095-Youth-Examines the functions and design features, both diesel and nuclear, and focuses on tactics, missiles and torpedoes

Submarines-by Grady, Sean M-Lucent Books-1994-96p-Youth-Probing the ocean depths

Submarines-by Graham, Ian-Franklin/Watts-Glouchester-1989

Submarines-by Hervey, JB Adm-Brassey's-1994-289p-150 illustrations-ISBN 0080409709

Submarines-by Humble, Richard-Watts, NY-1985

Submarines-by James, Alan-Blackwell, Oxford-1973-61p-ISBN 0631069402

Submarines-by Jameston, Mary Ethel-1918-97p-A list of References in the New York Public Library

Submarines-by Lenton, HT-Doubleday-1973

Submarines-by Maynard, Christopher

Submarines-by Norman, CJ & F Watts-1986

Submarines-by Peterson, David-Children's Press, Chicago-1984-Presents a history of underwater boats and describes various kinds of submarines and their parts and crews

Submarines-by Petty-1986

Submarines-by Preston, Anthony-Octopus Books-1975-The history and evolution of underwater fighting vessels

Submarines-by St. Lawrence, William P-Nelson Doubleday-1959-64p

Submarines-by Stephen, RJ-Watts, UK-1990-29p-Youth

Submarines-by Thomson, George Pirie-Muller, UK-1959-144p-Detailed description of the working of a submarine

Submarines-by Van Tol, Robert-Watts, UK-32p-1984-Presents a brief history of submarines and describes various types

Submarines-by Zim, Herbert S-Harcourt, Brace-1942-306p-The story of the undersea boats

Submarines-Vol 402-by Taylor

Submarines-by Dadin-1963

Submarines-by James-1973

Submarines-by Saint Lawrence, William P-Doubleday-1959-64p

Submarines-by Casing, James-Macmillan-1951

Submarines Admirals and Navies-by Mayers, Colin-Assoc Publications, LA-1940-280p-Former officer in British Sub School

Submarine and 18-Hour Shift Work Schedules-by Kelly, Tamsin Lisa-Naval Health Research Center-1996-

Submarines and Other Underwater Craft-by Weiss, Harvey-Crowell, NY-1990-64p-Youth

Submarines and Seapower-by Domville-Fife, Charles W-G. Bell & Sons, Ltd-1919-250p

Submarines and Ships-by Humble, Richard-1995

Submarines and the War at Sea-1914-1918-Compton-Hall, Richard Macmillan, London-1991 345p-ISBN 0333443454

Submarines and the Electric Boat Company-by Horn, John H-1948-104p

Submarines and Torpedoes-by Hinkamp-1914

Submarines and Zeppelins in Warfare and Outrage-by Hurd, Archibald-Causton, London-1916-22p

Submarines at War-by Hoyt, Edwin-Stein & Day-1983-329p-ISBN 081282833X An authoritative history of the U.S. submarine service from Robert Fulton's first designs to the nuclear-powered and nuclear-armed vessels of today, full of dramatic stories and little-known facts-Jove pocketbook edition 1992

Submarines Attacking-by Cocchia, Aldo-W. Kimber, London 1956-204p-The author, an Italian admiral, tells the exploits of the Italian Naval Services from the convoy battles to the Italian human torpedoes

Submarines For the 21st Century-by Fuller, Geoffrey

Submarines: Hunter/Killers & Boomers-New York, N.Y.: Beekman House-1990-192p

Submarines in Arctic Waters-by Kolyshkin, Ivan-Progress-Moscow-1966-253p

Submarines in Color-by Gunston, Bill-Arco-1977

Submarines in Combat-by Icenhower, Joseph B-F Watts, NY-1964-180p-Young

Submarines in Periodical Literature 1911-1917-by Hosmer, Helen R-Franklin, Philadelphia-1917

Submarines in WW II-by Germinsky, Robert A-GPO-1994

Submarines Lake and Holland-by Lan, Luis A-US Navy Dept-1904-40p-Report of Commander LA Lan, Argentine Navy

Submarines: Men and Ships of the U.S. submarine Fleet-by Colby, CB-Coward-McCann, NY-1953

Submarines, Mines and Torpedoes in the War-by Domville-Fife, Charles W-Macmillan, NY-1920

Submarines of the 20th Century-by Chant, Christopher-Tiger Books International, Twickenham, England-1996-144p-ISBN 1855018047 -Large format-178 pictures and illustrations

Submarines of the 21st Century-by Khudiakov, Lev U-St. Petersburg-1994-61p-Russian

Submarines of the Imperial Japanese Navy-by Carpenter, Dorr P & Polmar, Norman-USNIP-1986-176p-ISBN 0870216821-line drawings, detail of many submarines. The history covers the period 1904 to the end of WW II

Submarines of the Royal Navy-1964

Submarines of the Royal Netherlands Navy, The-See Ik Nader Ongezien

Submarines of the Russian and Soviet Navies-by Polmar, Norman &Noot Jurrien-USNIP-1990-370p-ISBN 0870215701-1718-1990-The first comprehensive treatment of the development of Russian and Soviet submarine development and operations. 300 illustrations detail technical developments in design and construction

Submarines of the Tsarist Navy-Polmar, Norman (Ed) of English version-144p-ISBN 1557507716-75 photographs

Submarines of the US Navy-by Terzibaschitsch, Stephan-Arms & Armour-1992-216p

Submarines of the World-Miller, David-Orion Books-1991-ISBN 0861015622-A complete illustrated history 1888 to the present

Submarines of the World's Navies-by Domville-Fife, Charles W-G. Bell, UK-1910-150p

Submarines of Wings-by Treadwell, Terry C-Conway-1985

Submarines of World War Two-by Bagnasco, Ermino-Arms & Armour, UK & USNIP-1977   ISBN 0870219626-494 illustrations-This the record of 2500 submarines of all nations that were involved in WW II

Submarines Since 1919-by Preston, Anthony-Pheobs Pub. Co., UK-1974

Submarines Under Ice-by Williams, Marion-USNIP-1998-200 p-The U.S. Navy's Polar Operations

Submarines versus U-Boats-by Jones, Geoffrey-W. Kimber, London-1986-ISBN 0718306260

Submarines Vol III-Operations in Far Eastern Waters-HMSO-1955

Submarines With Wings-by Treadwell, Terry C-Conway Maritime Press-1985

Submarines: Disarmament and Modern Warfare-by Groeling, Dorothy T-1935-199p

Submarines: Diving and the Underwater World-by Anderson, Frank J-Archon-Hamden, Ct-1975-238p-A bibliography

Submarines: Hunter/Killers & Boomers-by Lightbody, Andy-Beekman House, NY-1990-192p

Submarines: Mines & Torpedoes in the War-by Domville-Fife, Charles W-1914-192p

Submarines, Leviathans of the Deep-by Francis, TL-Friedman /Fairfax Pub-1997-144p-ISBN 156799427X

Submarines-Shark of Steel-by Stillwell-Kaufman-1992

Submarines, Submariners, Submarining-by Anderson, Frank J-Shoestring Press-1963-140p Rewritten 1975 as Submarines, Diving and the Underwater World. A checklist of submarine books in the English Language

Submarines: Their mechanism and operation-by Talbot, Frederick A-Lippincott-1915-274p

Submarines-The Monge-by Milanesi, Guido-Alfieri & Lacroix-Milan-1916

Submarines Under Ice-by Williams, Marion-USNIP-1997-200p-ISBN 1557509433-The U.S. Navy's Polar Operations written by a member of the submarine service

Submarining-by Paine, TO-Tempo-1971-414p-Three thousand books and articles

Submarinos-by Genova, Arturo-Saturnino Calleja, Madrid-1922-203p

Submerged-A Tragedy in One Act-by Cottman, HS & Shaw, L-Row, NY-1929

Submerged Arc Welding-by Houldecroft, PZ-Abington Pub-1989-103p

Submerged Arc Welding-Australia Welding Institute-1981-71p-Basic Training Manual

Submersible, The-by Appleton-1910

Subs Against the Rising Sun-by Milton, Keith-Yucca Free Press-2000-368p-ISBN 1881325458-A detailed analysis boat by boat of all the boats in WWII and their actions. Not listed in this books bibliography, however, is the latest information available and that is Alden's Oct 1999 work: United States and Allied Submarine Successes in the Pacific and Far East During World

War II. A picture of each boat is included which are hard to come by and a complete list of all U.S. wolfpacks.

Subs and Submariners-by Whitehouse, Arch-Doubleday-1961-335p-A brief history of the submarine service

SubRon Five's Equatorial Cruise-by Hackerl, CJ-Sugar News Press, Manilla-1938

Subsmash-by MacDonnell, James E-Constable, UK-1960-288p

Subsunk-by Shelford, WO-Harrap, UK-1960-248p-Submarine Escape stories with drawings of submarine escape chambers and of escape devices

Subsurface Warfare-by Harrick, John Origen-DOD-1951-135p

Suicide Squads-by O'neil, Richard-Lansdowne Press

Suicide Submarines-by Yokota, Yukata & Harrington, JD-Ballantine-1962-255p

Sultan's Gold, The-by McLeod-1988

Summary of War Damage-by US Navy Staff-GPO-1989

Sun Beneath the Sea-by Piccard, Jacques-Scribner's Sons, NY-1971-405p

Sunk-by Busch, Harald-Ballantine Books-1955-Translation from the German-176p-German submarines in action 1939-1945

Sunk-by Hasimoto, Mochitsura EHM Colegrave & Henry Holt, NY-1954-276p-Avon abridgment in 1954 of 190p-The author was in command of I.58. The story of the Japanese submarine fleet 41-45

Sunk in Action: The United States Navy in World War II-by Freeman, Robert H ed.-Shellback Press, 1986

Sunken Nuclear Submarines-by Eriksen, Oliver-Norwegian U. Press-1990-176p Using available information this book examines some of the 200 known accidents involving nuclear submarines. The author has a degree in nuclear physics and covers collisions, groundings, loss rate of US, Soviet, UK and French designs. Potential factors influencing accidents involving nuclear submarines. Pressurized-water reactor propulsion plant, liquid-metal cooled propulsion shown with graphs and drawings

Sunken Submarine-by Danrit, Captain-Little, Brown, Boston-1912-308p-A man trapped for

Super Submarine, The-by Briggs, Raymonde-Dancy Printing Co, NJ-1942-29p-

Superwarriors, The: The Fantastic World of Pentagon Superweapons -by Canan, James-Weybright and Talley-1975

Supplying War-by Crefield, M-CUP, UK-1977-Logistics

Supreme Gallantry-by Spooner, Tony-358p-Malta's Role in the Allied Victory

Surface at the Pole-by Calvert, James-McGraw-Hill-1960-220p-The Voyage of the Skate

Surrender at Sea: A Compilation of the Stories of the Surrender of the Nazi Submarines-by Gray, Charlie-19454

Survey by Starlight-by Neville, Ralph-Hodder and Stoughton, London-1949-206p-A True story of Reconnaissance Work in the Med

Survival of Seaman Izzi-83 Days in 1942-by Murphy, Mark-Dutton-1943-124p

Survivor-by Herlin, Hans-Leo Cooper, UK-1995-True Story of the Sinking of the Doggerbank

Swastika at Sea-by Bekker, Cajus (pseud)-See "Defeat at Sea"

Sword of Damocles-by VADM Hugh Mackenzie RN-Royal Navy Submarine Museum-1995-ISBN 0952669609

Symposium on Underwater Physiology-Ed. by Lambertsen, CJ-Williams and Wilkins, Baltimore-1967-517p

Sythese del guerre sous-marine-by Caster, Capitaine-A. Challamel-Paris-1920-228p-WW1 A tactical view of the submarine threat and way to oppose it by then Cdr Castex, a well known French naval tactician

T

T-Class Submarine, The-by Kemp, Paul J-USNIP-1990-192p-ISBN 1557508267-200 illustrations

Tactical and Strategic Antisubmarine Warfare-by Tsipis, Kosta-MIT-1974-148p

Tactics and Technology of Underwater Warfare-by Compton-Hall, Richard-Orion, UK-1988

Take Her Deep-by Galantin, IJ-Algonquin Books-Chapel Hill-1987-ISBN 0912697644 The author, captain of the submarine USS Halibut, tells of his war in the Pacific between August 1943 and November 1944 against the Japanese-Paperback edition by Pocket Books in 1988

Take Her Down-by Thompson, Cmdr TB-Sheridan House, NY-1937-317p-A submarine Portrait of the L-9

Taranto e i suoi Sommergibile-by Lo Martire, NB-Schena, Fasano-1990-Taranto and It's Submarines

Task Force 57-by Smith, Peter-Crezy-1994-The British Pacific Fleet-The Forgotten Fleet

Tatsachenbericht enines U-Bootfahrers 1942-1945-by Ludes, Willi-Brunckhaus Verlag, Rossdorf 1983-132p-ISBN 3888990017-**Report of a U-boat man 1942-1945**

Tauchboote Tauchfahrzeuge aus aller Welt-by Gierschner, Norbert-by Transpress Verlag Verkehrswensen, Berlin-1980-308p

Technikmuseum U-Boot Wilhelm Bauer-Anonymous-Bremerhaven-1990-ISBN 3927857181

Technology and the Evolution of Naval Warfare 1851-2001-by Lautenschlager, Karl-National Academy, Washington-1984-59p

Ten Miles High, Two Miles Deep-by Honour, Alan-Brockhampton, UK-1957

Tenth Fleet-by Farago, Ladislas-Astor Honor-1962 366p-Anti-Sub Activity against Nazi Wolf-packs

Terrible Hours, The-by Maas, Peter-Harper Torch-2000-309p-ISBN 0061014591-The story of the Squalus and Swede Momsen

The Other Enemy-by Calhoun, CR-USNIP-1981

The Sea Our Shield-by Fell

The Year That Doomed the Axis-by Adams, Henry-Paperback Library-1969

Their Secret Purpose-by Bywater, Hector-Constable, London-1932

Theory of Gyroscopic Compass and its Deviations-by Rawlings, AL-Macmillan, NY-1944-182p

They Came to Fish-by Brighton, Ray-Portsmouth, NH-1974-2 Vol-History of Portsmouth including the Navy Yard and it's submarines

They Came to Kill-by Rachlis, Eugene-Random House-1961-305p-true story of 8 Nazi saboteurs in the U.S. planted by a U-boat

They Fought Under the Sea-by Editors of Navy Times-Stackpole-1962-182p-40 Photos

Thirty Years of Submarine Humor-by Dolphin Scholarship Foundation-1992-A collection of cartoons that were submitted for the Foundations annual calendar.

This Peoples Navy: The Making of American Sea Power-by Hagan, Kenneth-The Free Press- 1991-434p

Those in Peril on the Sea-by Ellis, Richard-Dial Press-1962

Thousand Mile War, The-by Garfield, Brian-1995 (Paperback of 1969 edition)-456p-B&W Photos—WWII in Alaska and the Aleutians

Threat to the SSBN, The-by McCue, Brian Gerald-1980-144p-Thesis

Three Before Breakfast-by Coles-1979

Three Japanese Submarine Developments-USNIP-1952

Thresher Disaster, The-by Bently, John-Doubleday-1974-372p-ISBN 0385099096-The most tragic dive in submarine history

Threshold-by Coulter, Stephen-William Morrow & Co, NY-1964

Threshold of War-by Heinrich, Waldo-Oxford U. Press, NY-1988

Through a Canadian Periscope-by Ferguson, Julie H-Dundurn Press Ltd-1995-ISBN 1550022172

Through Hell and Deep Water-by Lockwood, Charles & Hans Christian Adamson-Greenberg 1956-317p-The story of the USS Harder

Thunder Below-by Fluckey, Adm. E-U of Illinois Press-1992-ISBN 0252019253-USS Barb in WW II-Author was CO of USS Barb and won the MOH for his actions

Torpedo War-by Fulton, Robert-Swallow Press-Chicago-1971 (Reprint of 1810 edition)-60p-ISBN 1804005338

Torpedo War, and Submarine Explosions-by Fulton, Robert-Swallow, Chicago-1971 reprint of 1810 edition-60p

Torpedo!-Stories of the Royal Navy-Hackforth-Jones-1943

Torpedoboat Sailor-by Blackford, Charles-USNIP-1968

Torpedoes A List of Reference Material in the New York Public Library-Ellis, William A-1917

Torpedoes and Torpedo Vessels-by Armstrong, Sir George Elliot-Bell, London-1896-287p-Second edition 1901

Torpedoes and Torpedo Warfare-by Sleeman, Charles W-Griffin & Co, UK-1880-309p

Torpedoes Away-by Olsen, Robert I-Dodd, Mead & Co-1957-247p

Torpedoes Away!-by Shirreffs, Gordon D-Westminster John Knox Pr-1967-ISBN 066432407X

Torpedoes Away Sir!-by Hawkins, Maxwell-Holt-1946-268p-30 photos and maps-The story of our submarines in the first 18 months of WW II. Gives a clear and accurate description of an actual submarine

Torpedoes in the Gulf-by Wiggens, Melanie-Texas A&M U Press-265p-ISBN 890966273-It describes WWII from the perspectives of the Gulf Coast community of Galveston and of the German submariners sent to attack the city's busy shipping lanes. Interviews an diaries from former U-boat commanders and veterans of the US Navy and Merchant Marine recount German submarine attacks on some 70 American and Allied ships between 1942-43

Torpedoes, Mark 15 Type-by USN, Bur. of Ordnance-Washington-1945-279p

Torpedos der deutschen U-boote, Die-by Rossler, Eberhard-Koehler Verlag, Herford-1983-272p, 220photos-**The Torpedoes of the German U-boats**

Torpedy-by Komorowski, Antoni-Warsaw-1977-174p

Torpilles et Torpillieurs des Nations Etrangeres-by Buchard, Henri-Berger-Levrault, Paris-1889-222p

Torpillieurs et Sous-Marins-by Pouleur, Hector-Dosoer, Leige-1904-74p

Total War-by Calvocoressi, Peter Wint-Viking, UK-1989-The Causes and Courses of the Second World War

Totentanz der Siebenmeere-Death Dance of the Seven Seas-by Busch, Harald-Erich Pabel- 1960

Touching the Adventures of Merchantmen in the Second WW-by Kerr, JL-Harrap-1953

Track of the Gray Wolf-by Gentile, Gary-Avon Books-1989-U-Boat war on the East Coast

Tragedy of the Lusitania, The-by Ellis, Frederick D-National Publishing-Phila-1915-324p

Trager des Ritterkreuzes des Eisernen Kreuzes der U-Boot-Waffe-by Kurowski, Franz-Podzun-Pallas-Verlag-Friedberg-1987-80p-ISBN 3790903213-**Knights Cross recipients of the U-boat arm**

Trapped on Timor-by Humphris, Colin-Hyde Park Press, Australia-119p-ISBN 0646055194-The store of 30+ Australian Air personnel trapped on Timor Island and their eventual rescue by a Submarine

Traite de Plongee-by Guillerme, Jacques-Dunod, Paris-1955-213p

Trial of Heinz Eck-by Cameron, J-Wm. Hodge-1948

Trial of the German, The-by Davidson, Eugene-Macmillan Co.-1966

Trident-by Dalgliesh, DD & Schweikart, L-Sou. Ill. Press-1984-ISBN 0809311267-Chapters include: The Ultimate Weapon, A Description of Trident, Trident's Budgetary Birth, Adolescence and Maturity, The Trident Construction Process, Trident and Quality Control, Support Bases, Capability and Trident Operational Survivability, Technological Advances and more..

Trident Construction Program-by U.S. Senate-GPO-1985-91p

Trident Weapons Systems-by Dalgleish, Douglas-ISBN 0809311267

Triumph in the Atlantic-Nimitz, Chester, ed, Adams, Henry, ed, Potter, EB, ed-Prentice Hall-1960-188p

Triumph in the Pacific-by Potter, EB, ed & Nimitz, Chester, ed-Prentice Hall-1963-186p-The Navy's struggle against Japan

Triumph in the West-by Bryant, Arthur-William Kimber, UK-1958

Troopships of World War II-by Charles, Roland W-Army Transportation Assn.-1947

True Book about Submarines, The-by Hackforth-Jones, Gilbert-F. Muller, London-1955-141p

True Glory-by Arthur, Max-290p-The Royal Navy 1914-1939

Turk Denizalticilik Tarihi-by Metel, Rasit-Istanbul-1960-16p-Turkish submarine history

Turn of the Tide-by Bryant, Arthur-Doubleday & Co-1957

Tutte le Navi Militari d'Italia 1861-1986-by Bargoni, F-USMM, Rome-1990-All Italian Naval Ships 1861-1986

Twenty First Century Submarine-by Herbert, Frank-Avon, NY-1956 (Paperback version of Dragon in the sea)

Twenty Million Tons Under the Sea-by Gallery, Daniel V-Regnery-Chicago-1956-Tells of the Submarine War in the Atlantic and the unique capture of the U-505 off the coast of Africa by the US Navy-Republished 2001 by USNIP

Twilight of the Sea Gods-by Tuleja, Thaddeus V-WW Norton & Co-1958-German Navy

Two Hours to Darkness-by Trew, Antony-Random House-1963

Two-ocean War, The-by Morison, SE-Little, Brown & Co-1963-A short history of the US Navy in WW II

Type IX-by Stern, Robert-USNIP-1991

Type VII U-Boat, The-by Westwood, David-Conway Maritime Press-1984-95p-ISBN 0851773141

Type VII U-Boats-by Stern, Robert-USNIP-1991-160p-ISBN 1854090119-160 Photos-Over 700 submarines of this type were built, and pack attacks were to be one of the features that the Nazis decided upon for WW II. Good technical data

Type XXI U-Boat, The-by Kohl, Fritz, & E. Rossler-USNIP-1991-128p-ISBN 1557508291 100 photos

Typhoon: The Other Enemy-by Calhoun, CR-USNIP-1977

U

U-21-Rettet die Dardanellen-by Hersing, Otto-Hase & Koehler, Leipzig-1932-151p-Liberator of the Dardanelles-Also in Italian

U-31-das Schiff aus dem Jenseits-by Koebsell, Eberhard-Verlag Die Wehrmacht, Berlin-1937 187p

U-35-Das Erfolgreichiste Unterseeboot der Welt-by Herzog, Bodo-Ruhl, Krefeld-1964-Forward by Adm Lockwood

U-38-by Valentiner, Max-Ullstein-Verlag, Berlin-1934-269p, 23 photos

U-41-der Zweite Baralong-fall-by Crompton, Iwan-Scherl, Berlin-1917-116p

U-48-by Alman, Karl-1986-300p-The most successful boat in WWII

U-250-by Karschawin, Boris-St. Petersburg, Jena-1994-71p, 25 photos

U-333-The Story of a U-Boat Ace-Peter Cremer-by Cremer, Peter-Bodley Head-1984-244p-The author's account of his war as one of the three senior U-Boat commanders to survive, finishing the war as Admiral Doenitz's bodyguard. Later title of this book is U-Boat Commander

U-352-by Carain, Ed-1987-The sunken German U-boat in the Graveyard of the Atlantic

U-505-by Gallery, Daniel V-Paperback Library, NY-1955-Paperback edition 1971-Captain Gallery's story of the capture of the U-505 which now is in Chicago

U-524-Das Driegstagebuch eines U-Bootes-by Reintjes, Karl Henrich-Knoth-Verlag Melle-1994-229p-ISBN 3883682632-**U-524, the War Diary of a U-boat**

U-69 Sehrohr Sudwarts-by Mielke, Otto-A. Moewig Verlag, Munchen-39p-WWII

U-69-Die lachende Kuh-by Metzler, Jost-Ravensburg-1954-**U-69 the Laughing Cow** Autobiography of the U-69 Commander

U-668-Die Unternehmungen eines Nordmeer U-Bootes-by Scherzer, Veit-Patzwall, Verlag-1997-84p-ISBN 3931533344-**U-668, The patrols of the Arctic Sea U-Boat**

U-977 66 Tage Unter Wasser-by Schaeffer, Heinz-Limes-Verlag, Wiesbaden-1974-263p-ISBN   3809020494-U-977-66   Days Submerged. Autobiography of the commander

U-1105-The U-1105 survey: a report on the 1993 archaeological survey of 18ST636, a second world war German submarine in the Potomac River, Maryland-by Pohuski, Michael & Shomette, Donald-Annapolis, Md.: Maryland Historical Trust-1994-59p

U-Batar och I Tyska Fanglager-by Christiernsson, Nils Henrick-Norstedt, Stockholm-1917-93p

U-Boat-1939-1945-by Dallies-Labourdette, J-Histoire & Collections-144p-A pictorial account which contains many previously unpublished photographs from French and German archives, including 16 pages of color photographs

U-Boat-The Secret Menace-by Mason, David-Pan/Ballantine-1968-160p-ISBN 0345249887

U-Boat-by Sharkhunters-1997-Chapters by former submarine commanders, including Kretschmer, Topp, Hardegen, Gallery, Giese and many more

U-Boat 202-by Spiegel-Melrose, London-1919-170p

U-Boat 977-by Schaffer, Heinz-W. Kimber-1952-260p-Geheimnis um U-977 in German-Written by the CO of the U-977. The author rose from cadet to the command of this submarine To avoid surrender at the end of hostilities, he crossed the Atlantic making for Argentina. He was charged with helping Hitler to escape

U-Boat Ace-by Vause, Jordan-Airlife-1992-256p-ISBN 087021666X-35 illustrations-Story of Wolfgang Luth-The story of an ardent Nazi ideologue who could be a saint or sinner, but was a very successful commander-Also in USNIP Bluejacket edition 2001

U-Boat Aces-by Jones, Geoffrey-W. Kimber-1988-ISBN 0718306856-The author investigated the loss of many large ships of the Royal Navy and the careers of their commanders. He discovered fascinating new insights into these dramatic events in the first two years of WW II

U-Boat Adventures-by Wiggins, M-USNIP-1999-Firsthand accounts from WWII

U-Boat Command-Showell, Jak P. Mallmann-Conway Maritime Press-1989-ISBN 0851774073

U-Boat Commander-U-333-by Cremer, Peter-USNIP-1984-244p-ISBN 0870219693 Story of a U-Boat Ace written by himself. One of the few German Aces to survive the war. First printed in England as U-333 in 1984

U-Boat Commander-by Prien, Gunther-1969 English Translation-Award Books/paperback-158p-

U-Boat Commanders and Crews-by Showell, J.M.-SPCK & Triangle-1998

U-Boat Commander's Handbook-by Coates, EJ-Thomas Pubs-1943

U-Boat Commanders Handbook, The-by Kelshall, Gaylord TM-Thomas-120p-30 U-boat photos

U-Boat Crews-by Williamson, Gordon-Reed Consumer Books, London-1995-64p-ISBN 1855325454-Softcover-Uniforms, hats and insignia-1914-45

U-Boat Devilry-by Bateman, Charles T-Hodder & Stoughton, London-1918-175p-Illustrating the heroism and endurance of merchant seamen

U-Boat: Evolution and Technical History-by Rossler, E-USNIP-1989-The design and construction of U-Boats from the inception. Glossary of German technical terms. The definitive book on the subject.

U-Boat Fact File-by Sharpe, P-1998-1100 boat details

U-Boat Far From Home-by Stevens, David-Allen & Unwin-1997-304p-ISBN 1864482672 An account of the German Plan for an underwater offensive against Australia. The author covers the operation's planning and rationale, its implementation, and Australia and the allies responses. The author focuses in particular on U-862 and its young crew which survived the mission.

U-Boat Hunter, The-by Milner, Marc-USNIP-1994-326p-Royal Canadian Navy and the Offensive against German subs-ISBN 155750-8542

U-Boat Hunters, The-by Connolly, James B-Schribner's, NY-1918-263p

U-Boat Hunters, The-by Watts, Anthony-Macdonald & Janes-1976-192p-Anti-Submarine Warfare in WW II

U-Boat in Action-by Stern-1977

U-Boat Intelligence-by Grant, Robert M-Hamden: Archon Books-1969-192p

U-Boat Killer-by Macintyre, Donald-Norton, NY-1956-239p-The author commanded Escort Groups in the Battle of the Atlantic-he won the DSO three times. In this grim struggle his ships accounted for 7 U-Boats

U-Boat Offensive, The-by Tarrant, VE-Arms & Armour Press & USNIP-1989-192p-ISBN 087021764X-70 illustrations-1914-1945-Chronicles the strategic and tactical evolution of submarine warfare in the North Atlantic

U-Boat Operations of the Second World War-by Wynn, Kenneth-USNIP-1998-368p-A rapid reference source for every aspect of a boat's activities, from the laying of the keel to her ultimate fate, this is Vol 1 of 2 and covers case studies of U-1 through U-510

U-Boat Peril, The-by Whinney, Bob-Blandford Press-1986-160p-ISBN 0713718218-The author, Captain of the destroyer HMS Wanderer, relives his struggle against the U-Boat threat in the Atlantic and English Channel

U-Boat Prisoner-by Gibbs, Archie-Houghton, NY-1943-208p-Life story of a Texas sailor

U-Boat Secret Menace, The-by Mason, David-Ballantine, NY-1968-160p-Pictorial record of German submarines

U-Boat Stories-by Bergen, Claus & Neureuther, Karl-Constable & Co, London-1931-207p-Narratives of German U-Boat sailors

U-Boat Tankers-by White, John F-Cassell-1999-Submarine suppliers to the Atlantic wolf packs

U-Boat War-by Buchheim, Lothar Gunther-Collins, UK-1978-ISBN 0394414373-The author was an official German war artist. He served on a U-Boat and this is a record of part of what he saw. 205 photos form this epic essay of the world on board Germany's U-Boats at war. No comparable record of this war at sea exists anywhere-Buchheim pictures are unique .

U-Boat War in the Atlantic, The-by Hessler, Gunter-HMSO-1989-442p-ISBN 0117726036-1939-1945

U-Boat War in the Caribbean, The-by Kelshall, Gaylord TM-USNIP-1994-544p-ISBN 1557504520-27 photos-11 maps

U-Boat Warfare-by Guitard, Pierre-Pallas, UK-1939-80p

U-Boat Wars, The-by Hoyt, Edwin-Robert Hale, UK-1984

U-Boat Wars, The-by Terraine, John-1989

U-Boat, The-by Rossler, Edward-USNIP-1981-384o-ISBN 0870219669-447 illustrations

U-Boats-by Keatts, Henry C-Dive into History-Vol 3

U-Boats-by Hoyt, Edwin P.-McGraw Hill-1987-289p-A Pictorial History

U-Boats-by Preston, Anthony-Arms & Armour, London-1978-192p-ISBN 0853681929-

U-Boats, The-by Botting, Douglas-Time-Life-1979-ISBN 080942757-German U-Boats from WW I through WW II

U-Boats Against Canada-Hadley, Michael-McGill Queens U Press-1985-360p-ISBN 0773505849-German Submarines in Canadian Waters

U-Boats and T-Boats 1914-1918-National Archives USGSA-1985-355p

U-Boats at War-by Busch, Harald-Putnam, London, McClelland, Toronto-1955-286p

U-Boats at War-by Mallman-Showell, Jak P-USNIP-2001-160p, 170 photos-ISBN 155750864X-Many photos unpublished in this WWII history of the U-Boats written by a son of a U-boat Commander

U-Boats at War: That's the Way it Was-Busch, Harald-Ballantine-1955-176p

U-Boats Command and Battle of the Atlantic-by Showell, Jak-Conway, UK-1989

U-Boats Destroyed-by Grant, Robert M-Putnam-1964-172p-The effect of ASW 1914-1918

U-Boats in Action 1939-1945-by Herzog, Bodo-Ian Allen-1970 (see U-Boote im Einsatz 1939-1945)

U-Boats in Action-by Stern, Robert C-Squadron Signal-50p-ISBN 0897470540-110 photos

U-Boats in the Atlantic-by Beaver, Paul-Pat. Stephens, Ltd-1979-With over 150 official German photographs it analyses U-Boat convoy routes, insignia and operations

U-Boats in the Bay of Biscay-by McCue, Brian-National Defense U Press-1990-206p

U-Boats of World War Two-Vol 1-by Stern, Robert-Arms & Armour-1988

U-Boats Offshore-When Hitler struck America-by Hoyt, Edwin P-Stein & Day-1978-278p The dramatic story of the near disaster when U-Boats were sent to the East Coast and raised hhavoc

U-Boats to the Rescue-by Peillard, Leonce-Jonathan Cape-1963-The unique story of the dilemma facing a U-Boat commander in 1942 after he had sunk the liner Laconia in the South Atlantic with 1,800 Italian prisoners on board

U-Boats Under the Swastika-by Showell, Jak P-Mallmann-1973-167p-ISBN 0870219707-USNIP-Reprint 1987-1935-1945-German title, U-Boote Gegen England

U-Boats Westward!-by Hashagen, Ernst-Putnam, NY-1931-247p-Log of a U-Boat Commander

U-Boat!-by various-Sharkhunters-1997-21 chapters by U-Boat commanders of all nations.

U-Boot-by authors of 3 other books-Heyne Verlag, Munchen-1996-ISBN 345309560-This book contains: Graue Wolfe in Blauer See, Die Nacht der U-Boote, Haie im Paradies

U-Boot Abenteuer-by Spiess, Johannes-1940-See Six Years of Submarine Cruising

U-Boot ahoi!-by Von Forstner, Geroge Gunther-G. Weise, Berlin-1937-123p-**U-Boat Ahoy!**

U-Boot Alarm-by Krause, Gunter-Brandenburgisches Verlagshaus, Berlin-1998-255p-ISBN 3894881267

U-Boot Asse-by Alman, Karl-Prisma-Verlag, Wien-1980-239p-ISBN 3570072142

U-Boot auf Feindfahrt: Bildberichte vom Einsatz im Atlantik-U-Boat on Patrol-by Busch, Harald Bertelsmann-94p, 89 photos-1942-Most of photos where probably taken on U-101

U-Boot Bunker-by Becker, Fabian-Edition Temmen, Bremen-1996-ISBN 3861082888

U-Boot Direction Centre Atlantique (in French and German)-by Alaluquetas, Jacques-LOKI-Paris 1977-200 photos

U-Boot-Ehrenmal Moltenort, Das-by U-Boat Kameradschaft Kiel-Kiel-1990-80p, 76photos-U-Boat Memorial Motenort

U-Boot Fahrer-by Buchheim, Lothar-Gunther-Bertelsmann Verlag-1985-307p-ISBN 3492040446-An illustrated book concerned with the crews of U-boats

U-Boot Fahrer von heute-by Schepke, Joachim-Deutscher Verlag, Berlin-1940-136p-The author was a U-boat commander and describes life on the U-Boat

U-Boot Fahrer und Kamelsreiter: Kriegsfahrten enis Deutschen Unterseebootes-by Dinklage, Ludwig-Franckhsche, Stuttgart-1939-212p

U-Boot Friede?-by Moller, Wilhelm-Mitteldeutsche Verlag, Dresden-1918-71p

U-Boot Fahrer und Kamelsreiter: Kriegsfahrten enis Deutschen Unterseebootes-by Dinklage, Ludwig-Franckhsche, Stuttgart-1939-212p

U-Boot Friede?-by Moller, Wilhelm

U-Boot Gruppe Eisbar-by Pfitzmann, Martin-Moewig Verlag, Rastatt-1986-160p-ISBN 3811843516-**U-boat Group Polar Bear**-Covers the first operation of U-boats U-68, 156, 159, 172, 179, 504 in South African waters

U-Boot im Fegefeuer-by Spiegel, von und zu Peckelsheim, Edgar-Scherl, Berlin-1930-210p-**U-Boat in Purgatory**-The commander of U-32 and U-93 describes his war patrols

U-Boot Kommandant Wolfgang Luth, Der-by Vause, Jordan-Motorbuch Verlag, Stuttgart-1999 268p-ISBN 361301937X-**U-Boat Commander Wolfgang Luth**

U-Boot Krieg-by Buchheim, Lothas-Gunther-Piper Verlag, Munchen-300p-ISBN 3492022162 This is part three of Buchheim's photo essay. Many photos from his time aboard U-96 when he was a war correspondent

U-Boot Krieg 1939-1945-by Busch, Rainer and Roll, Hans-Joachin. Vol 1 1996-Die Deutschen U-Book Commandanten 344p, Vol 2 1997-Die U-Boot Bau Auf Deutchen Werften 545p-Both only in German

U-boot Krieg 1939-1945-by Padfield, Peter-Ullstein-Verlag, Berlin-1996-496p-ISBN 3550070934-Covers submarine conflict 1939-1945, across all theatres and nations but mainly focusing on German, British, US and Japanese operations with some on Italian boats

U-Boot Krieg 1939-1945 in der Literatur, Der-by Schlemm, Jurgen-Elbe-Spree-Vlg., Hamburg-2000-212p-ISBN 3931129241-**The U-boat War 1939-1945 in Literature**: An annotated bibliogra-phy-An annotated bibliography covering hundreds of books, articles and pamphlets relating to the U-boat war

U-Boot Krieg in der Karibik-by Kelshall, Gaylord TM-ES Mittler & Sohn, Hamburg-1999-336p-ISBN 3813205479-Covers the entire war in the theatre in detail. This book translated for English The U-Boat War in the Caribbean

U-Boot Krieg und Volkerrecht-by Sohler, Herbert-ES Mittler & Sohn-1956

U-Boot Minaccia Segreta-by Mason D-E Albertelli, Parma-1970-U-Boat Secret Menace

U-Boot Tanker 1941-1945-by White, John F-Koehler Verlag, Herford-2000-256p-ISBN 3782207904-In English as U-Boat Tanker-Translated from English by Wenke, Carsten

U-Bootbau-U-Boat Construction-by Gabler, Ulrich-Wehr & Wissen-Bonn-1978

U-Boot und Luftbook-by Kirchhoff, Hermann-Marinedank, Berlin-1915-30p

U-Boot und U-Boot-Krieg-by Walderyer-Hartz, Hugo-Westermann, Braunschweig-1917-252p

U-Boot und U-Jagd-by Krause, Gunther-Militarverlag der DDR, Berlin-1986-263p, 171 photos ISBN 3327000824-**U-Boat and Sub Hunting**

U-Boot und Weltwirtschaft-by Thielemann, Walter-Haase, Prague-1916-279p

U-Boot vor dem Feind-by Von Forstner, George Gunter-G. Weise, Berlin-1939-64p-**U-Boats in Battle**

U-Boote-1935-1945-by Labourdette, J Dallies-Philippe-1996-144p-Also by Motorbuch Verlag, Stuttgart in German-1998

U-Boote-by Lakowski, Richard-Militarverlag˙ Berlin-1985-355p, 52 photos-**U-Boats**

U-Boote am Feind-by Langsdorff, Werner von-Bertelsmann, Dutersloh, -1943-367p-WW I German Submarine operations

U-Boote der US Navy-by Terzibashitsch, Stefan-Koehels Verlagsgesellschaft

U-Boote, Deutschlands Schaarfe Waffe-by Glodschey, Erich-Stuttgart -1943-239p

U-Boote: Eine Chronik im Bildern-by Rohwer, Jurgen-Stalling, Hamburg-1962-96p

U-Boote England's Tod!-by Steinwager, Leonhard-Lehmann, Munich-1918-48p

U-Boote gegen England-by Busch, Harald-Berlin-1939-**U-Boats Against England**

U-Boote gegen England-by Showell, Jak P. Mallmann-Motorbuch Verlag, Stuttgart-1987-189p ISBN 3613010097-Good bibliography included, list of all U-boats and their fates, technical data on all types and good glossary. **U-boats Against England**

U-Boote Gegen U-Boot-by Heimburg, Heino von-Scherl, Berlin-1917-124p

U-Boote im Duell-by Bendert, Harald-Mittler & Sohn Verlag, Berlin-1996-190p-ISBN 3813205169-**Submarines in Duel**

U-Boote im Einsatz-by Herzog, Von B-Podzun-Verlag-1970-256p-**U-Boats in Action**

U-Boote im Eismeer-by Ost, Horst-Gotthard-Franz Schneider Verlag, Berlin-1943-112p-**U-boats in the Arctic Sea**-covers patrols of U-88 and U-435

U-Boote Superwaffe der Zukunft?-by Whitestone, Nicholas-Lehmanns Verlag, Munchen-1973 - ISBN 3469005346

U-Boote vor dem Feind-by Forstner, Georg-Weise, Berlin-1939-64p

U-Boote vor New York-by Beckmann, A-Franckh, Stutgart-1931-54p

U-boote Westwards-by Hashagen, Ernst-Mittler & Sohn Verlag, Berlin-1931-219p-**U-boats Westward**

U-Boote Wilhelm Bauer-by Schneider, Gerd Dietrich-Technikmuseum, Bremerhaven-1994-126p, 132 illustrations-A short history of German submarines and type XXI

U-Booterfolge der Achsenmachte-by Rohwer, Jurgen-Lehmann Verlag, Munchen-1968-380p, 10 grid maps-Contains data on which U-boats sank which ships and where. Very well researched-**Axis Submarine Successes**

U-Bootfaher von heute: Erzahltund Gezeichnet voneinen-by Schepke, Joachim-Im Deutchen 1940-Submariners of Today: Narrative by a U-Boat Cmdr

U-Bookkrieg 1914-1918-by Kaulisch, Baldur-VEB Deutscher Verlag der Wissenschaften, Berling-1976-39p, 48 photos-Published in East Germany-**U-Boat War 1914-1918**

U-Bootkrieg 1939-1945 Band 1, Der-by Busch, Rainer and Roll, Hans Joachim-Mittler & Sohn Verlag, Berlin-1996-320p, 96 photos-ISBN 3813204901-**The U-Boat War 1939-1945: The Commanders** -This book details the service records of 1411 officers of the

German Kriegsmarine know to have commanded a U-Boat from U-1 in 1935 to August 1945.

U-Bootkrieg 1939-1945 Band 2, Der-by Busch, Rainer and Roll, Hans Joachim-Mittler & Sohn Verlag, Berlin-1997-545p-U-boat construction at German Shipyards from 1939-1945

U-Bootkrieg 1939-1945 Band 3, Der-by Busch, Rainer and Roll, Hans Joachim-Mittler & Sohn Verlag, Berlin-2000-400p-ISBN 3813205134-**The U-Boat War 1939-1945: German U-Boat successes from September 1939 to May 1945**

U-boots Taten-by Busch, Fritz Otto-Keimer Hobbing, Berlin-125p-**U-boat Actions-**The U-boat in World War 1

U-boots-Kommandanten und Kriegsverbrecher-by Von Forstner, George Gunther-Frundsberg-Verlag, Berlin-1936-297p-**U-boat commanders and war criminals**

U-Boots-Leben-by Forstner, Georg-Velhagen and Klasing-1916-32p

U-Boots-Liste-by Zeissler, Herbert-Hamburg-1956-129p-**List of U-boats**

U-Boots-Maschinist Fritz Kasten: Das Frontbuch der Deutschen Kriegsmarine-by Freiwald, Ludwig-Lhemann, Munich-1933-327p

U-Boots-Taten-by Busch, Fritz Otto-Hobbing, Berlin-1934-125p

U-Bootsarbeit und ihr Erfolg-by Pechmann, WE-Phoebus, Wein-1918-19p

U-Bootsfallen-by Rehder, Jacob-Lehmann, Munich-1935-159p

U-Bootsgeist: Abenteuer und Fahrten im Mittelmer-by Ritter, Paul-Koehler, Leipzig-1935-246p

U-Bootsfahrten. Buchschmuck von Werner Chomton-by Busch, Fritz Otto-Schneider, Berlin-1938-95p

U-bootskrieg, 1914-1918, Der-by Michelsen, Andreas-KF Koehler, Leipzig-1925-207p

U-Bootswaffe, Die-by Donitz, Karl-Mittler & Sohn Verlag, Berlin-1939-96p-**The U-boat force**

U-Boottaktik-by Jeschke, Hubert-Verlag Rombach, Freiburg-1972-120p-ISBN 3793001687

U-Boat Tactics-And combat instructions for the type XXI U-boat

U-Boottyp XXI-by Roessler, Eberhard-Lehmann, Munich-1968-160p-Republished in 1986 as ISBN 3763758062-161p, 54 photos

U-Boottype XXIII-by Roessler, Eberhard-Lehmann, Munich-1968-116p-38 drawings

U-Flotille Der Deutchen Marine-by Everth, Hannes-Koehlers Verlagsgesellschaft, Hereford-1988-106p, 100+photos-ISBN 3782203984-**The German U-boat Flotillas**

U-Kreuzer 151 Greift An-by Plath, Karl-Voggenreiter, Potsdam-1937-128p

Uboot Type VII-by Westwood, David-Neckar Verlag, Villingen-1986-95p-ISBN 3788301317 Many scale line drawings, useful for modeling purposes

Uboote gegen Kanada-by Hadley, Michael L-Mittler & Sohn Verlag, Berlin-1990-352p, 50 photos-**U-Boats Against Canada**

Uboote im 2. Weltkrieg-by Bagnasco, Erminio-Motorbauch Verlag, Stuttgart-1994-304p-ISBN 3613012529-**Submarines in World War II**

Unheimliche See, Die-by Puttkamer, Karl Jesko von-K. Kuhne, Wien-1952-64p-**The Eerie Sea**

Unser Recht auf den U-Bootskrieg-by Hollweg, Karl-Ullstein Verlag, Berlin-1917-242p-**Our Justification of the U-boat war**

Unter Nippons Sonne-by Thomer-Kohler Verlag Minden-1959-248p, 32 photos-**Under the Rising Sun-**About the U-843

Unterseeboote der Kaiserlichen Marine, Die-by Rossler, Eberhard-Hernard & Graefe Verlag, Berlin 1997-232p, 350 illustrations and photos-ISBN 3763759636-**The Imperial Navy U-Boats**

US Army Air Force in the World War II-by Warnock, Timothy-Center for Air Force History-1993-29p-The Battle Against the U-Boat

US Naval History Sources in the United States-by Allard, Dean & Crawley, Martha & Edmison, Mary-Naval History Division-Washington-1979-235p

US Naval Hull Numbers-by Shirlaw, David-Lexinton Media, 1955-298p-Arranged by Name, by Type, by Hull Number and also contains a Ship Classification guide

US Navy: An Illustrated History-by Miller, Nathan-American Heritage-1977-416p

US Sea-Based Strategic Force:-Cost of the Trident-by Davison, Richard H.-USGPO-1980-62p

US Ship Scorpion SSN-589 in Memoriam-USGPO-1969-64p

US Sub-A Bibliography-Low & Muche-1986

US Submarine Losses in World War II-US Naval History Division-1963

US Submarine Losses World War II-NavPers-1949

US Submarine Production Base-by Birkler, John-Rand Corp-1994

US Submarines-by Lenton-1973

US Submarines in Action-by Penfield, Thomas-Whitman-Racine, WI-1944-24p-A fact story of the U.S. submarines in the Pacific

US Submarines in World War II-by Kimmett, Larry & Regis, Margaret-Navigator Publishing 1996-159p-ISBN 1879932016-Paperback or Hard-An Illustrated History

Uberfall auf die Altmark, Der-by Frisch, Friedrich-Berlin-1940-64p-**The Attack on the Altmark**

Udar Pod Vodoi-by Perlia, Zigmund N-Moscow-1945-Torpedoes and mines

Ufficio Storico Della Marina Militaire-by Somergibili, Baldina & Cocchia-Rome-1966-Vol XII (Italian only)

Ugroza iz Glubiny Sostoanie I Perspektivy Razvitia Atomnykh Podvodnykyh Lodok za Rubezhom-by Droblenkov, VF-Moscow-1966-306p-In Russian

Ultra Americans, The-by Parrish, Thomas-Stein & Day-1986-Cooperation between British and American codebreakers

Ultra And Mediterranean Strategy (1941-1945)-by Bennet, Ralph-William Morrow, NY-1980

Ultra At Sea-Breaking of the U-Boat Code-by Winton, John-Leo Cooper-1988-ISBN 0850528836

Ultra Goes to War-by Lewin, Ronald-McGraw Hill, NY-1978

Ultra in the Pacific-1941-45-by Winton, John-Lee Cooper, UK-1993-ISBN 0850522773

Ultra in the West-by Bennett, Ralph-Charles Scribner's Sons, NY-1979-From Normandy to V-E Day

Ultra Secret, The-by Winterbotham, FW-Harper & Row-1974-286p-ISBN 0440190614

Ultra-Magic Deals, The-by Smith, Bradley F-Presidio-1993-1940-1946

Un sommergibile nonae rientrato alla bases-by Maronari, Antonia-3ed by Libreria Rizzoli-1951-335p-44 p of plates-A Submarine has not returned to Base

Un Sous-Marin Attaque-by Romat, Etienne-Gigord, Paris-1946-63p-WW II submarine operations

Unbroken-by Mars, Alastair-Frederick Muller, UK-1953-224p-The Unbroken was the only submarine operating in the Mediterranean, whilst Malta was reeling under bombardment and Rommel was heading for Egypt. The Captain is the author

Undeclared War-by Langer, William L & Gleason, SE-Harper Bros-1953-1940-41

Under Ice-by Leary, William M-Texas A&M University Press 1999-320p-Biography of Dr. Waldo Lyon—Development of the Arctic submarine

Under the Black Ensign-by Gwatkin & Williams-Hutchinson, London-1922-238p

Under the Jolly Roger-by Quigley, Dave J-Maritime Books, UK-British Subs at War 39-45

Under the North Pole-by Wilkins, George Hubert-Warren & Putnam, NY-1931-347p-A converted O-type submarine names Nautilus peeks under the ice-

Under the Ocean to the South Pole-by Rockwood, Roy-Cupples & Leon, NY-1907

Under the Periscope-by Bennett, Mark-Collins, UK-1919-254p-Also printed in 1930-Personal Narratives from WWI

Under the Red Sea Sun-by Ellsberg, Edward-Dodd, Mead-1946-500p

Under Two Flags: The American Navy in the Civil War-Fowler, William M Jr-WW Norton, NY-1990

Undersea Fleet-by Pohl, Frederick & Williamson, Jack-Gnome Press-1956

Undersea Machines-by Pick-1979

Undersea Machines-by Stephen-1986

Undersea Patrol-by Young, Edward-McGraw Hill-1952-298p-WWII submarine warfare

Undersea Raiders-by Shapiro, Milton J-D McKay, NY-1979-56p-Accounts of actual submarine adventures in WW II-youth

Undersea Vehicles and Habitats, the Peaceful Uses of the Oceans-by Ross, Frank X-Crowell, NY-1970-183p

Undersea Vehicles Directory-by Busby-Busby Associates-VA-1990

Undersea Victory-by Holmes, WJ-Doubleday-1966-505p-Allied Subs in the Pacific-Also published as two paperbacks in 1979 by Zebra Books.

Undersea War, The-by Compton-Hall, Richard-Poole, Dorset; Blandford-1982

Undersea Warfare-by Humble, Richard-Basinghall Books-1981

Undersea Warfare and Allied Strategy in World War 1-by Lundeberg, Philip K-Smithsonian Journal of History-1966-2 Vol

Undersea Warriors-by Schwab, Ernest Louis-Crescent Books: Publications International-1991-256p

Underseas!-by Cheney, Cora-Coward & McCann-Toronto-1961-121p-Submarines, diving and Oceanography written for early teens

Understanding Soviet Naval Developments-5th Edition-by CNO-USGPO-1985-152p

Underwater Acoustic System Analysis-by Burdic, William S-Prentice Hall-1984

Underwater Attack-by McManners, Kelsey-Burcett Co-1978-47p-The First Submarine

Underwater Defense Handbook-by Callahan, Vincent-Callahan Pub.-1963-138p

Underwater Exploration-by Diole, Philippe-Messner, NY-1954

Underwater Explosions-by Cole, Robert Hugh-Princeton U. Press-1948

Underwater Medicine-by Miles, Stanley-Lippincott-1962-328p-A Psychological approach-2nd edition 1966, 3rd edition 1969

Underwater Mosquitos-by Voyenzidat, M-1969-A Soviet book on midget submarines, their development and military use

Underwater Signal and Data Processing-by Joseph C. Hassab-CRC Press-1989

Underwater Torpedo-Boats-by Lake Torpedo Boat Company-1906-116p

Underwater War-by Compton-Hall, Richard-Banford, Poole-1983-160p-The author writes from a submariners viewpoint about the way they lived and fought during WW II. Photos are drawn from exclusive archives in many countries, very few have previously been published and the renowned artist John Batchelor has contributed his meticulously researched artwork

Underwater War, The-Submarines 1914-1918-by Gray, Edwyn-Chas Scribner's Sons-1971- 259p-ISBN 684126974

Underwater Warfare in the Age of Sail-by Roland, Alex-Indiana U. Press-1978-237p

Underwater Warriors-Story of American Frogmen-by Best, Ailena C-McKay, NY-1967-152p-For the young reader

Underwater Warriors-by Kemp, Paul-USNIP-1996-192p-ISBN 1557508577-60 photos-Looks at the daring sorties made by one- and two-man submarines during WW I and II, examining the craft that were built and the missions that were attempted by both Allied and Axis powers

Underwater Weapons-by Beloshitskiy, VP & Baginskiy YM-Military Publishing House, Moscow-1960-In Russian or English

Unholy Three-by Nagle, Jimmy

Uniforms and Insignia of the Navies of World War II-by Naval Intelligence-USNIP-1991

Union and Confederate submarine warfare in the Civil War-by Ragan, Mark K-Mason City, Iowa: Savas Publishing, c1999-310p

United States & Armaments, The-by Tate, Merze-Howard U. Press-1948

United States and Allied Submarine Successes in the Pacific and Far East During World War II-by Alden, John-Pub: John Alden-1999-409p-This book is a revision of his earlier (1989) work entitled U.S. Submarine Attacks During World War II. It contains information from Freedom of Information Act declassification. The definitive work on every action by U.S. Submarines

United States in the World War 1918-1920-by McMaster, John B-D. Appleton and Co-1920-510p

United States in World War I-by Lawson, Don-Scholastic Book Services, NY-1964-152p

United States Naval Academy Readings in the History of Sea Power-by Kirk, Neville, ed-1971-2Vol

United States Naval Administration in World War II-Copies at Submarine Force Library & Museum-Groton and Navy Library-Submarine Commands, Vol 1&2

United States Naval History: A Bibliography-by Lynch, Barbara & Vajda, John-USGPO-1993

United States Naval Submarine Force Information Book-by Christley, James-Graphic Enterprises of Marblehead-1996-198-Also 1997 and 1995 (80p)

United States Naval Vessels-Official US Navy Reference Manual-by Division of Naval Intelligence 1945-4 manuals reprinted-1996-672p-Detailed information includes relevant data of the period, silhouettes, line drawings and indexes.

United States Navy At War-by King, Ernest J-United States News, Washington-1945-48p

United States Navy in the Pacific-1909-1922-by Braisted, WR-U. of Texas Press-1971

United States Navy in World War II-by Smith, SE-William Morrow-1966-Ballantine Paperback in 1969 with 1128 pages and 64 pages of photos

United States Navy Patches: Submarines-by Roberts, Michael L-Schiffer-174 pages-Identifies more than 1,000 insignias in full

color used by the Navy's submarine service, indexed for easy
access of specific subs

United States Nuclear Navy, The-Gimpel, Herbert J-Watts, NY-1965-
199p

United States Ship Thresher (SSN-593)-In Memoriam-by US Navy-
1964-146p

United States Ship Scorpion (SSN-589)-In Memoriam-by US Navy-
1969-64p

United States Submarine Data-by General Dynamics-1958 3rd edi-
tion-23p-Lists of all submarines, name, number, design, yard,
dates, sponsor, commissioning and disposal

United States Submarine Operations in World War II-by Rosco,
Theodore-USNIP-1949-ISBN 0870217313-Publishable portion
of the US Navy's Operational History

United States Submarine Veterans, Inc 1999 National Roster-90p-
Indexed by Last name and then by Hull number sequence

United States Submarine Veterans of World War II-by US Sub Vets
WWII-Turner Publishing, 1991-4 vols+an Index volume. Many
photos of boats, commissioning and decommissioning crews
and between for all the boats in WWII. Also many bios of
members of the Organization at time of publishing.

United States Submarines-by Barnes, Robert H-Morse, New Haven-
1946 (3rd ed)-221p

Unlucky in June-Hiyo meets Trigger-by Beach, Edward L-USNIP

Unrestricted Warfare-by DeRose, James F-John Wiley & Sons-2000-
310p-ISBN 047138495X-U.S. Submarine CO's in WWII

**Unser Boot und Wir im Mittelmeer-Our Boats and us in the
Mediterranean**-by Brennecke, Hans Jochen-Otto von Holten-1943

Unser Rect auf den U-Bootskrieg-Ullstein, Berlin-1917-242p

Unsinkable Fleet, The-by Davidson, Joel-USNIP-1996-224p-ISBN
1557501564-20 photos The Politics of U.S. Navy Expansion in
WW II

Unterseeboosbau-by Gabler, Ulrich-Bernard & Graefe Verlag,
Koblenz-1987-150p, 42 photos U-boat Construction

Unterseeboote-by Brase, WAH-Duisberg, Hannover-1933

Unterseeboot, Das-by Neureuther, Karl-Hertz, Munich-1915-23p

Unterseeboot, Das-by Raver, Herman-ES Mittler & Sohn-1931

Unterseeboot im Kampfe, Das-by Otto, Freidrich-Ameland, Leipzig-1915-157p

Unterseeboote Ostereich-Ungarns, 1 Band-by Aichelburg, Wladimar-1981

Unterseeboote Ostereich-Ungarns, 2 Band, Die-Aichelburg, Wladimar -1982

Unterseeboot: Seine Bedeutung als Teil Enier Flotte, Das-by Bauer, Hermann-ES Mittler, Berlin 1931-140p

Unterseeboote und Torpedoes mit Kreislaufantrieb-by Kurzak, KH & Roessler, E-Private-1969-162p

Unterwasserschalltechnik, Grundlagen, Ziel und Grenzen-by Aigner, Franz-Krayn, Berlin-1922-322p

Uomini contro Navi-by Pegolotti, B-Vallechi, Firenze-1960-Men Against Ships

Uomini dell' Atlantico-by Raiola, G-Longanese & C, Milano-1973- Men of the Atlantic

Up Periscope!-by Masters, David-Dial, NY-1943-275p-Also 1992 edition-A saga of British Submarines and the indomitable spirit of the seamen who operated them

Up Periscope-by White, Robb-Doubleday, Garden City-1956-251p

US Ballistic Missile Subs In Action-by Adcock, Al-Squadron/Signal Publications-many photos and drawings-50p-Warships In Action Vol 6-ISBN 0897472934

US Merchant Vessel Casualties of World War II-by Browning, Robert M-USNIP-1996

US Military Medals 1939-1994-by Foster, Col. Frank & Borts, Larry-80p

US Military Online-by Arkin, William-Brassey's-1997-256p-ISBN 1574881434-The first directory of its kind to assist you in locating online military information

US Military Operations Since World War II-by Anderson, Kenneth-Brompton Books Corp-1984

US Naval Academy Archives-Photos of Graduating Classes

US Naval Hull Numbers-by Shirlaw, David-Self

US Naval Logistics in the Second World War-by Ballantine, Duncan S-Princeton U. Press-1947

US Naval Submarine Base New London, CT-1959-36p-General information pamphlet

US Naval Vessels-1943-US Navy-1986-288p-ISBN 0870217240-679 photos

US Naval Weapons-by Friedman, Norman-USNIP-1987-Every weapon used by the Navy from 1983 to present

US Navy-by Miller, Nathan-USNIP-312 p-ISBN 1557505950-A standard text at the Naval Academy, it is known as the best available brief history of the U.S. Navy-ISBN refers to 1997 paperback edition

US Navy-by Silverstone, Paul-96p-ISBN 0853689210-195 illustrations-1945 to the Present

US Navy, The-200 Years-by Beach, Edward-Henry Holt & Co-1986-564p

US Navy at War-by King, Fleet Admiral Ernest-US Navy Dept-1946-U.S. Navy at War 1941-1945: Official Reports to the Secretary of the Navy

US Navy Bureau of Ordnance in WW II-by Rowland, Boyd & Buford-USGPO-1943

US Navy in the 1990s: Alternatives for Action-by George, James L-USNIP-1992-ISBN 1557503265

US Navy in the Pacific-1909-1922-by Braisted, William R-U. of Texas Press-1971-2 vol

US Navy Research and Development Since World War II-by Allison, David K-MIT Press-1985

US Navy, Vietnam-by Moeser, Robert D-USNIP-1969-247p

US Navy War Photographs: Pearl Harbor to Tokyo Bay-Steichen, Edward, ed-Crown, NY-1956

US Navy Yard Portsmouth-by Boyd, David F-1931

US Nuclear Submarines-by Meisner, Arnold-Concord-1990

US Shipbuilding Industry: Past, Present and Future-by Whitehurst, Clinton-USNIP-1986

US Submarine Attacks During WW II-by Alden, John D-USNIP-1989-285p-The most complete compilation of data ever presented on U.S. and Allied submarine operations in the war against Japan. Includes a full chronological listing of attacks and matches and evaluates the data against Japanese and other sources-Updated with new information in October 1999-400p+ but officially published yet. The update is a large 8 ½ X 14 softcover.

US Submarine Losses in World War II-by Holmes, Wilfred J

US Submarine Losses in World War II-USN-Washington-1949-174p-Includes crew lists of the 52 lost submarines

US Submarines-by Barnes, Robert Hatfield-HF Morse Assoc-1944-195p

US Submarines-by Keats, Henry & George C Farr-Pices Books-1991-221p

US Submarines in Action-by Stern, Robert C-Squadron-Signal-1979-45

US Submarines since 1945-by Friedman, Norman-USNIP-1994-280p-ISBN 1557502609 An Illustrated Design History

US Submarines Through 1945-by Friedman, Norman-USNIP-1994

US Submarines, A Bibliography-by Law, Lani & James Muche-Fathom Eight-1986-196p

US Subs in Action-by Stern, Robert C-Squadron Signal-1979-ISBN 0897470850-52p-100 photos

US Warships of WW I-by Silverstone, Paul H-1970

US Warships of WW II-by Silverstone, Paul H-Ian Allen-1971-444p-A complete and detailed survey of all the major ships and support vessels of both the Navy, and the Coast Guard. List of war losses. Data on each ship, with many photographs

Use of Emergency Evacuation Hyperbaric Stretcher in Submarine Escape-by Latson, Gary W-Navy Experimental Diving Unit-1999-

US Warships since 1945-by Silverstone, Paul-1987-240p-ISBN 0870217690-194 photos

Use of Japanese Midget Submarines at Pearl Harbor, The-by Allen, Stewart J-1974

USS Balao-by US Navy-1957-The ship's history

USS Barb-by Cracknell, William H-Culver City, CA-1973-23p

USS Billfish (SSN 676): Departure Ceremony, 12 August 1998, Naval Submarine Base, New London, Groton, Connecticut.-1998-329

USS Bowfin-by Lott, Arnold S & Sumall, Egan-Leeward Pubs-1975-ISBN 0915268051

USS Cod-Oxford Museum Press-1999-80p-Photo Museum Guide

USS Grouper-by Hodgdon, Roland W-Hampden, MA, 1996-121 p-

USS O's Submarine Log Book-1918

USS Pampanito Killer Angel-by Michno, Gregory-U. Of Oklahoma Press-2000-445p-ISBN 0806132051

USS Razorback SS394-Cruise Book-by Aubrey-1945-30p

USS Scorpion in Memoriam-USGPO-1964-64p

USS Sea Cat SS-399: 1944-1968 The Boat and the Men-by Winburn, Robert-Robert H. Winburn Pub-2001-239p-200 photos-Crew list from 44-68-500 printed

USS Seawolf-Submarine Raider of the Pacific-by Frank, Gerold & Horan, James D-GP Putnams 1945-197p

USS Spadefish SS411-by Scanlon-1988-in WW II

USS Thresher-USGPO

USS Triton-by Beach, Edward L.-USGPO-1960-80p-The official log of the cruise around the world submerged

USS Tunny SSN 682-Inactivation ceremony, September 2 1997, Naval Submarine Base, Pearl Harbor, Hawaii-1997-32p

U-X stand im Mittelmeer-by Schoder, Edgar-Steiniger-Verlag, Berlin-1943-95p, 48 photos-

U-X stations in the Mediterranean

V

Vagabunden auf See-by Weyher, Durt & Ehrlich, Hans Jurger-Katzmann-Verlag, Tubingen-1953 301p-**Vagabonds at Sea**

Vakhtenn's Zhurnal (The Log)-by Chernavin, Vladimir N (Adm)-Russian

Vanguard to Trident: British Naval Policy Since World War II-by Grove, Eric J-USNIP-1987

Vedetta Atlantica-by Betasom-Betasom, Boreaux-1970-Atlantic Lookout

Veetig jaren Onderzeedienst 1906-1946-by Comite Voor De Viering-Scheltens & Giltay, Amsterdam-1947-208p-Commemorating 40 years of the Dutch submarine service

Veil, The Secret Wars of the CIA, 1981, 1987-by Woodward, Bob-Simon & Schuster-1987

Venetia, Avenger of the Lusitania-by Greene, Clay-San Diego-1919-45p-Only 300 copies of this book. The Venetia was responsible for the sinking of U-39, the German submarine thought to have sunk the Lusitania

Vengeance in the Depths-by Steele, George-Dutton, NY-1963-183p-Young

Verdammte See-by Bekker, Cajus-E.S. Mittler & Sohn, Herford-1998-First published in 1971. ISBN 382890307X-The author served on the Kriegsmarine staff in WWII

Verdammter Atlantik: Schicksale deutscher U-Boot-Fahrer-by Herlin, Hans-Nannen, Hamburg, 1959-Leo Cooper-1994-426p

Verdreven Doch Niet Verslagen-by Bezemer, K.W.L.-W. de Haan N.V., Hilversum-1967-Dutch-War history (WWII) of the Royal Netherlands Navy

Verrantene Flotte, Die-by Freiwald, Ludwig-Lehmann Verlag, Munchen-1831-298p-**The Betrayed Fleet**

Versunkene Flotte, Die-by Bekker, Cajus-G. Stalling, Oldenburg-1961-80p-**The Sunken Fleet**

Verticalnoye Vspleteeye (Vertical Dive)-by Mikhailovski, AP-(Russian only)-St Petersburg Naooka-1995-534p-ISBN 5020282723

Very Special Intelligence-by Beesly, Patrick-Hamish Hilton, UK-1977-Doubleday (78)-ISBN 0385132069-Story of the Admiralty's Intelligence Center (39-45)

Vessels for Underwater Exploration-by Limburg, Peter R-Crown Publishers, NY-1973-154p-ISBN 0517505347

Victoria and the Triton-by Dibner, Bern-Burnby Library-1962-58p

Victory At Sea-The Submarine-by Parrish, Thomas P-Ridge Press-1959-60p

Victory At Sea-WW I-by Sims, William S-Doubleday, Garden City-1920-410p-Written by Adm. Sims who was CO Naval Atlantic in WW I

Victory At Sea-by Dunnigan, James & Nofi, Albert-Quill-1996-624p-Softcover-World War II in the Pacific

Vietnam: The Naval Story-by Uhlig, Frank-USNIP-515p-Fifteen essays by key naval officers and staff present eyewitness commentaries on U.S. naval operations in Vietnam, from the Tonkin Gulf in the north to the Gulf of Thailand in the south, covering operations afloat, aloft and ashore.

Vita di Marinaio-by Birindelli, G-Vito Bianco, Rome-1991-Life of a Sailor

Viviamo Ancora-by Neureuther, C-A. Salani, Firenze-1036-We Still live

Voenno-Morski Flot-by Kolbasev, Sergei-Leningrad-1926

Vom Orignal Zum Modell-by Kohl, Fritz-Bernard & Graefe Verlag, Koblenz-1988-64 p, 91 photos-ISBN 3763760008-**The Original to scale model: Type XXI U-boat**

Vom Orignal Zum Modell-by Kohl, Fritz-Bernard & Graefe Verlag, Koblenz-1997-64p-ISBN 3763760024-Type VIIC

Vom Orignal Zum Modell-by Kohl, Fritz-Bernard & Graefe Verlag, Koblenz-1990-68p-ISBN 3763760059-Type IXC

Vom Orignal Zum Modell: Uboot Type II-by Rossler, Eberhard-Bernard & Graefe Verlag, Bonn-1999-88p-ISBN 3763760237

Vom Orignal Zum Modell: Uboot Type XVII-by Rossler, Eberhard & Kohl, Fritz-Bernard & Graefe-1995-80p-ISBN 3763760091

Vom Orignal Zum Modell: Type XVIII unde Type XXVI-by Rossler, Eberhard-Bernard & Graefe Verlag, Bonn-1998-88p-ISBN 3763760199-Many plans and drawings

Vom Seeflieger zum Uboot-Fahrer-by Just, Paul-Motorbuch, Verlag-1982-220p-**From Naval Aviator to U-Boat Skipper**

Vom Segelschiffe Zum U-Boot-by Scheer-1924

Vom U-Boot-Offizier zum Passionierten Jager-by Deutschmann, Fritz-Frieling, Verlag-1996-224p-From U-boat officer to enthusiastic hunter-Served on U-18, U-3034, U-3505

Von Kolberg uber La Rochelle nach Berlin-by Marbach, Karl-Heinz-Haag & Herchen Verlag-1994-276p-From Kolberg via La Rochelle to Berlin-Autobiography of Karl-Heinz Marbach, commander of U-953

Von U-Boot Zur Kanzel-by Neimoller, Martin-Warneck, Berlin-1934-210p-From U-boat to Pulpit

Voyage of the Deutschland-by Koenig, Paul-Hearst International-1916-247p-The First Merchant submarine-Reissued as a Classic of Naval Literature Series book by USNIP in 2001-ISBN 1557504245

Voyage of the Hunley-by Hoyt, Edwin-Burford Books, Inc-2001-192p-ISBN 1580800947

Voyenno-morskoy Flot SSSR 1945-1991-by Kuzin, VP & Nikolskiy, VI-St. Petersburg-1996-The Navy of the USSR 1945-1991

W

Waffe Unter Wasser-by Wiedemeyer, Gerhard-Kyffhauser-verlag, Berlin-1940-160p, 30 photos-Underwater Fleet

Wahoo-by O'Kane, Richard H.-Presidio Press-1987-376p softcover-ISBN 0891413014

Wake of the Wahoo-by Sterling, Forest J-Chilton Books-1960-210p-From a crewmember-Reissued by RA Cline Publishing ISBN 0966323521-1999

Walker RN-by Roberston, Terence-Evan Brothers, UK-Kimber-1955-Captain Walker won three DSO's, and his task was to beat the awful menace of the German U-Boats in the Atlantic

Walker's Groups in the Western Approaches-by Wemyss, Cdr DEG-Liverpool Daily Post-1948

Walter Uboote-by Kruska, Emil-Lehmann, Munich-1969-216p-A technical book on all designed and projected Walther hydrogen peroxide high speed u-boats

Walter Uboote-by Rossler, Eberhard & Fritz Kihl-Bernard & Graefe Verlag-Bonn-1995-80p ISBN 3763760091-Written in German

War and Peace in the Nuclear Age-by Newhouse, John-Alfred A. Knopf-1988

War at Sea-by Cant, Gilbert-John Day Co-1942

War at Sea-by Rohwer, Jurgen-USNIP-1996-192p-ISBN 1557509158-250 photos-A visual history of naval operations in WW II, archival photographs create a stark picture of the realities of war at sea and a running narrative covers every aspect of the naval war

War at Sea 1939-1945-by Hamilton, John-272-176 Paintings

War at Sea, The-by Roskill, SW-HMSO-1960-3 vols

War at Sea, The: The British Navy in World War II-by Winton, John-William Morrow & CO, NY

War Beneath the Sea-by Brou, Willy-See "Combat Beneath the Sea"

War Comes to Dutch Harbor-by Rourke, Norman-White Mane-1996-144p

War Damage Report #58-by Navy Department-USGPO-1949-In particular Appendix #1: Briefs of War Damage incurred by U.S. Submarines during WWII

War Diaries of the U-764, The-Guske, Heinz-Thomas-192p-A submariner's critical analysis of the exploits, command and subsequent surrender of Captain von Bremen's U-Boat

War Diary, Easter Sea Frontier-Morison, Elting E

War Diary, North Atlantic Naval Coastal Frontier-by Morison, Elting E

War Diary of the Operations Division German Naval Staff-Also known as KTB-1/SK1-Located at U.S. Naval Historical Center

War Fish-by Grider, George & Lytel Sims-Little Brown-1958-Pyramid-1961-Ballantine-1973-282p-Adventures in the U.S. submarine service. Captain Girder served in four submarines which included the Wahoo and commanded the Flasher

War in the Atomic Age-by Karig, Walter-WH Wise & Co, NY-1946-63p

War In the Boats-by Ruhe, Capt William J-Brassey's-1994-ISBN 0028810848-Paperback 1996-ISBN 1574880284-One of the most inclusive descriptions of the undersea war against Japan. "This is an extraordinary account of our submarine war in the steaming tropics of the Pacific. It is unlike other World War II submarine books and much can be learned from it about submarines and the character of submariners, a unique breed

War in the Deep-by Hoyt, Edwin P-GP Putnam's-1978-Pacific Submarine Action in WW II

War in the Pacific-by Winton, John-Sidgwick & Jackson-1978-193p

War in the Southern Oceans-by Gordon-Cumming, HR & Turner, LCF & Betzler, JE-Oxford U. Press-1961-1939-1945

War in the Underseas-by Wheeler, Harold FB-Geo. Harrap, London-1919-320p

War of the Submarines, The-by Casey, Robert J-Bobbs-Merrill-1945

War on German Submarines, The-by Carson, Edward H-TF Unwin, London-1917-8p

War on the High Seas-Time-Life Books-1990

War on the Sea-Harper's Pictorial Library of the World War, in several volumes-Harper Bros, NY-1920

War on the Sea: Strategy and Tactics-by Darrieus, Gabriel, USNIP-1908

War Patrols of the USS Flasher-McCants, William-Self-1994-465p

War Plan Orange-by Miller, Edward S-USNIP-1991-The US strategy to defeat Japan

War Under the Pacific-by Wheeler, Keith-Time Life-1980-280p

War Under the Waves-by Warshofsky, Fred-Pyramid-1962-157p

War on German Submarines, The-by Carson-1917

War Under the Pacific-by Wheeler, Keith-Time-Life Books-1980-208p

War Under the Waves-by Warshofsky, Fred-Pyramid Books-167p-Stories of the Turtle, the Holland, Gunther Prien and other early submarine heroes.

War Without Mercy-by Dower, John W-Pantheon, NY-1986-ISBN 0394751728

Warlords, The-by Carver, Michael-Little, Brown & Co-1976

Warring Seas, The-or **Dynamite for Hire**-by Selwood, AV-T. Werner-1956\

Warrior in White-by Jopling, Lucy W-Watercress Press, San Antonio-1990-133p-ISBN 0934955182 (HB)...204(paper). The story of the eleven nurses on Corregidor that escaped via the USS Spearfish

War Damage Report #58 Jan. 1949-Appendix 1, Briefs of War Damage Incurred by U.S. Submarines During WWII. Dept. of Navy and reprinted by Floating Drydock, 1976

War's New Weapons-by Dewitz, Hrolf von-Dodd & Mead, NY-1915-295p

Warship 1990-Conway Maritime Press-USNIP Publisher in U.S.-1990-255p-ISBN 1557509034-This book is published yearly and not exclusively submarine. This particular issue, however, contains: Russian 'Lake' Type Submarines and the Baltic War 1914-1919 and The Midget Submarine Attack on the Tirpitz

Warship Losses of World War Two-by Brown, David-USNIP-1990-256p-ISBN 0853688028

Warships and Naval Battles of the Civil War-by Gibbons, T-Dragon's World-1989-176p, 180 color illustrations-ISBN 1850280940

Warships in Profile-by Preston, Anthony-Doubleday, NY-1974-152p-One of the six chapters-concerns "Rubis" French Free submarine

Warships of the 20th Century-by Chant, Christopher-Tiger-144p.

Warships of the Imperial Japanese Navy-by Hansgeorg & Jentschura-Jung & Mickel-1976-284p-ISBN 087021893X-350 illustrations

Warships of the World-by Galuppini, Gino

Warships of the World-by Ireland, Bernard-I Allan, London-1980-160p-ISBN 0711009767-Submarines and Fast Attack Craft

Warships of the World-by Preston, Anthony-Biston Books, Greenwich, CT-1983-399p-ISBN 0861241029

Warships of World War I-Submarines-by LeFleming, HM-Ian Allan, UK

Warships of World War II-by Lenton, HT & Colledge, JJ-Ian Allen-638p-This book presents a complete record of all known vessels of the Royal and Dominion Navies which participated in the Second World War

Wartime Passenger Ship Disasters-by Williams, David-Haynes-1997-192p-400 stories from-both wars

Wartime Transportation Convoys History-by Komamiya, Shinshichiro-Japanese only as Senji Yuso Sendan Shi

Was Jeder vom Deutschen U-Boot Wissen Muss-by Bartsch, Max-Limpert, Berlin-1940-40p What everyone should know about the German U-Boat

Washington Command Post: The Operations Division-by Cline, Ray S-OCMH-1951

Washington Goes to War-by Brinkley, David-Alfred A. Knopf Inc.-1988

Washington Papers-by Leitenberg, Milton-1987-Soviet Submarine Operations in Swedish Waters

Watchdogs of the Deep-by Jones, Thomas M-Angus, Sydney-1935-224p

Water Baby-by Kaharl, Victoria-Oxford U. Press-1990-356p-The Story of Alvin

Water Losses From Submarine Storage Batteries-by Kirkpatrick, J-1929

We Band of Angels-The Nurses on Bataan and their escape-by Norman, Elizabeth-Random House, 1999

We Captured a U-Boat-by Gallery, Daniel V.-Sidgewick & Jackson-1957-Capture of the U-505

We Dive At Dawn-by Edwards, Kenneth-Reilly & Lee, Chicago-1941-412p-Royal Navy submarine warfare during WW I and post war submarine service up to WW II

We Dive the Sub-by Reeman, Douglas-Putnam, NY-1961

We Were There on the Nautilus-by Webb, Robert N-Grosset and Dunlap, NY-1961-178p-Young

We Work for Freedom-by Hopkins, John Jay-Newcomen Soc, NY-1950-28p-Transcript of an address by the Electric Boat President

Weapons of War 1916-John Heywood, Ltd-1916-164p

Weapons that Wait-by Hartman, Gregory K & Turner, Scott C-USNIP-1991

Wegduiken: De Nederlandse Onderzeedienst 1906-1966-by Stok, MC-Holland-1966-633p-Issued to commemorate the 60th anniversary of the Dutch submarine service

Weimar Hitler und die Marine-by Dulffer, J-Droste, Dusseldorf-1973

Wer Das Schwertninmt-He Who Takes Up the Sword-by Kleneck, Walter-Universitas-1987 1940-45

What a Wonderful Machine Is the Submarine-by Bate, Norman-Schribner's, NY-1961-For young children 4-8-The Submarine Picture Story

What About Submarines-by Care-1982

What the Citizen should know about Submarine Warfare-by Woodbury, David Oakes-Norton, NY-1942-231p-Later reprints titled: What You Should Know About Submarine Warfare.

When the U-Boats Came to America-by Clark, William Bell-Little, Boston-1929-359p

Where Are the Submarines-by Breemer, Jan S-USNIP-1993

Who Killed Surcouf?-by Young-1988

Who Really Invented the Submarine-by Wyckoff, James-Putnam, NY-1965-95p

Who Sank Surcouf?-by Rusbridger, J-Century-1991

Who Was Who in American History-the Military-Marquis, Chicago-1975

Will Not We Fear-by Warren, CET & James Benson-Panther (Harrap in 1961) 1964-228p-The authors, themselves submariners, tell the story of HMS Submarine Seal which was lost. They were subsequently captured

Winning Edge, The-by Poolman, Kenneth-USNIP-1997-240p-ISBN 1557506876-Naval Technology in Action-1939-1945. Allied navies deployed new weapons like ASDIC, RDF, direction finding equipment along with acoustic torpedoes and snorkel development.

Winning the War With Ships-by Land, Emory S-Robert M. McBride Co-1958

Wir an den Maschinen: Kriedsfahrten auf und Unter See-by Reinhard, Wilhelm-Hase & Koehler, Leipzig-1940-256p

Wir Leben Noch!-by Neureuther, Karl-Union Deutche, Stuttgart-1930-206p-We still live! German heroes of the U-boat war

Wir U-Bootfahrer sagen: "Nein! So war das nicht!"-by Merten, Karl-Friedrich & Baberg, Kurt-1986-We U-boat men say: "No, it wasn't so!"

Wireroping the German Submarine-by Roebling, John-Roebling's, NY-1920-37p

With the Red Fleet-Putnam, London-1965-247p-The Memoirs of Adm Golovko

Wizard War, The-by Jones, R-Coward, McCann & Geohegan-1978

Wolf-by Vause, Jordan-USNIP-1997-256p-ISBN 1557508747-U-Boat Commanders in World War II. Examines the lives of many U-boat officers following their careers from their initial training through the war and into the post-war period. Draws heavily on primary sources and interviews with surviving U-boat personnel

Wolf Pack-by Kaplan, Phillip & Currie, Jack-USNIP-1997-240p-ISBN 1557508550-245 photos-U-Boats at War 1939-1945-In German as Wolfsrudel-ISBN 3813205401

Wolf Packs Third Reich-by Constable, George-Time Life-192p-Covers U-Boat development and wartime operations through World War II. Includes a room by room tour of U-505 with color photos

Wolfe der Meere-by Wiedemeyer, Gerhard-K Curtius, Berlin-1941-47p-Wolves of the Sea

Wolfgang Luth-by Alman, Karl-Podzun-Pallas-Verlag, Friedberg-1988-288p-ISBN 3860708546-U-boat Commander

Wonders of the Submarine, The-by Corbin, Thomas W-Seeley Service-1918-163p

World At Arms; A Global History of World War II-by Weinberg, Gerhard-Cambridge-1994-1172p

World At War-by Arnold-Forster, Mark-Stein and Day-1973

World Beneath the Sea, The-by Barton, Otis-Crowell, NY-1953-246p

World Beneath the Waves, The-by Doukan, Gilbert-Allen & Unwin, London-Nelson, Toronto-1957-301p

World in the Balance-by Weinberg, Gerhard-U. Press of New England-1981-Behind the scenes of WW II

World Naval Weapons Systems-1991-1992-by Friedman, Norman-USNIP-1991-928p ISBN 0870212885-800 illustrations

World Naval Weapons Systems Update-by Friedman, Norman-USNIP-1994-168p-ISBN 1557502595-150 photos/drawings

World War II at Sea-by Smith, Myron J-Scarecrow, NJ-1976-A Bibliography of Sources in English, 3 vols

World War II: Battle at Sea-by McIntyre, Colin-Mallard-176p-Text and photos chronicle the great naval engagements, from the sinking of the Bismarck to the battles of Midway and Leyte Gulf, with detailed reappraisals of tactics and intelligence that shed new light on the outcomes.

World War II in the Atlantic-by Messenger, Charles-Gallery Books, NY-1990-80p

World War II in the North Pacific-by Hutchison, Kern Don-Greenwood Press-1994

World War II-by Ellis, John-1993-300p-A statistical Survey

Worldwide Submarine Challenge-ONI-GPO-US Government-1996-32p

Wreck Information List-US Hydrographic Office-USGPO-1945

WTEC Panel Report on Research Submersibles and Undersea Technologies-by Seymour, RJ, ed-Loyola College, 1994-315p

Wunderwaffe Elektro-Uboot Typ XXI-by Breyer, Siegfried-Podzun, Pallas-1996-48p-ISBN 3790905879-The Wonder Weapon-Electric Boat XXI

X

X-craft Raid, The-by Gallagher, Thomas-Harcourt Brace-1971-170p-ISBN 0151997268-WW II mission to sink the Tirpitz

X-Men-by Bekker, Cajus D-George Mann Ltd.-1973

Y

Yankee, RN-by Cherry, Alex-Jarrolds, UK-1953

Year That Doomed the Axis-by Adams, Henry-Paperback Library-1969

Years of Deadly Peril-by Adams, Henry-David McKay Co-1969

Yesterday's Heroes-by Jordan, Kenneth-Schiffer-1996-614p-This book contains all 433 Medal of Honor citations, along with Official Communiqués from the front, and newspaper accounts of various battles. This is a dramatic look at the courage of the American soldier in World War II

Young Naval Captain, The-by Bonehill, Ralph-Thompson & Thompson-Chicago-1902

Z

Z dejin Ponorky-by Kamil, Lhotak-Sti Nakl detsle Lmoju, Pravda-
1956-185p
Zehn Jahre und Zwanzig Tage-Ten Years and Twenty Days-by
Doenitz, Karl-1958-Autobiography from 1934 forward
Zerstorer unter deutscher Flagge 1934-1945-by Harnack, Wolfgang-
1978
Zoomies, Subs, and Zeros-by Lockwood, Charles A-Greenberg, NY-
1956-301p-Rescues in World War Two by the Submarine
Lifeguard League

Fiction

A Fiction

20000 Leagues Under the Sea-by Verne, Jules
21st Century Sub-by Herbert, Frank-Avon, NY-1956-190p
A Dawn Like Thunder-Reeman, Douglas-Pan Books-1997-338p-ISBN
    0330341952-A 2-man mini submarine is used off Burma
A Drowning War-by Winton, John-Ulverscroft Large Print Books-
    1992-286p-ISBN 070891621X-Originally published 1985
A House at War-Dorfman, Allan-Xlibrus Publishing-492p-ISBN
    0738822019-A Ship and a family do battle against the sea and
    the Nazis
A Sailor of Austria-by Biggins, John-St. Martin's Press, NY-1994-396p-
    ISBN 0312105347 This book is a very good read. A lot of detail
    is given, so one can get the feel for life in the service of the
    Hapsburg submarine corps of the First World War. The novel is
    told from the point of view of a surviving U-boat commander,
    who is Czech, and is reminiscing about his career in the
    Adriatic from an old folks' home. The novel gives one a good
    feeling for life aboard WWI U-boats, starting with adventures
    aboard a Holland-class boat, and then moving on to U-boats
    that Austria-Hungary had purchased from Germany.
A Share of Honor-by Fullerton, Alexander-1982

A Stillness at Sea-by Aasheim, Ashley-Bell/Banbury Books, Wayne, Pa-1983-358p-Subject: Lusitania

A Time of Killing-by Hardy, William M-Dodd, Mead, NY-1962-186p-It's the end of the war, and sub skipper hasn't yet avenged lost crewmen with just a few hours left

A Twist of Sand-by Jenkins, Geoffrey-Fontana/Collins, UK-1959-252p-

Action Atlantic-by Gray, Edwin-1975-U-Boats in WWII-2nd in a series by Gray centering on 1941

Adolph Hitler and the Secrets of the Holy Lance-by Buechner, Howard A & Bernhart, Wilhelm   Thunderbird Press

Albatross Run-1986-US war correspondent hitches ride on ship commanded by mad captain. While in convoy, unstable captain runs amuck

America-by Coonts, Stephen-St. Martin's Press-2001-ISBN 0312253419-400 p-An experimental American submarine is hijacked

An Operational Necessity-by Griffin, Gwyn-GP Putnam's Sons-1967-Harvill Press reissue in 1999-ISBN 186046596X-Paperback, 416 pages-This book deals with the subject of the (U-996 in the book) which sank a ship and then fired on the wreckage killing many of the ship's crew. The book covers this incident, the later sinking of the U-boat, and the war crimes trial but in novel form with fictional crew members. The title comes from the claim that destroying the wreckage was an "operational necessity" to avoid Allied aircraft. Originally published 1967. U-Boat machine guns helpless survivors of freighter, and crew is brought to trial after the war. Based on true incident

Anitov-by Deremer, Robert E-Burke Publishing Co, San Antonio-1999-ISBN 0967603811-A Russian agent in put in a shipyard to destroy the U.S.S. Thresher.

Aquarius Mission-by Caidin, Martin-Bantam Books-1978-213p-ISBN 0533112678-US sub investigates disappearance of 2 nuclear subs, finds strange world miles deep

Arctic Mutiny-by Horst, Karl-Corgi, London-1981-174p-ISBN 0552117218

Arctic Submarine-by Mars, Alistair-Elek, UK-1955-191p

Assault on a Queen-by Finney, Jack-Simon Schuster-1959-A sunken U-Boat is raised and used to rob the Queen Mary at sea

Assignment Sulu Sea-by Aarons, Edward S-Fawcett, Greenwich-1964-159p

Atlantic Run-by Davis, Bart-Pocket Books-1993-288p-ISBN 0671769049-Captain Peter MacKenzie who is the hero in all of Davis's submarine books takes a group of undersea "top guns" to a mission to stop a top Soviet submarine captain from delivering a high-tech submarine to Cuba.

Atlantikwölfe-See Grey Wolf

Attack of the Seawolf-by DiMercurio, Michael-Berkley Books-1993-412p-ISBN 0451180518-USS Tampa, on spying mission, is captured by Chinese. USN sends maverick captain in new, untried sub to steal it back. Author was Lt Engineer on real SSN USS Hammerhead.

Attack on the Queen-by Henrick, Richard P-Avon-1997-401p-ISBN 0380790270-A terrorist group attacks the Queen Mary and is holding all the world's leaders who were meeting there. Two brothers set out to reverse the damage

Avenge the Belgrano-by Langley, Bob-Walker and Co, NY-1988-267p-ISBN 0802710301

B Fiction

Barracuda-by Greenfield, Irving A-Charter, NY-1978-America's best sub is lost at sea and the forgotten until she is spotted half the world away. The hunt begins anew

Barracuda: Final Bearing-by DiMercurio, Michael-1996-427p-ISBN 0451407423-Japan attacks Manchuria. The US calls on Michael Pacino to destroy the Japanese fleet.

Bear Island-by MacLean, Alistair-Doubleday, Garden City-1971-243p-ISBN 0449200361 This novel deals only indirectly with U-boats, with the action taking place a quarter century after the end of World War II.

Bedford Incident, The-by Rascovich, Mark-Pocket Books-1963-291p-USS Bedford versus a Soviet submarine in the Cold War era-A movie made from this book

Beneath the Silent Sea-by Henrick, Richard P-Zebra Books-1988-414p-ISBN 0821740083-Beneath the waves, three great super-powers class in the first battle of the final war

Blake of the Rattlesnake-by Jane, Fred T-Fiction

Blow Negative-by Stephens, Edward-Doubleday-1962-Dell-1963-466p-Hardback and then 3 different paperback editions. This story is a satirical story paralleling Adm. Rickover and his work in starting the Nuclear Program.

Boat, The-Das Boot-by Buchheim, Lothar Gunter-Piper & Co, Verlag, 1973, Knopf, NY,1975, Dell, 1988-463p-ISBN 039449105X-Dell ISBN 0440200636-The classic of German submarine warfare from which the movie Das Boot was made.

Boomer-By Taylor, Charles D.-Pocketbooks-1990-335p-ISBN 067167630X -Twenty years ago the KGB planted an agent in the U.S. Navy. Today he is the commander of an American SSN and he's setting out to destroy the U.S. fleet.

Bone Collectors, The-by Callison, Brian

Boy Allies with the Navy Series-by Hayes, Clair W-Burt, NY-1915-22-Three books in this series concerned submarines including "With the Flying Squadron" 1915

Bowmanville Break, The-Shelley, Sidney-Fitzhenry & Whiteside, Ltd., Toronto-1968-Loosely based on a rebellion and escape attempt orchestrated by Otto Kretschmer the Bowmanville prison camp in Canada. Based on fact as Kretschmer was in fact a prisoner there.

Bridge of Magpies-Herst, Roger E-1974-Search for lost underwater city off coast of Africa turns up a missing U-Boat, presumed sunk in 1943

Bright Shark-by Ballard, Robert & Tony Chiu-Island Books by Dell-1992-ISBN 044021405X In 1968 the Israelie sub Dakar sunk. In 1988 hints are uncovered as to it's location but other terrorists actions are at work

Brink, The-by Gallery, Daniel V-Paperback Library-1969-255p-Accident aboard Polaris sub 100 fathoms down in Norwegian Sea threatens to start WWIII. The author was the U.S. Navy capturer of the U-505

Bucke of Submarine V2-by Walker, Roland-SW Partridge & Co-1916 & 1931-256p

Brutus Lie, The-by Gobbell, John-Charles Schribner's Sons, NY-ISBN 0684192497

C Fiction

Cabot Station-by Schaill, William S-Avon-1992-238p-ISBN 038071714X -Small, forgotten North Atlantic listening post hears Soviet subs kill unknown submarine nearby. Now the post is under attack

Capture of the Swordray-by Blair, Clay

Cardinal of the Kremlin-by Clancy, Tom-GP Putnam's Sons, NY-543p-ISBN 0399133453

Cayman Gold-by Hankins, John-ISBN 1889260002

Chain of Deceit-by McIntosh, DA-Xlibrus Publishing-444p-ISBN 0738802387

Chasing the Wind-by Elmer, Rob-Bethany House-1996-187p-3 Danish children are trapped aboard a 1945 German submariner attempting to escape to South America with Nazi treasure

Chains-by Scott, Douglas-1984-WWII merchant captain is torpedoed and picked up by U-Boat and escapes from prison camp just prior to Allied invasion of Italy but is accuses of being collaborator

Churchill's Gold-by Follett, James-Mandarin, London-1993-223p-ISBN 0749304960-In early 1941, an American whaleman whose wife was killed in the sinking of the Athenia takes his revenge by sinking a U-boat by ramming. He is then persuaded to use his ship to carry the last of England's wealth, $240 million in gold, from South Africa to England. Through information supplied by a double agent, the Germans learn of this plan and send out a U-boat to waylay the whaler. The rest of the novel is a suspenseful account of the chase. Originally published 1980.

Circle, The-by Poyer, David C-St Martins Press-1992-ISBN 0312929641 -Fresh officer on first cruise on old WWII destroyer headed for Arctic to test new sonar gear in rough weather. They find rogue Soviet sub.

Clammer and the Submarine, The-by Hopkins, William J-Houghton Mifflin, Boston-1917-346p-Fiction re German submarine off East Coast of USA

Clearwater-by Buchanan, Bill-Berkeley Fiction-2000-475p-ISBN 042517364X-A new USS nuclear submarine is hijacked and disappears. A new technology that can track a trail of clear water in the ocean might help find the Maine before it's weapons are used

Clear the Decks-by Gallery, Dan-Paperback Library-1967-223p-A humorous look at the war but all tales are based on fact. The author was the man to captured the U-505 in real life

Code Name Nimrod-by Leasor, James-Houghton Mifflin-1981-ISBN 0395302285

Cold is the Sea-by Beach, Edward L-Zebra, NY-1978-413p-ISBN 0821725076-Advanced nuclear sub Cushing collides with another sub of USSR coast and the duel begins-Author is Captain Ned Beach who truly has BTDT on submarines.

Cold Warriors-Pub. By Graphic Enterprise of Marblehead-1997-182p

Command-Ross, Melville-Collins, London-1985-156p-WWII action

Commander-by Gerson, Noel B-Delacorte Press-1965

Convoy-by Pope, Dudley-USNIP-1988-ISBN 0802709605-A wounded British naval officer begins a second career as intelligence expert in a section charged with coming up with anti-U-boat strategy. The problem is that convoys seem to be attacked by assailants that appear out of nowhere. A traitor within is suspected.

Counter Force-by Henrick, Richard P-Zebra Books-1987-ISBN 0821720139-In the Pacific, an enemy holds target cards for U.S. targets. The only chance to prevent the launch is betrayal of some Russian hierarchy member

Crash Dive-by Leyland, Eric-Ward, UK-1961-128p

Crash Dive 500-by Gray, Edwyn-Walker Publishing Co-1985 (1981 London)-WWII Action in a British Submarine

Crimson Tide-by Henrick, Richard-Avon Books, 1995-239p-ISBN 0380783231-The novel based on the screenplay

Cruel Coast, The-by Gage, William-Signet, NY-1966-278p-A crippled U-Boat slips into a neutral Irish harbor of a small island and the 19 people who are drawn in to save their lives and their honor

Cry of the Deep-by Henrick, Richard P-Zebra Books-1989-ISBN 0821725947-Escorted by the advanced attack sub Kirov, the invincible Russian warship Caspian is headed toward the Caribbean, its devastating nuclear weapons locked on strategic targets in the U.S. Only a cranky thirty-year-old diesel boat can stop them.

Cryptonomicon-by Stephenson, Neal-Avon Books-1999-ISBN 0380973464 -This is a high-tech novel which has its roots in WWII German U-boats and crypto technologies. Roughly half the book takes place in WWII with the rest in current times.

Cuban Bluff-by Weber, Joe-1990-Novel bases on true story of Cuban missile crisis

D Fiction

Dangerous Waters-by Collins, Paul-Jesperson Pub-St Johns, Newf.-1996-164p

Das Geheimnis von U 180-by Higgins, Jack-Bertelsmann-1994-346p-ISBN 3570120317-A British intelligence agent dives a U-boat in the Caribbean believed to be carrying the names of Nazi sympathizers

Das Letzte U-Boot nach Avalon-by Guenther, CH-Ullstein-Verlag, Berlin-1996-Volume 1-Einsatz im Atlantik (patrol in the Atlantic)-240p-ISBN 3548239250-Volume 2-U-136 in Geheimer Mission (U-136 on secret mission)-240p-ISBN 3548239269

Day of Fate-by Cheney, Theodore A Rees-Popham Press-1981-259p-ISBN 0441139086-A Chinese sub copied from American plans places some missiles. An American goes after them as well as a Russian

Dead Sea Submarine-by Caillou, Alan-Pinnacle-1972 2nd ed-Arabs are moving a submarine across the desert to the Dead Sea and commandos are sent to stop it.

Decoy-by Pope, Dudley-Hamlyn, London-1983-323p-ISBN 0708912710 -Drifting in the winter Atlantic, hoping to be picked up by a U-boat, a group of British Marines and other adventurers hope to capture an Enigma and confidential books. Excellent description of the insides and operations of a U-boat.

Deep Chill-by Slater, Ian-Worldwide Library-1989-378p-The USS New York lays on the bottom in the icy North Pacific disabled. A famous oceanographer is sent to help. One the Russian's submarine commander has dealt with before

Deep Core-by Adair, James B-Berkley-1991-280p-ISBN 0425130290-A fully integrated spy system that tracks vessels above and below the surface is guarded by the U.S. A high-tech naval force is on it's way to destroy it

Deep Core Crash Dive-by Adair, James B-1992-247p-ISBN 0425132676-In the Atlantic a Deep Core team is trying to recover a huge gold treasure at 1000'. A Japanese war lord has his own ideas

Deep Core Boomer Down-by Adair, James B-1992-247p-ISBN 0425131807-A British sub lies hurt by a mine. Deep Core is called in but a 3rd world country also wants the weapons on the British sub

Deep Flight-by Carpenter, M Scott-Pocket Books-343p-ISBN 0671759035-Written by the astronaut Scott Carpenter along with the book The Steel Albatross. Rick Tallman, a Lt Cmdr USN is recalled to duty on the Steel Albatross, a sonar-proof stealth sub in to action chasing a Japanese relic with huge political overtones.

Deep Gold-by Amberg, Jay-U-Boat torpedoes cruiser containing 13 tons of Russian gold. 50 years later, UK, USA and Russians try to salvage it jointly, but there seems to be a killer curse

Deep is the Blue-by Ehrlich, Max-Pocket Books, NY-1964-299p-The ghost of the Thresher hangs over the nuclear sub USS Cody

Deep Lie-by Woods, Stuart-Harper Paperbacks-1986-401p-ISBN 0061044490-A secret Baltic and a renegade Soviet submarine commander vs the CIA

Deep Silence, The-by Reeman, Douglas-Berkley, NY-1967-ISBN 4250402519

Deep Sound Channel-by Buff, Joe-Bantam-2000-351p-ISBN 0553801333-

Deep Sting-by Taylor, Charles D-Pocket Books-1991-While the superpowers relax under the spirit of glasnost, a Soviet strategic and technical genius, is on a mission to neutralize the vital U.S. Trident missile submarines forever.

Deepwater Showdown-by Clark, Halsey-Dell, 1983-335p-ISBN 0440018404-2nd in a series of 5 books from this author. A story of a U.S. submarine commander to attacks the submarine pens on the coast of France

Defcon One-by Webber, Joe-1989-Clancy-like story involving subs, fighters, bombers, aircraft carriers, CIA and last throes of Russian military

Defector, The-by Reynolds, Howard-Penquin-1988-ISBN 05148800395 -A Soviet physicist defects to the West but the Russian begin putting pressure on his family. A test of a new device capable of crippling the Russian submarine.

Die Insel-by MacLean, Alistair-W. Heyne, Munchen-1980-303p-ISBN 345300647X-The Island

Die U-boot Jager-by Kent, Alexander-Ullstein-Verlag, Berlin-1999-367p-ISBN 3548246370-The U-boat Hunters-A novel about a British destroyer on a mission to sink the U-234

Depth Force-by Greenfield, Irving A-Zebra Books-Build in secrecy and manned by a phantom crew, the Shark is American's unique high technology submarine whose mission is to stop the Russians from dominating the seas. If in danger of capture the Shark must self-destruct—meaning there's only victory or death

Depth Force #2 Death Dive-by Greenfield, Irving A-Zebra Books, 1984-235p-ISBN 0821714724-The Shark, racing toward an incalculable fortune in gold from an ancient wreck, has a bloody confrontation with a Soviet killer submarine. Just when victory seem assured, a traitor threatens the survival of every man aboard-and endangers national security.

Depth Force #3 Bloody Seas-by Greenfield, Irving A-Zebra Books, 1985-252p-ISBN 0821715410-Under the ice in the Soviet Arctic, American's top secret high-tech submarine, the Shark is about to blast its way to the surface. Up above, in a cove on the Russian mainland, a special six-man undercover unit is counting on the American sub to save them from capture. The Shark is the only vessel who can get them out but they didn't count on a Soviet killer sub.

Depth Force #4 Battle Stations-by Greenfield, Irving A-Zebra Books, 1985-255p-ISBN 0821716271-Russia's most lethal submarine lies crippled at the bottom of the ocean. The U.S. sends the Shark to complete the job. But it's a trap.

Depth Force #5 Torpedo Tomb-by Greenfield, Irving A-Zebra Books-1986-236p ISBN 0821717693-Commander Boxer and the crew of the Shark are assigned a new experimental submarine. This sub can travel on ground as well and they head into Libya to bring out some captives.

Depth Force #6 Sea of Flames-by Greenfield, Irving A-Zebra Books-254p-ISBN 0821718509-A renegade naval force steals the Shark. The North Atlantic becomes a launching pad for WWIII with missiles aimed at the Soviet Union. Jack Boxes the captain of the Shark takes another SSN after the Shark.

Depth Force #7 Deep Kill-by Greenfield, Irving A-Zebra Books-1986-286p-ISBN 0821719327-A Russian invasion fleet is headed for Arabia. The new Barracuda stalks the armada waiting for the word to fire but know a monster Russian boat is following them

Depth Force #8 Suicide Run-by Greenfield, Irving A-Zebra Books-1987-254p-ISBN 082172018X-A Russian sub glides through Antarctica's to control the continents mineral wealth. The Barracuda comes in to stop this plan. The Russian's commander is Viktor Borodine who Commander Boxer has fought with and even saved once years before.

Depth Force #9 Death Cruise-by Greenfield, Irving A-Zebra Books-1988-253p-ISBN 0821724592-Faced with trumped up charges, now Admiral Boxer has to chose between imprisonment or almost certain doom beneath the waves as the Russians and Iranians have built a undersea haven for deadly mini-subs.

Depth Force #10 Ice Island-by Greenfield, Irving A-Zebra Books-1988-254p-ISBN 0821725351-In the Arctic, two awesome subs stalk each other. The new S99 is commanded by AdmiralBoxer. A Russian scientist stranded on the ice is wanted by both countries.

Depth Force #11 Harbor of Doom-by Greenfield, Irving A-Zebra Books-1989-253p-ISBN 0821726285-The new U.S. Manta under

Boxer's command chase three stolen Chinese subs. They plan to hold the world hostage with missiles while re-destroying Pearl Harbor.

Depth Force #12 Warmonger-by Greenfield, Irving A-Zebra Books-1989-255p-ISBN 0821727370-Russia has a new sub, but a mutineering officer threatens to decimate the West with it. Admiral Boxer heads for the base where the sub was made and sits but meets a Soviet surface craft also trying to recapture the base.

Depth Force #13 Deep Rescue-by Greenfield, Irving A-Zebra Books-1990-224p-ISBN 0821732390-A new American sub is crippled and down. Boxer heads for her. The sub has sent out a distress call which is intercepted by old friend and Soviet captain Victor Borodine. As if that isn't enough, there are saboteurs around.

Depth Force #14 Torpedo Treasure-by Greenfield, Irving A-Zebra Books-1991-208p-ISBN 0821734229-On a pleasure cruise with friends, Admiral Boxer is captured by an old Nazi U-Boat XO with a tale of sunken treasure. Victory Borodine is called in by Boxer to help find the Russian ship carrying 500 million in Russian Gold. But Iranian pirates wish death to both.

Depth Force #15 Hot Zone-by Greenfield, Irving A-Zebra Books-1992-223p-ISBN 0821736663-Aboard the new SSN-S1, Admiral Boxer intercepts a distress signal. A Soviet SSN is down in the North Pacific. When he arrives to help he finds the crew dead and the boat radiated by an illegal nuclear waste dump. The Admiral and Victor Borodine set out to destroy the site yet have company.

Depth Force #16 Rig War-by Greenfield, Irving A-Zebra Books-1992-223p-ISBN 0821738518-An American company finds a huge new deep-sea oil reserve. Sabotage plays a hand and the Navy discharged Boxer is called out the President to help. With his new business partner Borodine, Boxer takes on mercenary subs who are trying to destroy the oil site.

Depth Force Project Discovery-by Greenfield, Irving A-Kensington Publishing, 1988-397p-ISBN 0821723529

Depths of Danger-by Clark, Halsey-Dell/Emerald-1983-286p-ISBN 0440018889

Destroy the Kentucky-by Davis, Bart-Pocket Books, NY-1992-371p-ISBN 0761696645-Central Asian nationalists seeking independence from the Soviet Union seize the USS Kentucky and they plan to launch the missiles on Russia. A U.S. Navy Captain comes in to help.

Devil Flotilla-by Gray, Edwin-Pinnacle Books, 1979-183p-ISBN 0523414056-Aboard UK sub HMS Rapier, leading a pack of Allied subs on a series of daring missions into German territory in WWII

Devils Voyage-by Chalker, Jack L

Die for the Queen-by Scott, Douglas-William Collins, London-1981-ISBN 0436444267-A novel that tells the story of the sinking of Royal Oak by *Prien*. It also describes his personal life (most likely imaginary) with *Kretschmer* and a few others.

Die Heimfahrt der U-720-by Lehnhoff, Joachim-Kindler-Verlag, Munchen-1956-288p-The Return of U-720

Dive in the Sun-by Reeman, Douglas-Berkley, NY-1961-257p-Four men in the RN's smallest submarine must get in and sink a German dry dock

Dive Into Terror-by Cruts, Randy-Black Forest Press-348p

Dive to Oblivion-by Henrick, Richard P-Zebra Books-1993-ISBN 0821740261-A US boat dives and then surfaces moments later half way across the world. The cold war is not over as a group of Russian dissidents try to control the destiny of the free world

Down the Hatch-by Winton, John-1961-204p-Humorous

Down to the Sea-by Robertson, Morgan-Harper & Brothers, NY-1905-312p

Duel Mit dem Nassen Tod-by Maasch, Erik-Ullstein-1999-330p-ISBN 354824632X-Duel with Wet Death-A novel about a Fahnrich (Ensign) zur See who ships aboard a U-Boat as a last minute substitute in 1944

Dust On the Sea-by Beach, Edward L-Holt, Rinehart & Winston-1972-351p-ISBN 0030763908-USS Eel, Whitefish, & Chicolar form a wolfpack on a mission of deadly peril in the Bungo Suido

E Fiction

Ecowar-by Henrick, Richard P-Harper Books-1993-ISBN 0061006491-A US sub with a Dr. aboard who is a dolphin expert is headed for Japan waters to investigate reports of a marauding sea monster

Eighth Trumpet, The-by Land, Jon-Fawcett-1989-400p-ISBN 0449133982-

Eine Frau War an Bord-by Lebert, Norbert-Heyne Verlag, Munchen-1981-268p-ISBN 3453014847-Fictionalized story of a submerged snorkel cruise of U-977 to South American

Emerald Decision-by Thomas, Craig-Harper Books-1987-513p-ISBN 0061000671-An American author uncovers a 40 year old deadly secret

Emma Tupper's Diary-by Dickinson, Peter-Little Brown, Boston-1971-212p-Youth Fiction While visiting her Scottish cousins, Emma becomes involved in a plot to hoax the news media by changing the appearance of an old submarine into a sea monster

Enemy Below, The-by Rayner, DA-Henry Holt-1957-191p-WW II Battle of the Atlantic pitting HMS destroyer Hecate against a German U-Boat

Enigma-by Harris, Robert-Random House-1995-Fiction but highly accurate

Enigma, The-by Barak, Michael-William Morrow-1978-Fictional spy story with references to Enigma

Evasive Action: The Hunt for Gregor Meinhoff-by Reisinger, John-iUniverse-2001-300p-ISBN 0595184839

Event 1000-by Lavallee, David-Holt, Rinehart & Winston-1971-ISBN 030859697-Sub sunk after collision is trapped 1300 feet down while everyone tries to help. Movie Grey Lady Down was made from this book. Author was actual submarine officer, diver and underwater technician

Extinction Cruise-by Price John-Allen-Zebra-1987-496p-ISBN 0821720392 -A mutiny aboard a Russian subs needs help from the US to move the submarine 12,000 miles away.

F Fiction

Fackeln der Vernichtung-by Schulz, John-Gebr. Zimmermann Verlag, Balve-**Torches of Destruction.** Fiction account of U-522 under the real Erich Topp

Fathom-by Hammond, Marc-Jove Fiction-1979-367p-The worlds most sophisticated mini-sub is missing as is a nuclear warhead.

Fathoms Deep-Dawson, Michael-Sheridan House, NY-1948-187

Fighting Submarine-by Gray, Edwin-Pinnacle Books, 1978-182p-ISBN 0523413998-WW II RN Submarine warfare

Fighting Temeraire, The-by Windon, John-1971

Final Crossing- by Ardman, Harvey-As WW II looms, a luxury liner crosses the Atlantic carrying the likes of Mrs. Hearst, Marlene Dietrich, Sonja Henie, Cole Porter, plus France's gold reserves, a German bomb and a US secret agent. U-Boats on the trail!

Final Harbor-by Homewood, Harry-McGraw-Hill-1980-ISBN 0070296944 -A US sub's mission is to seek out and destroy Japan's ships.

Final Voyage of the S.S.N. Skate-by Cassell, Stephen-Pinnacle Books, 1989-383p-ISBN 1558171576-The "leper" of the SSN fleet, the sub Skate is way past scrap time yet is sent to do an act of piracy against the Soviet's elite. Carrying off this theft could doom the crew, while failure to do so could hasten America's ultimate destruction.

Fireplay-by Wingate-1977

Flight of the Condor-by Henricks, Richard P-Zebra Books-1987-ISBN 0821721399-The US loses is satellite eye and the Russians take advantage. The USS Razorback meets the threat.

Flucht und Uberleben-by Krutein, Eva-Ullstein-377p-ISBN 3454823151 -Flight and Survival

Flying Sub, The-by Snell, Roy-Reilly & Lee, Chicago-1925-282p

Foreign Spies-Doctor Doom and the Ghost Submarine-1939 Better little Book

Forty Fathoms Down-by Jones, J Farragut-1981-Dell-ISBN 044012655X -America's ultimate sub sinks during sea trials. Navy tries to rescue amid espionage

Free and the Brave-by Cornwell, John-1978-The hero joins the USN after Pearl Harbor, gets assigned to the ancient wreck of a destroyer and chases U-Boats

Full Alert-by Korel, Charles-Kensington Pub. Corp.-1989-286p-ISBN 0821726226-Soviet agents have their orders: seize America's most sophisticated submarine which is the commander center of the United States

Full Fathom Five-by Davis, Bart-Bantam Books-1987-311p-ISBN 055326205X-A Soviet nuclear boat has been stolen by Central American rebels. A U.S. Navy captain is assigned to recover the sub before it launches it's deadly missiles.

G Fiction

Gate Crashers, The-by Fullerton, Alexander-1984

Gemini Plot-Sequel to Ninety Feet to the Sun-by Collenette, Eric J-1985-

Ghost Boat-by Simpson. George & Berger, Neal-Dell-1976-412p-ISBN 05170358515-A WWII submarine missing for 30 years but returns in perfect order except for the crew is missing. Is there a Devils Triangle in the Pacific?

Ghost Sub-by Herst, Roger E-Zebra Books-1979-352p-ISBN 0890836558 -US missile sub cruising under ice pack in Russian waters is found and trapped.

Gironde Incident, The-by Hughes, Michael-Zebra Books-1984-317p-ISBN 0821714279

Gold Crew-by Scortia, Thomas & Robinson, Frank-Warner Books-1980-435p-ISBN 0446835226-An American nuclear submarine is put the test. It's crew is led to believe the USSR has attacked the US. What is their response?

Golden U-Boat, The-by Henrick, Richard P-Zebra Books-1991-ISBN 0821733869-In the final days of WWII, a U-Boat carrying the Nazi's last hope for world domination is sunk. 50 years later a fugitive SS officer is raising the boat. A U.S. boat hears the surfacing as does a Russian boat.

Go in and Sink!-1973-British captain command German U-192 on mission into the Med

Great Stone of Sardis-by Stockton, Frank-Harper & Bros-1898

Greatest Enemy, The-by Reeman, Douglas-Jove Books/GP Putnam's Sons, 1970-317p-ISBN 0515070874-A frigate in the South Seas finds a German U-boat being re-fueled

Grey Wolves-by Kent, Alexander-Ullstein-Verlag, Berlin-1989-270p-ISBN 3548221513-About a submarine commander in 1944 German title: **Atlantikwölfe**

Greyfox Underway 1944-by Levin, B.L.-Premier Books On-Demand-1992-323p-ISBN 1885101767

H Fiction

Hatteras Blue-by Poyer, DC-St. Martin's Press-1989-288p-A German U-boat is lost in 1945, yet bodies are washed up in 1985. Was the boat sunk or is it used now for drug dealings

Heimfahrt der U-720, Die-by Lehnhoff, Joachim-Kindler-Verlag, Munchen-1956-288p-A U-boat leaves port with six frogmen aboard. The CO recognizes their leader as the man involved with his wife. Scenes shift between boat and shore throughout. **The Return of U-720**

Hell Below-by Ellsberg, Edward-Grossett, NY-1933

Hero in a Bottle-by Walker, Norman H-Rainbow Books-1988-ISBN 0935834699

His Majesty's U-Boat-by Reeman, Douglas-GP Putnam's Sons-1973-A British crew in a German sub in WWII

Hitler's Last Gasp-by Krutein, Manfred-The Miracle Weapon-Amador Publishers-1995-193p-ISBN 0938513192-As the end of WWII approached, many Germans believed rumors about a Miracle Weapon. This novel shows a dramatic encounter between an American OSS officer, a German U-boat commander and a Nazi SS officer. They fight for control of the weapon, directed at the U.S. East Coast. At the end the action is declared a national secret, with all documents sealed for fifty years.

H.M. U-Boat-by Drummond, John D-W.H. Allen/Tattoo-1977-181p-Late in 1942 reports reached Germany that the lost U-Boat 570 was really captured by the British and was being used to sink U-Boats. Based on a true story

HMS Thule Intercepts-by Mars, Alastair-Elek, UK-1956

HMS Trigger-by Melvin-Ross, Antony-Ballantine-1982-281p-ISBN 0345301733-In the Med in 1943 a young submarine captain must follow orders from an agent in Germany.

HMS Ulysses-by Maclean, Alistair-William Collins, London-1959-ISBN 0385041837-This is a classic that tells the story of a convoy heading towards Murmansk in winter 1943. The book describes the conditions in which the convoy men had to survive

HMS Unseen-by Robinson, Patrick-Harper-2000-526p-ISBN 0061098019 -A HMS Nuclear submarine is missing. The planes start disappearing out of the sky. A terrorist is on the loose

Hollow Sea-by Jenkins, Geoffrey-1971

Homeward Run, The-by Lehnhoff, Joachim-Wyman & Sons Ltd-1957-224p-In this novel, Germany is on the eve of collapse. A U-boat slips its moorings at night with six frogmen on board. The crew look forward to a perilous journey, while the Captain recognizes the IWO as the man who has seduced his young wife. The main theme is a chance encounter between two young people. Many more characters make up the story line. Scenes on the boat are interspersed with scenes ashore.

Howard Had a Submarine-by Lawhead, Steve-Lion Publishing-1988-ISBN 074591179X

Hunt for Red October-by Clancy, Tom-USNIP and Berkeley as Paperback-387p-ISBN 0425083837-Somewhere under the Atlantic a Russian Commander decides to move west for good. The Americans want her, the Russians was her destroyed. What a chase develops.

Hunter-Killer-Jenkins, Geoffrey-GP Putnam's Sons-1967-A Nuclear sub chase but why has the sub skipper been declared dead?

I Fiction

Ice Station Zebra-by Maclean, Alistair-Fawcett-1981-224p-ISBN-0449205762-A SSN leads for Arctic to investigate problems at British meteorological station on polar ice cap. Russians have the same idea.

Ice Wolf-by Henrick, Richard P-Harper-1994-336p-ISBN 0061006483-The USS Springfield, a US 688 nuclear boat patrols off the Falklands with an English boat. A rogue Nazi type XXI U-Boat steals some lost treasure in an attempt to restore the Reich's power

Incident in Mona Passage-by Savage, Douglas-Avon-1995-386p-ISBN 0380724855-US sub conducts top secret biowar experiment that goes wrong. Sub seeks solution to sickness as another sub stalks her

In Deadly Waters-by Sasgen, Peter-Self published as a. pdf file via Net only-http://www.rollingthunderbooks.com

In Pursuit of the Awa Maru-by Inners, Joe W.-William Bunton-1980

In the Wake of the Leopard-by Frew, James-1990

Insel, Die-by MacLean, Alistair-W. Heyne, Munchen-1980-303p-ISBN
345300647X-**The Island**
Islands in the Stream-**by Hemingway, Ernest**-480 pages-ISBN 0684837870
-Many printings

J Fiction

Jimmy-the One-by Wingate, John-Newnes, London-1960-256p

K Fiction

Killing Ground-by Reeman, Douglas-1969-An ASW battle between a
HMS ship and the U-boats in the Atlantic
Kilo Affair-by Etka, Craig L-American Literary Press, Baltimore-1998-
A US Navy Captain sets out to destroy two Kilo Class boats
stolen by Columbian Drug traffickers. Scorpio Connection is
the first book in this series
Kilo Class-by Robinson, Patrick-Harper-1999-519p-ISBN 0061096857-
China has received three new Kilo's from Russia and 7 more
are due for delivery. SEALS and under ice action
Kilo Option-by Flannery, Sean-1996-383p-ISBN-0812550633-Iranian
terrorists get nukes and a Russian Kilo class sub, and our hero
has to find and stop them before they decide to launch missiles
Klebers Convoy-by Trew, Anthony-Popular Library-1973-ISBN
0002214156-221p-Kleber, commanding a 15-boat wolfpack, is
determined to destroy a 35-ship convoy to Murmansk. A
British Vice-Admiral with twenty-six escort vessels is equally
determined that he will not. The author commanded an escort
vessel on the Northern convoys.
Konvoi 1943-by Forester, CS-Eduard-Kaiser, Verlag-1970-416p-First
published in 1955-About a 37-ship convoy guarded by destroyers from Poland, British, American and a Canadian corvette

L Fiction

Last Command, The-by Gray, Edwyn-Pinnacle-1977-241p-In the final days of WWII, U-Boat skipper still hunts for prey, but the Fuhrer needs the boat to escape to Argentina 4th in Series of U-Boats in WW II-This book is the 4th in the series which includes No Survivors, Action Atlantic, and Tokyo Torpedo

Last Fathom, The-by Caidin, Martin-Meredith Press-1967-312p-ISBN 0523404522-Russians plant doomsday bomb in middle of Atlantic to destroy America and Europe, and secret US sub, controlled by only two men tries to stop it.

Last Lieutenant, The-by Gobbell, John J-St. Martin's Paperbacks-1995-448p-ISBN 04490300699-A story about the US breaking the code to discover an invasion on Midway. But a Nazi mole is there to insure the Japanese gain victory

Last Mayday, The-by Wheeler, Keith-Doubleday-1968-316p

Last Ship, The-by Brinkley, William-Viking-1998-616p-Similar to "On the Beach" in that a U.S. DD in an age of Nuclear holocaust and the eventual meeting up with a Russian submarine.

Last Voyage of the SSN Skate, The-by Cassell, Stephen-1988

Last U-Boat, The-by Sasgen, Peter-Self published as a. pdf file via Net only-http://www.rollingthunderbooks.com-available in fall of 2001

Le Jour ne se leve pas pour nous-by Merle, Robert-Plon, Paris-1986-The Sun Does Not Rise For Us

Letzte U-Boot nach Avalon, Das-by Guenter, CH-Ullstein-Verlag, Berlin-1996-Vol 1: Einsatz im Atlantik (Patrol in the Atlantic) ISBN 3548239250, Vol 2: U-136 in geheimer Mission (U-136 on secret mission) ISBN 3548239269

Living Torpedo, The-by Yates, Tom

Lodestar Project, The-by Bradley, David-Pocket Books-1986-279p-ISBN 0671604554-A Navy coverup, two missing subs and a big coverup over a super weapon

Log of the Flying Fish-by Collingwood, Harry-Scribner, NY-1886-384p

Lost Sentinel-by Hardy, Rene'-Doubleday-1960-A novel about the Italian sub Moro in the Med during WW II

Louisiana Blue-by Mounce, David R.-1994-Oil well work 1000' feet down

Lost Treasure of Rocky Cove, The See Speedwell Boys

M Fiction

Maitres de la Foudre-by Stepanov, Victor-Editions du Progres, Moscow-1987-237p

McKenzie Break-by Shelley, Sidney-Dell-1970-ISBN 44005128075-Originally published as The Bowmanville Break

Mermaid and the Major, The-by Melendez, Francisco-1972

Mismatch-by Pye, Lloyd-Dell-1988-342p-ISBN 04402022213-A computer hacker joins with the Russians to attack the US. A US sub must find the Russian boat-Reissued by iUniverse in 2000

Mission Tokyo Bay-by Blair, Clay & Joan-Bantam-1980-216-ISBN 0553134124-By the author of Silent Victory which is the bible of the submarine war in the Pacific. This story is great and tells of taking a boat right into Tokyo Bay which really didn't happened but the action is very real.

Murphy's War-Catto, Max-Dell Pocketbooks-1968-256p-Murphy lay in missionary's hospital sweating hate for the U-boat that destroyed his ship and his crewmates. The U-Boat is found hiding in a river near Murphy and he goes after it! Made into a movie also

Mystery of U-13-by Ralphson, GH-Donahue, Chicago-1915-252p-Young-Also knows as Boy Scouts in the North Sea

N Fiction

Neptune-by Gerson, Noel B-Dodd, Mead-1976-ISBN 0396073255-
Secret salvage and spy ship seeks sunken Soviet sub with
advanced atomic arsenal

Neptune's Lance-by Forbes, Stephen-Signet-430p-ISBN 0451171209-
The U.S. star sub, the USS Alaska is sunk. Then the truth comes
out, it wasn't sunk but it is in the volatile waters of the Persian
Gulf in the hands of someone who might destroy the earth

Night Boat, The-by McCammon, Robert R.-Avon Books-1990-261p-
ISBN 0671732811 A horror novel based on a Type VIIc on patrol
in the Caribbean. Basically the U-boat gets trapped underwater
and the crew are put under a curse by the local islanders. Forty
or so years later a diver finds a metal cylinder in the sand
which after a lot of uncovering becomes an unexploded depth
charge. Of course he lets it fall and tries to get away when the
ensuing explosion occurs and the night boat is jarred loose and
rises to the surface. Originally published 1980.

Nimitz Class-by Robinson, Patrick-Harper-1998-495p-ISBN 006109594X
-A U.S. Nuclear Carrier disappears at sea. An nuclear accident?
Or a rogue submarine?

Nine Lives of Alphonse-by Johnson, James L-Tydale House-253p-
1968-Rev. Raymond Sebastian attempts to rescue Cuban defec-
tors using untested midget sup

Ninety Feet to the Sun-by Collenette, Eric J-Walker Publishing, 1985-
180p-North Atlantic Action

No Less Renowned-RN Subs in 11 Short Stories-by Hackforth-Jones,
Gilbert-1939-306p

No Survivors-by Gray, Edwyn-Seeley, Service & Co. Ltd., London-
1974-Edwyn Gray, author of several U-boat books wrote a
series of novels with Konrad Bergman as the main character.
The four novels ("No Survivors" in 1974, "Action Atlantic" in
1975, "Tokyo Torpedo" in 1976 and "The Last Command" in
1977) follow Bergman's U-Bootwaffe career from his pre-war

training, through the war as a U-boat commander, culminating in his part in an attempt to smuggle Hitler to Argentina. His obvious disenchantment with the Nazi regime ensures that the missions assigned him are suicidal.

Normandie Triangle-by Scott, Justin-Arbor House-1981-ISBN 0877953465

North Star Crusade-by Katz, William-Jove Books, NY-1976-A mutinous patriot steals a nuclear sub and has a master plan for world domination

Norton Book of the Sea-by Coote, John-1989

Not Thinking of Death-by Fullerton, Alexander-Warner Books-1995-409p-ISBN 0751513520-Based loosely on the real loss of the HMS Thetis in 1939, this story is about the testing of a new class of submarine. Fullerton was a submarine officer in real life.

O Fiction

O God of Battles-by Homewood, Harry-McGraw-Hill-1983-ISBN 0688019153-Two brothers, one on the subs and the other a fighter pilot fight the war in the Pacific

Ocean Black-by Bostrum, Hank-Pinnacle-1995-445p-ISBN 0786001968 -In the depths a high-tech killing duel has begun. Manned with submarines and remote controlled missile robots, two men are after each other. Greed of a mother lode of Manganese and a threat to the west coast to get it are the problems.

Off-Islanders, The-by Benchley, Nathaniel-Mitchell-238p-Movie-The Russians are coming!

Omega Deception-by Bayer, John F-Broadman & Holman-2000-In 1942 a U.S. man who wants to get even with Nazi Germany. To do that he has to join them. A deadly weapon is going to be unleashed on the U.S. He must stop it.

Omega Sub-by Cameron, JD-Avon, NY-1991-1st in the series-249p-
ISBN 07100100295   They survived Armageddon to sail the
oceans of a ravage nightmare world

Omega Sub: Blood Tide-by Cameron, JD-Avon, NY-1991-219p-4th in
series-ISBN-380763214-In a nuclear-devastated tomorrow only
the "Liberator" stands between a crazed warlord and his dark-
dream of global domination

Omega Sub: City of Fear-by Cameron, JD-Avon, NY-1991-215p-3rd in
series-ISBN 0380760509-In the nuclear-wasted jungles of
Central America terror lives on after civilization has died

Omega Sub: Command Decision-by Cameron, JD-Avon, NY-1991-
246p-2nd in series-ISBN-380762064-The nuclear holocaust dec-
imated mankind but the war isn't over for the USS Liberator

Omega Sub: Death Dive-by Cameron, JD-Avon, NY-1992-214p-5th in
series-ISBN 07100100350-On the East Coast of a nuclear-deci-
mated America, the Liberator sails into a savage zombie hell

Omega Sub: Raven Rising-by Cameron, JD-Avon, NY-1992-214p-6th
in series-ISBN 07100100350-In the grim aftermath of a nuclear
nightmare, the Liberator is trapped in lethal tides of treason
and terror

On the Beach-by Shute, Nevil-Ballantine-1974-Movie by same name-
Adm Lockwood served as advisor to the movie made from this
classic book. The story basically is about a nuclear war and the
survivors in Australia and their struggles with death they
know is coming. First published in 1957

Operation Cuttlefish-by Mounce, David R-Pyramid Books-1970-
222p-ISBN 0515034754Canadian spies in the Bahamas try to
solve mystery of Soviet submarine spy network

Over the Brink-Greenfield, Irving A-Zebra Books-1990-287p-ISBN
0821731238-A Russian sub is down which threatens a proposed
Russian invasion of South Yemen. A US sub sets out to on a
deep water rescue mission. However, the Russians send
another sub to destroy their submarine and anything near it.

Overdue and Presumed Lost-byMacMahan, H. Arthur-1st Books Library-2000-306p-ISBN 1588201074-From Submarine School to the war in the Pacific against a carrier and 4 Japanese destroyers, the story follows one enlisted man from liberty to war.

P Fiction

Pacific Standoff-by Clark, Halsey-Dell-1983-286p-ISBN 0440067804-WW II Pacific submarine action-1st in a series of 5

Pandora Secret, The-by Forrest, Anthony-1983

Passage, The-by Poyer, David C-1994

Pearl Harbor Periscopes-by Jones, J Farragut-1981-Dell

Pentagon Country-Blair, Clay Jr.

Periscope Red-by Rohmer, Richard-Beaufort Books-1980-ISBN 0825300207

Phantom Submarine-Bantam Books-1989 re-issue-ISBN 0553236350

Phoenix Odyssey-by Henrick, Richard P-Zebra Books-1986-ISBN 0821717898-A Trident boat loses communications after a war alert. The US cannot reach her to cancel a missile launch.

Phoenix Sub Zero-by Dimercurio, Michael-Onyx Books-1995-460p-ISBN 0451406038-A middle east country has the best sub oil money can buy and it's broken into the Med and on the way to the American shores. Captain Pacino and USS Seawolf searches for it

Pigboats-by Ellsberg, Edward-Dodd, Mead, NY

Piranha Firing Point-by Dimercurio, Michael-Onyx Fiction-1999-400p-ISBN 0451408764 Japanese subs are attacked and believed destroyed. But the US knows that the old guard from Red China has stolen them to war against Free China. The author's 5th book and series hero Pacino is given command of a new SSNX.

Pirate Submarine-by Westerman, PF-Musson, Toronto-1945-251p

Poseidon's Shadow-by Kobryn, AP &Rawson, Wade-1979-ISBN 0892560878-Renegade US ballistic sub Adresteia goes up against the Pentagon, the Soviets and the American Sub killer. Skipper intends to expose nasty military scandal, but must try to stay alive first

Pre-empt-by Vorhies, John R-Henry Regnery Co-1967

Pressure Point-by Couch, Dick-Berkley Books-1993 edition of the original 1992 G.P. Putnam's 1992 edition-370p-ISBN 042513900X-Written by a former SEAL. A U.S. nuclear boat is abducted.

Pursuit of the Seawolf-by Mack, William P-The Seawolf was the largest German submarine ever made. An old US destroyer takes up the chase of the boat that is sinking a lot of ships

Q Fiction

Quecksilber-by Lehnhoff, Joachim-Bastei Lubbe, Bergisch Gladbach-1998-415p-ISBN 35482444750-The story of the U-859, it's sinking and it's raising in the 1980's. Also published in 1984

R Fiction

Race against the U-boats-by-Bateman, Robert-J. Cape, London-1963-111 pages-When he is orphaned during the Second World War, an English youth signs on as cabin boy with a convoy of tramp steamers bound for Canada and experiences tense moments when German submarines threaten. For younger readers. **Rage Under the Arctic**-by Jackson, Basc-WW Norton-1974-ISBN 0393083799

Raise the Red Dawn-by Davis, Bart-Pocket Books, NY-1991-339p-ISBN 0671696637-An old Russian diesel submarine is trapped under the ice under escort by an Akula. A U.S. sub goes in to salvage the secrets but is met by the Akula determined to keep the U.S. away.

Raven's Nest-by Snow, Dave-iUniverse-2000-416p-ISBN 059512934X After 27 years of knowing little of her orphan past, the heroine is surprised to find she is the daughter of a modern submarine operating pirate.

Red Phoenix-by Bond, Larry-Warner Books-1990-ISBN 0446359688- How the second Korean War might proceed on land, sea and air. Tom Clancy collaborated on this work.

Red Sky at Morning-by Garrison, Paul-Harper Torch-421p-ISBN 0380802201

Red Storm Rising-by Clancy, Tom

Red Tide-by Largent, R. Karl-Leisure Suspense-1992-442p-ISBN 0843933666-Russian old leaders and leaders of the US are meeting. Someone knows of the meeting and wants to destroy them.

Rendezvous-by Hudson, Alec-USNIP-1992-Reprinted by USNIP as Up Periscope and Other Stories in 1992.

Rendezvous South Atlantic-by Reeman, Douglas-Jove Books/GP Putnam's Sons, 1972-341p-ISBN 0515057177-An old cruiser chases German wolfpacks in the North Atlantic

Return From the Deep-by Trimble, Hugh J-McHew-Indiana-1958- Quasi-fictional story of the Squalus and her career as the Sailfish

Rig for Depth Charges!-by Hazlett, Edward E-Dodd, Mead-1945-269p

Rites of War-by Mobley, CA-Jove Books, NY-1998-342p-ISBN 0515122254-A new Germany tries to draw the U.S. into a war with Korea while it goes after England and using a NATO exercise as a cover. While the US is placating the Koreans, it's left to a NSA agent and former USN Commander lady to prevent the war.

Rockets of the Reich-by Kinrade, Kim-Bainbridge Books-1999-250p- ISBN 1891696149-In this fast paced novel, Hitler has conceived a plan to launch a nuclear attack against the United States through rockets fired from an island off the coast of Nova

Scotia. An officer of the US Coast Guard and a Canadian army veteran find an unlikely ally in a German U-boat commander as they struggle to foil the plan before it's too late.

Run Silent, Run Deep-by Beach, Edward L-Holt, NY Pocket Books-1955-364p-The classic submarine novel by Captain EL Beach who truly was there.

S Fiction

Satam der Tiefe-by Koizar, Karl Hans-Omnibus Verlag, Wien-1979-237p-ISBN 3570004325

Saturn Experiment-by Sheperd, Peter-Warner Books-1989-218p-ISBN 0446354856-A NATO nuclear sub and a Russian battleship meet in Russian waters in a mission gone wrong. The sub is sunk but not dead. She has one option which is to fight back

Scanlon of the Submarine Service-by Senseney, Dan-Doubleday & Co-1963-142p-Youth Oriented

Schwarzer Mai-by Gannon Michael-See Black May

Scorpion in the Sea-The Goldsborough Incident-by Deutermann, Peter T.-George Mason University Press/St. Martin's Paperback edition-1992-582p-ISBN 0312951795-Technothriller about antisubmarine warfare, written by ex-Navy CO of a destroyer squadron

Scorpius Connection, The-by Etka, Craig L-American Literary Press, Baltimore-1994

Scourge of Scapa Flow-by Jones, J Farragut

Sea, The-by Largent, R. Karl-Leisure-1999-362p-ISBN 0843944951

Sea Above Them, The-by Wingate, John-St Martin's Press-1985

Sea Devil-by Henricks, Richard P-Zebra Books-1990-ISBN 0821730894-A new Russian super sub wants to destroy the US's Navy base at Holy Loch.

Sea Glow-by Schaill, William S-Leisure-1998-360p-ISBN 0843944293-A sunken Russian submarine's nuclear reactor becomes unstable threatening the East Coast with contamination. The Russians hire an American to help, but the US military, the Russian mob and Saddam Hussein get into it.

Sea Guerrillas, The-by Ballenger, Dean W-Signet-1998-188p-ISBN 0451114132-The Wasp was a decrepit Portuguese fishing vessel familiar to the German U-Boats. But U-Boats began disappearing. What were the 7 man crew of the Wasp doing?

Sea Leopard, The-by Craig, Thomas-Viking Press-1981-514p-ISBN 0670626228-A secret weapon is a board a British nuclear submarine. The inventor is missing and the Russian and US intelligence communities are out to get it

Sea of Death-by Henricks, Richard P-Zebra Books-1992-ISBN 0821737422 -A Ninja is threatening to unleash a biological weapon. A group of nuke trained submarine sailors have only a diesel boat to stop this action

Sea Leopard, The-by Thomas, Craig-Bantam Book-1982-316p-ISBN 0553209035-British sub Sea Leopard possesses secret sonar invisibility, so Soviets spring trap and seize sub. USN expert is sent after it

Sea Wolves, The-by Leasor, James-1980

Seawolf-Shark Africa-by Krauss, Bruno-Zebra, NY-1978-156p-ISBN 0890838712-#5 in Series-Men of Hitler's U-Boats on deadly and devastating missions

Seawolf-Shark Hunt-by Krauss, Bruno-Zebra, NY-1980-160p-ISBN 089083833X-#4 in Series

Seawolf-Shark North-by Krauss, Bruno-Zebra, NY-1978-#2 in Series

Seawolf-Steel Shark-by Krauss, Bruno-Zebra, NY-1978-175p-ISBN 0890837554-First Mission of new U-42 supersub and Captain Baldur Wolz earns them the name, "Sea Wolf." #1 in series

Seawolf-Shark North-by Krauss, Bruno-Zebra, NY-1978-Wolz and the Sea Wolf on mission to land spy in Norwegian Fjord, winds up in command of another submarine U-55 #2 in series

Seawolf-Shark Pack-by Krauss, Bruno-Zebra, NY-1978-156p-ISBN 0890838178-#3 in Series

Sea-Wolf Hunter-by Collenette, Eric J.-William Kimber, Wellingborough-1989-176p-ISBN 0718307259 A story of hunting U-boats in British submarine Tarantula. Hero is Ben Grant.

Secret of the Sunken Sub-by Roddy, Lee-1990-148p-A 12-year old witnesses the sinking of a Russian robot sub and gets in the middle of Russian spies and the US Navy

Send Down a Dove-by MacHardy, Charles-Coward-McCann-1968-351p-Adventures of UK sub Scorpion as it fights mines, mutiny, Germans and each other on patrol in the North Sea in WW II

Sentinels-by Smith, Derek-Frederic C. Beil-2001-Concerns the sinking of the Confederate submarine Hunley and it's relationship to contemporary murders in Charleston, SC

Seraphim Code, The-Liston, Robert A-Thomas Doherty Assoc, Inc., 1988-343p-ISBN 0812506162-While a retired spy runs for his life on land, a Russian submarine, carrying a full load of nuclear missiles, runs silently beneath the Atlantic

Shadow in the Sea, The-by Owen, John-Dutton, NY-1972 p-British secret service vs a Russian submarine

Shadow of Peril-by Zhadanov, Aleksandr-Doubleday-1963-Russian author claims all this is true. Story of Soviet sub espionage and interference in U.S. space program.

Shark-by Smith, Bernard K-iUniverse-2000-232p-ISBN 0595150853-A submarine adventure utilizing a retired Trident boat, a retired CO and a new power plant.

Shark Mutiny-by Robinson, Patrick-Harper Collins-2001-ISBN 0060196319-463p

Sharks and Little Fish-by Ott, Wolfgang-Ballantine-1982-428p-ISBN 3807500030-This highly acclaimed novel realistically describes the life of a German U-boat officer in WWII. The first 300 pages focus on minesweepers, at which point the main character transfers to U-boats. His commander is hard and bitingly sarcastic, feared by the crew, but has already racked up 100,000 tons of shipping sunk and bears a grudge against the British because he once observed through his periscope a British surface ship machine gunning survivors of a sinking U-boat. The remainder of the book is a succession of hellish experiences-North Atlantic storm, Caribbean heat, on shore a gruesome revenge attack by the Marquis, torpedo tubes used as not-so-cold storage for the bodies of fallen crewmen, and various mutilations suffered by the crew in the line of duty. A movie based on the book was released in 1957. First published in 1957 by Pantheon Books. Published in German by Hervig Verlag, Munchen in 1958 as Haie und Kleine Fische

Sharuq-by Keith, Bill-Harper-313p-ISBN 0061006149-An Arab terrorists has gained control of a Russian SSBN and starts cutting the US's oil supply

Ship of Gold-by Allen, Thomas & Norman Polmar-1987-366p-Subs seek sunken ship as 40-yr old mystery surrounding a sunken Japanese vessels unfolds.

Show of Force-by Taylor, Charles-Ace Charter/St. Martin's Press, 1980-346p-ISBN 0441761976

Siege of Ocean Valkyrie, The-by Price, John-Allen-Zebra-1992-351p-Arab terrorists want to destroy a North Sea Oil platform. A submarine near mothballs is called back by it's daring captain to prove the submarine is not done yet

Silent Descent-by Couch, Dick-Berkley-1994-382p-ISBN 042514335X-In the frozen wastes of northern Russia, an American mole gathers proof of an illegal nuclear weapons trade. Now she has disappeared. The U.S. wants her. Five Navy Seals are sent in after her. One submarine can get her out—in a daring rendezvous in Russian-occupied waters.

Silent Hunter-by Taylor, Charles D-Jove Books, NY-1987-ISBN 0515098140-A super large submersible cruises the ocean floor with all the latest weapons. The Russians are going after it in the Arctic

Silent Sea-by Homewood, Harry-McGraw-Hill-1981-354p-ISBN 0070296952-Aboard the USS Eelfish in the Pacific with Captain Mike Brannon and a young crew. WW II action

Silent Service-by Chambliss, William C-Signet-9/1965-190-True exploits of actual WWII submarines with dialogue added. Perch, Sculpin, Harder, Thresher (old), Bergall, Seahorse

Silent Service Grayback Class-by Riker, H. Jay-Avon-2000-421p-ISBN 0380804662-A platoon of SEALS aboard an near obsolete Grayback Class boat has to get in to the port of Russia's new Akula submarine

Silent Service Los Angeles Class-by Riker, H. jay-Avon-2001-410p-ISBN 0380804670-2nd in the series. Similar to the first book but with some twists. The commanding officer from the Grayback now has a new LA class boat and is trying to get a SEAL team into Russian territory only the Russians now it because of a plant

Silent Warriors-by Henrick, Richard P-Zebra Books-1985-ISBN 0821716751-The Russian Sub commanders have orders to launch. It comes down to one US SSN to fight one Russian boat.

Sounding-by Searls, Hank-Ballantine-1985

Speedwell Boys in a Submarine or The Lost Treasure of Rocky Cove-by Rockwood, Roy-Cupples & Leon Co, 1913

Spy on the Submarine, The-Parker, Thomas D-W.A. Wilde Co/Boston, 1918

Spy Story-by Deighton, Len-Ballantine-1985-288p

SSN-by Clancy, Tom-Berkeley Books-1996-350p-ISBN 0425173534-China has invaded the Spratley Islands for their oil. The third world war opens. The USS Cheyenne is sent to\protect a carrier group, but a full blown war soon erupts. Obviously the language/terms used by Clancy are very accurate.

Status 1SQ-by Herst, Roger-Doubleday-1979-ISBN 0385142420

Steel Albatross, The-by Carpenter, Scott-1991-371p-ISBN 0671673149-A fighter pilot signs up with the Nave SEALS so he can "pilot" super-secret sub that works like a glider. Untested sub is rushed into action against Russian threat. Author is the ex-astronaut.

Strike From the Sea-by Reeman, Douglas-William Morrow, NY-1978-ISBN 0688033199-A group of RN and Free French are going to try an capture the German's largest submarine in the South Pacific in WWII

Sub Sailor-by McLeod, Grover S-Manchester Books-Alabama-1964-315p-Novel of WW II in the Pacific by a man who served in subs during the period

Sub Wars #1: Target SUSUS-by Good, James-Zebra Books-1982-223p-ISBN 0821710923

Sub Wars #2: Target Delta V-by Good, James-Zebra Books-1982-216p-ISBN 082171046X

Sub Wars Target Delta V-by Good, James-Zebra Books-1982-216p-ISBN 082171046X

Sub Zero-by Campbell, John-Avon, NY-1996-340p-ISBN 07100100599-Hostile forces are making a brazen grab for the U.S. most devastating military secrets. A heavily armed assault team dispatched for a North Korean Kilo class sub is about to shift the balance of power.

Submarine-by Wingate, John-1984

Submarine Adventures of Little Jinks-by Jewett, HK-Wetzel, LA-1930-79p-Humor

Submarine Alone-by Hackforth-Jones-141p-A Story of H.M.S. Steadfast

Submarine at Bay-by Mars, Alastair-Elek, UK-1956-164p

Submarine Boys and the Middies-by Durham, Victory G-1909

Submarine Boys Final Trip-by Durham, Victor G-1909

Submarine Boys For the Flag: or, Deeding their lives to Uncle Sam-by Durham, Victor G (pseud) Altemus, Philadelphia-1910-247p-This is a one in the series of books, six of which were republished in London by Saalfield 1933-1937

Submarine Boys' Lightning Cruise ; or, the Young Kings of the Deep-by / by Durham, Victor

Submarine Caper-The Hardy Boys Series-by Dixon, Franklin-Pocket Books-Reissue-1986   ISBN 067142338X-Also known as "The Deadly Chase"

Submarine Captain-by Irvine, AT-Anchor Publications

Submarine Mystery, The-by Robeson, Kenneth-Bantam Books-1971-121p-Doc Savage

Submarine Rendezvous-by Icenhower, Joseph B-Winston, NY-1957-182p-Young

Submarine Rescue-by U. of California-Harr Wagner Publishing Co, San Francisco-1967-73p Youth oriented

Submarine Sailor-by Felsen, Henry-Literary Guild of America, NY-1929-208p

Submarine Treasure-by Ellsberg, Edward

Submarine U-137-by Topal, Edward-Berkley-1983-357p-ISBN 0424097188-CIA tries to find out the true mission of secret Soviet sub by sending spy aboard. As usual, everything gets fouled up and entire world is held hostage

Submarine Wolfpack-by Hardy, William M-1961

Submarine Z-1-by Chanoukoff, Lon-Citadel, NY-1960-221p

Submariner-by Coote, John C-W W Norton & Co-1992-ISBN-393030741

Submariner, The-by Stephens, Edward-Doubleday-215p-ISBN 0385088841 -A diesel sub is assigned to attack a nuclear enemy boat that has sank two U.S. subs.

Submariner Sinclair-by Wingate, John-Newnes, UK-1959-255p

Sultan's Gold, The-by McLeod, Grover S

Summit-by Taylor, Charles D-Pocket Books-1996-355p-ISBN 0671875795 -Fourteen world leaders are meeting aboard a high security yacht. A ruthless submarine commander wants to take them down

Sun Does Not Rise For Us, The-by Merle, Robert-French only-1986

Supersub-by Clark, Halsey-Dell/Emerald-1983-317p-ISBN 0440084032 -A young WWII maverick submarine genius struggles to bring the nuclear submarine to life. As the story moves to the 60's he finds new opposition from his son and daughter who have a growing anti-nuclear twist. He deadliest WWII U-Boat commander surfaces as a Soviet agent with plans to steal the new supersub's secrets. This book is the 5th in the series.

Surface!-by Fullerton, Alexander-1953 & 1984-Academy Chicago-224p-ISBN 0583122957 Describes several patrols of an S-type British WWII submarine, based at Trincomalee, on the Far East front. First published 1953. After Germany surrenders, UK sub Seahound joins war against Japanese. Author is ex-sub officer in RN

Surface with Daring-by Reeman, Douglas-Berkley, NY-1976-ISBN 4250400612-A British mini-sub with four men must get past the nets and destroyer a German warship in a Norwegian\fjord

Swordray's First Three Patrols-by Blair, Clay-Bantam-1980-ISBN-0553136534-This fictional story tells of the boat that sank a carrier, two destroyers and 4 troop ships. But the CO faces an insubordination charge

T Fiction

Target 5-by Forbes, Colin-Dutton, NY-1973-256p-ISBN 0525214305

Target Mayflower-by Hirschhorn, Richard-Jove Books-1977-254p-In 1945, the Nazi's make one last gamble to win the war and land in Maine, liberate a POW camp an capture a uranium ore train

Target Susus-by Good, James-Kensington Pub. Corp, NY-1982-223p-ISBN 0821710923

Teodoro-by McLeod, Grover-Manchester Press, Alabama-1969-254p-USN submarines in Pacific. Philippines guerrilla operations

Those in Peril-by Follett, James-Mandarin-1994-ISBN 0749319631-The fictional epic journey of U-395's voyage home, including a spy story, U-boat combat and a dramatic rescue operation.

Those Who Serve-by Barton, AF

Threat Vector-by Dimercurio, Michael-Onyx-2000-555p-ISBN 0451409086-A old Russian submarine commander is called back to test a new weapon and in the process kill the entire US Navy upper echelon. A Navy CO in a new sub gives chase not knowing the Russian is heading for American shores

Three Boys on an Electrical Boat-by Trowbridge, John-Houghton, Mifflin, Boston-1896-215p

Threshold-by Coulter, Stephen-Heineman, London-1964-215p

Thunder of Erebus-by Harrison, Payne-Ivy Books-1991-498p-ISBN 0804108773-The Cold War is over and the US and Russia are partners in an Antarctic venture. That is until a new discovery of a power source is found. Who controls it controls the world.

Thunder Point-by Higgins, Jack-Berkley Publishing Group-1994-356p-ISBN 0425143570 Story of a British intelligence agent diving on a mysterious U-boat found in the Caribbean. The commander's briefcase, believed to hold incriminating documents listing prominent families supporting the Nazi party, is believed to be on board. As with all Jack Higgins novels it is fast-paced, and this one makes you want to go search for the sunken boats! A movie of the same title was made a few years later.

Thunderers, The-by Stepanov, Victor-Progress Pub Co-1986-ISBN-9997853423

Tiger Cruise, The-by Thompson, Richard-Knox Jones Enterprises-1999-280p-ISBN 0967561302-A LA Class boat leaves Norfolk with 14 civilians aboard, but is diverted to stop a Iraq mini-sub loaded with Anthrax spores

Tiger der Meere-by Schulz, Joh.-Gebr. Zimmermann Verlag, Balve-Tiger of the Sea-Fictionalized account of U-181 called U-861 in the book under Luth

Tinfish Run, The-by Bassett, Ronald-1942-An ancient RN DD fights U-Boats and planes while trying to protect a convoy

To Kill the Leopard-by Taylor, Theodore-Harcourt Brace & Co-1993-297p-ISBN 0151240973-From the publisher: "Aboard the tanker S.S. Galveston, American Sully Jordan has joined the vital dash across the Atlantic to a besieged Great Britain. Beneath the surface of those same chill waters, prowls the U-122—the invincible German U-boat commanded by a man known as "The Leopard." As the battle rages, these two men face off in a clash of explosive force." As he sets the scene, Theodore Taylor's action-packed narrative cuts swiftly between the German and Allied camps skillfully delineating each side's complex tactics in tracking the enemy's actions. Fascinating details of the British use of subtle psychological warfare, the French Resistance's intricate espionage network, American expediency, and Germany's advanced technology and single-minded determination to win the war take us gradually to the climactic denouement. 1993-US merchant skipper, torpedoed twice by U-boat Leopard gets Q-ship and goes sub chasing.

To Kill the Potemkin-by Joseph, Mark-New American Library-1987-ISBN 0451400399-319p-A US submarine sonar expert versus the Soviet's old guard in a new nuclear boat face each other

Todlicher Atlantik-by Schulz, Joh.-Wappertal-1962-Deadly Atlantic

Tokyo Torpedo-by Gray, Edwyn-Seeley, Service & Co. Ltd., London-1976-Author of several U-boat books wrote a series of novels with *Konrad Bergman* as the main character. The four novels ("No Survivors" in 1974, "Action Atlantic" in 1975, "Tokyo Torpedo" in 1976 and "The Last Command" in 1977) follow Bergman's U-Bootwaffe career from his pre-war training, through the war as a U-boat commander, culminating in his part in an attempt to smuggle Hitler to Argentina. His obvious disenchantment with the Nazi regime ensures that the missions assigned him are suicidal.

Tom Swift and His Submarine Boat-by Appleton, Victor (pseud)-Grosset & Dunlap, NY-1910-216p-Or: Under the Ocean for Sunken Treasure

Tom Swift and His Subocean Geotron-by Appleton, Victor II (pseud)-Collins, London-1969-160p

Torpedo!-by Homewood, Harry-McGraw-Hill-1982-ISBN 0070296987-Sleek and deadly, the ultra-silent Soviet missile sweeps through the depths to destroy the nuclear submarine USS Sharkfin. Admiral Mike Brannonis torn between two devastating choices. Admiral Brannon was the hero in the book Silent Sea also

Torpedo Alley-by Dowdell, EL-1988-414p-ISBN 1558170987-US sub Pocatello chases Russian supersub Suslov carrying stolen secrets that will render USN defenseless

Torpedo Run-by Reeman, Douglas-Hutchinson & Co., London-1981-290p-ISBN 688001335 In 1943It was 1943. On the Black Sea the Russians were fighting a desperate battle to regain control, but their naval defenses let them down. At last the British agreed to help their allies and sent a flotilla of motor torpedo boats under the command of John Devane

Torpedo Run-by White, Robb-Scholastic Book Services-1967-255p-WW II action

Torpedoes Away!-by Shirreffs, Gordon-1967

Torpedoes Away!-by Olney, Ross R-by Dodd, Mead, NY-1957-247p-WW II in the Java Sea

Torpedoman-by Smith, Ron-

Tracking the Wolfpack-by Jones, J Farragut--Dell-1981-319p-ISBN 0440185890-Germany's leading submarine ace versus a Royal Navy bent on revenge

Trapped-by Innes, Hammond-Ballantine-1940-Two journalists are missing along the English coast in prewar England

Treasure Below-by Ellsberg, Edward-Dodd, Mead, NY-1940

Trident Hijacking-by Steib, Dan-Fawcett by Ballantine, 1983-200p-044912388X

Trident Tragedy, The-by Monroe, Stanley C & Szilagye, Robert J-Dell-1983-272p-ISBN 0440187699

Triton Ultimatum-by Delaney, Lawrence-Thomas Y Crowell, NY-1977-ISBN 0690014902-Ten men steal Triton sub Lewis & Clark, demand ransom, create havoc with sino-soviet-US relations

Trojan Hearse, The-by Callison, Brian-Magna Print Books-1990-394p-ISBN 0002237857

Truk Lagoon-Rossi, Mitchell Sam-Pinnacle Fiction-1988-384p-ISBN 15581712125-An American sub in 144 laden with gems, lost secrets of civilization, covert government cover-ups all happen in this book

Twist of Sand-by Jenkins, Geoffrey-1959-Ulverscroft Large Print Books-1974-ISBN 0854562508-Experimental German U-boats in South African waters. Originally published\1961. A movie based on this book was released in 1968.

Two American Boys Aboard a Submarine-by Crockett, Sherman-Hurst, NY-1917-Two boys aboard a marauding German submarine and Greek blockade gun-runners during WWI

Two Hours to Darkness-by Trew, Antony--Random House, NY-1962-312p-Captain of UK sub goes mad while on patrol in Arctic

Typhoon-by Joseph, Mark-Simon & Schuster-1987-300p-ISBN 0671708651-USS Sub Reno watches two Russian subs stalk each other under polar ice cap and wonders which one to help

U Fiction

U-91 Satan der Tiefe-by Koizar, Karl Hans-Omnibus-Verlag, Berlin-1999-367p-ISBN 3570004325-U-91 Devil of the Deep

U-137-by-Topal, Eduard-London ; New York: Quartet-1983-278p

U-571-by Collins, Max Allan-Avon-2000-245p-ISBN 0380812908-Movie Tie-In

U-700-by Follett, James-Mandarin-1992-ISBN 0750504676-Novelization of the capture of U-570 and the attempt of the IWO to sink the surrendered vessel after his escape from a prison camp. Otto Kretschmer plays a part in the story as well.

U-713 ou Les Gentilhommes d'infortune-by Mac Orlean, Pierre-Editions d'aujourd'hui, Paris-1977-U-713 or the Mariners of Misfortune

U-Boat in the Hebrides-by Divine, David-Collins, London-1940-252 pages-A mystery novel.

U-Boot-Jager, Die-by Kent, Alexander-Ullstein-Verlag, Berlin-1999-367p-ISBN 3548246370-**The U-Boat Hunters**-A novel about a British destroyer out to sink the U-234

Under the Ocean to the South Pole-by Rockwood, Roy (pseud)-Cupples and Leon, NY-1907-248p-Young-Also known as The Strange Cruise of the Submarine Wonder

Ultimate Weapon, The-by Grant, Edward-Pinnacle Books, NY-1976-ISBN 0523008325- Russia vs USS Devilfish which is the best submarine in the world.

Ultra Deep-by Lovejoy, William H-1992-Soviet rocket with nuclear payload sinks deep into ocean, where it will melt down and poison sees unless the hero, with his robot submersibles can find and disable it in time

Unbroken-by Mars, Alastair-Elek, UK-1953

Under Pressure-by Herbert, Frank-Ballantine-1956-345p

Under the Freeze-by Bartram, George-Pinnacle Books, 1984-404p-ISBN 0523420552-US secret agent chases madman with stolen plutonium from Argentina to London, Paris, Moscow and finally aboard subs under the ice pack

Under the Ice-by Henricks, Richard P-Zebra Books-1989-ISBN 0821728083-A Russian Akula is sent to retrieve a down Russian plane under the Canadian pack ice. But the US has other plans

Undersea Victory II-by Holmes, W.J.-Zebra Books, 1966-271p-ISBN 0890834482

Up From the Deep-by Harmuth, Robert K-Compilation of SSG Class sea stories

Up Periscope!-by White, Robb-Scholastic Bookservice-1956-WWII submarine vs a Japanese DD

Up Periscope! & Other Stories-by Hudson, Alec(psued)-USNIP-ISBN 155750377X-248p-Written by J. Holmes a submariner who was forced to leave the submarine service because of an injury in 1935 although he worked in Navy Intelligence during the war. These stories appeared in the Saturday Evening Post and 5 of the 6 are about submarines. Holmes also wrote the book Double Edged Secrets about Ultra in WWII. This edition by USNIP in 1992 is a facsimile of the 1943 book Rendzvous and Other Long and Short Stories about Our Navy in Action.

USS Mudskipper-by Hardy, William M-Dodd, Mead, NY-1967-224p-Sub skipper decides to cap his career by sinking a Japanese train

USS Seawolf-by Robinson, Patrick-Harper Collins-2000-436p-ISBN 0060196300-The US sends a boat into China waters to spy on a new Chinese SSBN. One of the boats passengers is the son of the President. They boat is captured!

USSVI Membership Roster-by USSVI-The current membership roster of the U.S. Submarine Veterans Inc organization. Published in 1999 and 2001

Utmost Fish!-by McCann, Hugh W.-Simon & Schuster, NY-1965-384p

V Fiction

V-3-by Melchior, Ib-Charter Books, NY-1985-388p-ISBN 0441848095-A deadly gas is at the bottom of the Atlantic in a torn hull of a U-boat slowly corroding over the decades

Vengeance Reef-Waters, Don

Voyage of the Devilfish-Dimercurio, Michael-DI Fine Co, NY-1992-351p-ISBN 1556112912-Admiral of Russian fleet decides to force USA disarmament by deploying fleet within missile range. US killer sub Devilfish hunts Russian boomer flagship under polar ice. Author was Lt. Engineer on a U.S. nuclear SSN

Voyage of the Storm-Davis, Bart-Pocket Books, NY-1995-ISBN 0671769057-An old WWII British submarine which as has been on the bottom for years is all that is available find a cargo of Plutonium from Russia to Japan. But some Japanese terrorists hijack the cargo. Will the "Storm" be raised and can it help?

W Fiction

Waiting Game-by Fullerton, Alexander & Ives Washburn-1961-160p-Aboard sub HMS Setter in Arctic summer, where there's no nighttime, so subs shouldn't surface-Author was ex-sub officer in RN

War and Remembrance-by Wouk, Herman-Little, Brown-1978-ISBN 0316955019

War Beneath the Sea-by Bonham, Frank-Crowell, NY-1962-263p

Warhead-by Baker, F. Robert-Bantam Books-1981-281p-ISBN 0553147900 -A US boomer's family's are kidnapped by the Russians. The crew tells Russia to release them or suffer missiles. The US is trying to sink her.

Warhead-by Gerson, Noel B-Popular Library-1970-511p-This is a story of the men who run the yard where the Navy's newest subs are made. Demonstrators, unions, congressional committees and mad admirals all combine to make life miserable for the Yard CEO.

Warhead-by F. Robert Baker-Bantam-1981-291p-ISBN 0-553-14790-0- Terrorism strikes the families of the USS Montana's crew

Watering Place of Good Peace-by Jenkins, Geoffrey-William Collins Sons & Co, 1960-199p-ISBN 000616143X

Waters Dark & Deep-by Jones, J Farragut--Dell-1981-ISBN 0440194709- -Story of 2 sub skippers, one UK and one German come together in a huge battle

When Duty Calls-by Hendricks, Richard P-Zebra Books-1988-ISBN 0821722565-The world's first laser battle station is set to start operating on the Russian coast. A US SEAL team is sent in aboard a captured Russian submarine

Whirlwind Beneath the Sea-by Stanton, Ken-1972-Secret agent and the underwater service is off to Australia to solve mystery of undersea eruption, rising land masses and beautiful babes

Winner Take All-by Flannery, Sean-Forge-1994-378p-ISBN 0812522885 -The Cold War is over and the U.S. and Russia plan a large war game. However it becomes sabotaged as a U.S. spy sub is supposedly sunk by a Russian sub. Everyone heads for north Atlantic

With Blood and Iron-by Reeman, Douglas-1965-258p-WW II warfare in the Atlantic-Set in 1944, this novel deals with the U-991 and its commander, one of the old surviving aces. The plot revolves around the interaction of the officers and their reactions to the turning tide of the war, culminating in the July plot against Hitler.

With Honour in Battle-by McDaniel, J.T.-Writer's Club Press-2001-268p-ISBN 0595173527-At the end of 1944, Korvettenkapitän Hans Kruger, Germany's top U-boat ace, is exhausted and in need of rest. Instead, he is given command of U-2317, an experimental U-boat with a temperamental propulsion system that promises virtual immunity from attack, but also carries the potential of blowing up at any moment. Now Kruger must contend with a triumphant enemy, as well as jealous superiors and the intrusion of the war into his shattered personal life.

Wolfpack-by Hardy, William M-Dodd, Mead, NY-1960-Pacific action as a US wolfpack gets into a Japanese convoy and the books main character who is on his last patrol wants to make it memorable

World War III-by Fulgham, Joel-Writers Club Press-2000-ISBN 059509290X

Wotan Warhead, The-by Follett, James-Popular Library-1979-221p-ISBN 0445046295-Skipper of U-Boat carrying torpedo with

deadly warhead is pursued by Brits as he tries to carry out
secret mission

Wreckers Must Breathe-by Innes, Hammond-1940, 92-343p-ISBN
0854566449-A bit far-fetched story about a secret undersea U-
boat base in Cornwall, England(!) and its destruction by a
British Intelligence officer in 1939. Originally published 1967.

Y Fiction

Yashimoto's Last Dive-by Trew, Anthony-1987-Fiction

You Can Pilot a Submarine-by Bracken, Carolyn-Golden Press-1983-
ISBN 0307107639

Young Naval Captain-by Bonehill, Ralph-Thompson and Thomas,
Chicago-1902-221p-Young USN officer builds a Holland-type
submarine

Z Fiction

Zhukov Briefing-Trew, Anthony-Popular Library Press-1975-254p-
Russian supersub goes aground off Norway. USA and UK
want its secrets, Russians vow to protect it and Norway's
caught in the middle

Videos

41 For Freedom: Ballistic-Missile Carrying Submarines-30min-Heritage Press and Productions-Overview of the history of the construction, launchings and weapons systems of 41 nuclear powered submarines, as well as training facilities for submariners. Produced by the Navy in late 1960s. Clips of submarines include: USS Scorpion (re-christened USS George Washington) and USS Will Rogers.

Action in the North Atlantic (1943)-Starring: Humphrey Bogart, et al.-Number of tapes: 1-ASIN: 6302120454-This film, which takes place during WWII, provides a personal and professional insight into the unsung Merchant Marines, who risked their lives to bring supplies to the fighting soldiers. The story begins with the Merchant Marines' tanker being torpedoed by the Nazis. The surviving men are saved after 11 days adrift at sea, and return home. But soon, the men are called back into action with a new assignment—which forces them to confront the deadly Nazis once again. This film follows the exploits of the submarine, S.S. Seawitch, as they battle the Nazis in World War II. Academy Award Nominations: Best Original Story.

Anti-Submarine Ops 1950's-30min-Distrib: Traditions Military Videos, Escondito, CA

Anti-Submarine Ops 1960's-70's-60min-Distrib: Traditions Military Videos, Escondito, CA-Has footage of USS Scorpion

Atomic Submarine, The (1959)-Starring: Arthur Franz, et al, Director: Spencer Gordon Bennet-Number of tapes: 1-ASIN: 6305071519, DVD: 6305079722-An atomic sub is dispatched to the Arctic

North to search out and destroy an alien spacecraft which has been attacking the American fleet.

Bedford Incident (1965)-Starring: Richard Widmark, et al., Director: James B. Harris-Number of tapes: 1-ASIN: 0800106040-Strong Cold War story of authoritarian Navy captain (Widmark) scouting Russian subs near and determined to keep one down.

Big Submarine, The-Color, Youth oriented-50 min-1996-ASIN: 6304402635

Capture of the U-110-1hr by The History Channel-The story of the capture of the first Enigma coding machine

Challenge is Met, The-26min-Produced by Naval Submarine League-The conversion of 12 Poseidon missile boats to Trident types

Clay Decker: USS Tang-129min-Located at USNA/Nimitz Library

Crash Dive (1943)-Starring: Power, Baxter-Number of tapes: 1-ASIN: 6303102484

Crimson Tide (1995)-Starring: Denzel Washington-Director: Tony Scott-Number of tapes: 1 ASIN: 6303696813-DVD, 6304765258-Near future, Russian rebels have taken over one of the ICBM bases in the USSR. Alarmed by the prospect of a rebel strike, the U.S. sends the U.S.S. Alabama, a nuclear ballistic submarine, to watch over the base and retaliate in case they launch. While on patrol, the submarine is attacked and the radio systems are knocked out. An emergency message received during the battle is only partially recovered. Captain Ramsey believes it to be the order to launch on the rebels, while XO Hunter wants to wait for a confirmation message. The conflict escalates into mutiny as Ramsey and Hunter fight for control of the Alabama's nuclear missiles.

Das Boot-The Director's Cut (1982)-Director: Wolfgang Petersen-Number of tapes: 2-ASIN: 0800132343, DVD: 0767802470

Destination Tokyo (1943)-Starring: Cary Grant, Director: Delmer Daves-Number of tapes: 1-A ASIN: 6301967607-About a submarine that enters Tokyo to gather information for the upcoming Doolittle's Plane raid.

Down Periscope (1996)-Starring: Kelsey Grammer, Director: David S. Ward-Number of tapes: 1 ASIN: 6304107641

Enemy Below, The (1957)-Starring: Robert Mitchum, Director: Dick Powell-Number of tapes: 1-ASIN: 6301662954-Fine submarine chase tale, which manages to garner interest from usual crew interaction of U. S. vs. Germany in underwater action; the special effects for this earned Walter Rossi an Academy Award. The Enemy Below depicts a tense battle of wills between the commander of a U.S. Navy Destroyer and the captain of a German U-boat. The two men play this cat-and-mouse game as if their lives depended on it—which they do. For the German officer (a veteran who does not support the Nazis) must, however reluctantly, obey orders to blow the U.S. ship out of the water, while the American sailors will do everything they can to stop him. And when the winner is declared, both officers will have shown that they are, indeed, honorable opponents.

Escape from Submarines-1950's-30min-Distrib: Traditions Military Videos, Escondito, CA Fleet Ballistic Missile Man 1960s-Produced by the Navy, this video details the specialized training me received for working with the Polaris Missile System. Also good scenes of life aboard nuclear-powered submarines.

Flying Missile, The-Columbia, 1950-Glenn Ford Stars as a naval commander who develops the means to launch missiles from submarines

Forty-One For Freedom-29min-by Naval Submarine League

Gray Lady Down-Starring: Heston, Carradine-ASIN: B0000065MR-The Navy seeks to rescue the crew of the USS Neptune which sank off Connecticut coast after a collision

Great Ships: The Salvage Ships. Famed treasure hunter Mel Fisher is featured in this look at the men and machines that wrest sunken treasures and ships from their watery graves.

Great Ships: The Submarines-Slip beneath the waves with some of the deadliest and most technologically advanced ships ever made.

Great Ships: The Submersibles-From record-setting dives to deep-sea rescues, this is an authoritative look at these specialized vessels

Hell Below-1933-MGM-Director: Jack Conway

Hellcats of the Navy-Columbia 1957-Based on Admiral Lockwood's Book Hellcats of the Navy. It's about a group of U.S. submarines who enter the Sea of Japan. Ronald Regan and Nancy Davis

Hitler's Lost Sub (2000)-by NOVA-ASIN: B000053V72

Hostile Waters (1997)-Starring: Martin Sheen, Rutger Hauer, Director: David Drury-Number of tapes: 1-ASIN: 0783111037-Account based on an accident with a Russian missile sub off the coast of Bermuda in 1986 which actually happened. Based on book written in 1996

Hunley, The-TV, 1999-True story of the Confederate submarine Hunley, which became the first sub to sink a ship when it destroyed the USS Housatonic in 1863

Hunt for Red October, The (1990)-Starring: Sean Connery, Director: John McTiernan-Number of tapes: 1-ASIN: 0792139895-A Tom Clancy Thriller. Sean Connery is the Russian submarine commander trying to defect and is chased by both U.S. and Russian subs.

Killer Submarine-Cover up or accident? Explore the evidence surrounding the death of 13,000 people at the close of World War II

Koninklijke Marine-1924-1940-The Royal Netherlands Navy 1924-1940. Footage about many surface and submarine vessels K VI, K XVIII, K XIX, K XX, O 16, O 12, O 19 and O 20

Ice Station Zebra-MGM 1968-Cold War story about the nuclear submarine Tigerfish on a mission to rescue weather crew on an Ice station

Laconia Incident, The-For the first time on video, the complete story of one of the most dramatic and tragic stories of World War II, the sinking of the Laconia.

Lusitania: The Life, Loss and Legacy of an Ocean Legend-Sunk by U-20

Men Without Women-1930-20th Century-Director John Ford

Missile Navy-Produced by the Navy in the late 1960s and narrated by Chet Huntley, this film presents historical overview of the Navy missile program, as well as, a review of both tactical and strategic missiles in the Navy's arsenal

Modern Marvels: Deep Sea Exploration-Venture beneath the waves in the most advanced submersibles ever built and trace the history of man's adventures undersea.

Morning Departure-British, 1950-Released in U.S. as Operation Disaster. A WWII adventure about a group of British submariners waiting to be rescued in a sunken submarine

Morgenrot (German)-1933-About a crew trapped in a U-boat in WWI

Murphy's War-Starring Peter O'Toole-A U-boat sinks Peter O'Toole's ship and after recovering he finds it hiding in a deep river. He goes after it

National Geographics I-52-In Search of WWII Gold-ASIN B00004TX2K

New Explorers, The: Sounds of Discovery. Ride in a nuclear sub to see how formerly top secret technology is opening a new window into the world of the deep ocean.

On the Beach (1959)-Starring: Gregory Peck, Director: Stanley Kramer-Number of tapes: 1-ASIN: 6304111398-Stanley Kramer's 1959 anti-war movie looks like everything Kramer did: subtle as a car wreck but undeniably affecting. Gregory Peck plays a submarine commander looking for survivors in Australia after a nuclear holocaust. Ava Gardner is among them and, somewhat improbably under the circumstances, becomes his love interest. Fred Astaire and Anthony Perkins are among the characters awaiting death from the gradual spread of radiation from the north. One might scoff at Kramer's implicit finger-wagging about nuclear politics in his mad, mad, mad, mad world, but it is hard to stop watching this compelling drama all the same

Operation Pacific (1951)-Starring: John Wayne, Patricia Neal-Number of tapes: 1-ASIN: 0782006787-Overzealous Wayne is ultra dedicated to his navy command; the few WW2 action scenes are taut, and Neal makes a believable love interest.

Operation Petticoat-(1959)-Starring: Cary Grant, Tony Curtis-Number of tapes: 1-ASIN: 0782006787

Our Century: Death of the Wolf packs-Sail with the Allied convoys and slip beneath the waves with their Nazi foes in this comprehensive look at one of the most important battles of World War II

Polaris to Poseiden/Countdown to Trident-60min-Distrib: Traditions Military Videos, Escondito, CA-Two Navy films produced in the 1970s detailing missile and submarine programs. Clips of the following ships are included: USS Ethan Allen, USS James Madison, USS Observation Island, USS George Washington and USS Kamehameha.

Pride Runs Deep-28 1/2min-Produced by Naval Submarine League-Documents the rigors of submarine life in the 1960s. Lots of detailed footage of sub operations. Scenes were filmed at Holy Loch, Scotland, and New London and Groton, Conn., ballistic missiles are fired, and there is footage of the Los Angeles Class and Trident-class submarines

Raise The Hunley. Hear from divers and archeologists who helped salvage the first submarine to ever sink a ship in combat.

Run Silent, Run Deep (1958)-Starring: Clark Gable, Burt Lancaster-Director: Robert Wise-Number of tapes: 1-ASIN: 6304196954-Clark Gable goes after "Bungo Pete" who runs a Japanese destroyer which destroyed his previous submarine

Russians are Coming, The-Mirisch Corp, 1966-A comedy about a Russian submarine commander seeking help for his grounded submarine and the panic in the small Maine town

Salvage of USS Squalus-45min-Distrib: Traditions Military Videos, Escondito, CA

Sea Tales: The Secret of the U-110. Beneath the icy waters off Greenland, a top-secret Allied mission paved the way to victory in the Battle of the Atlantic.

Submarine-1928-Columbia-Frank Capra

Submarine Base-Starring: Litel, D'Orsay-ASIN: B000056AWR.

Submarine Command-Paramount, 1951-William Holden is a Korean War Submarine Commander who is haunted by his memory of the last day of World War II, when, as an exec, he saved his boat by crash diving while captain was on the bridge

Submarine D-1-1937-Warner Bros-Director Lloyd Bacon-A film showing a submarine rescue using the McCann Rescue Chamber and Momsen Lung

Submarine Officer-At Nimitz Library

Submarine Raider-Columbia, 1942-About a submarine that fails to warm Pearl Harbor of the impending attack then sinks a Japanese Carrier that launched it- John Howard, Bruce Bennett

Submarines, Secrets & Spies (1974)-by NOVA-ASIN: 6305373760

Submarine Service 1940's-1950's-40min-Distrib: Traditions Military Videos, Escondito, CA

Submarine: Steel Boats-Iron Men (1989)-Starring: Submarine, Tom Clancy, Number of tapes: 1-ASIN: 6302744490

Submarine Training & Submariners-1960's-30min-Distrib: Traditions Military Videos, Escondito, CA

Submarine War Against Japan-CAV Video Production-1992-Live Footage from 1946

Submarine Warfare-Starring Gene Kelly-Number of Tapes: 1-ASIN: 6301662954-Gene Kelly takes you under for a look at life aboard a fighting submarine during World War II.

Submarine Warfare: Navy's Most Deadly-ASIN: 6305828091

Submarine Warfare in WWII-60min-Distrib: Traditions Military Videos, Escondito, CA

Submarines: Sharks of Steel-Set of 4 tapes-192 min From deep within the belly of the beast comes an almost too-close-for-comfort look at the men and machines engaged in our country's "silent service. As early as the Civil War, a new breed of predator appeared in the seas and in one frightening instant changed the balance of world power. The submarine, by pure function of design and simplicity of purpose, evolved into the most terrifying weapon of mass destruction ever seen. The four programs in this collector's set are:

*Submariners—Go into the bizarre world of these undersea sailors, who not only operate a weapon but live inside it.

*In the Belly of the Beast—Operating on the vanguard of technology, there is no margin for error. Ocean floors are littered with the wreckage of those who failed.

*The Hidden Threat—Here are the massive SSBN "Boomers" and their SSN class "Hunter-Killer" shadows—missile and fast attack platforms capable of unleashing unimaginable destruction.

*The Hunters and the Hunted—From the very first sub to the German Wolf packs of World War II, trace the history of undersea warfare.

Submerged-TV, 1999-2 Hour show recreating the rescue of the USS Squalus

Suicide Missions: Deep Sea Rescue-Descend to the ocean floor with Navy divers trained to rescue sailors trapped in sunken subs

Tench Class Subs-60min-Distrib: Traditions Military Videos, Escondito, CA

Tora, Tora Tora-An epic about the attack on Pearl Harbor

Torpedo Alley (1953)-Starring: Dorothy Malone, Director: Lew Landers-Number of tapes: 1-ASIN: 630135852X-Typical Korean War action involving U. S. submarine offensives. Video Description: A guilt-ridden ex-Navy pilot applies for a treacherous submarine mission in order to overcome the lingering shame of the failed mission that killed his flight crew.

Torpedo Run (1958)-Starring: Glenn Ford, Director: Joseph Pevney-Number of tapes: 1-ASIN: 6301978625-Sluggish WW2 revenge narrative of sub-commander Ford whose family was aboard Jap prison ship he had to blow up.

U-Boat War-This is an extremely interesting and highly informative documentary in three parts. Each segment is roughly 50 minutes long and covers the broad history of U-Boats during WWII. There is much archival footage-ASIN: B00005BGQZ

Underway on Nuclear Power-by Naval Submarine League (NSL)-22 min-Focuses on the Engineering end but a good aid to introduce the submarine force to the public

Up Periscope-Starring: Garner, O'Brien-Number of tapes: 1-ASIN: 0790734907-Garner is Navy Lieutenant transferred to submarine during WW2, with usual interaction among crew as they reconnoiter Japanese held island. WarnerScope.

USS Robert E. Lee SSBN 601-1960's-30min-Distrib: Traditions Military Videos, Escondito, CA

Voyage to the Bottom of the Sea (1961)-Starring: Walter Pidgeon, Director: Irwin Allen-Number of tapes: 1-ASIN: 6302098416-Entertaining, colorful nonsense about conflicts aboard massive atomic submarine, with Pidgeon the domineering admiral trying to keep the Earth from being fried by a burning radiation belt. No deep thinking, just fun. Later a TV series

We Dive at Dawn/Submarine Alert-Number of tapes: 1-ASIN: 6305207917-Suicide Missions: U-Boats. German submarine commanders recall the deadly battle waged beneath the waves of World War II.

Weapons at War: Missile Submarines-Go on patrol onboard one of the most sophisticated and deadly ships ever built a nuclear-powered and armed "boomer."

Weapons at War: The Silent Service. This is the complete story of the U.S. submarines in the Pacific during World War II where they were responsible for 60 percent of all Japanese ships sunk

Weapons at War: Sub Hunters-Trace the deadly game of cat and mouse played out by German U-boats and allied ships in both world wars.

Weapons at War: Submarines-Go aboard a modern missile sub in this authoritative look at the vessels that have become the most important naval weapons in the world.

Appendix I

SUBMARINE MUSEUMS

DRUM (AGSS 228) USS Alabama Battleship Commission PO Box 65 Mobile, AL 36601 (205) 433-2703	**PAMPANITO (SS 383)** National Maritime Museum Association PO Box 470310 San Francisco, CA 94147 (415) 775-1943
NAUTILUS (SSN 571) Historical Ship Nautilus Submarine Force Museum NavSubBase New London Groton, CT 06349 (800) 343-0079	**ST. MARYS SUBMARINE MUSEUM** 102 St. Marys Street West St. Marys, GA 31558-4945 (912) 882-ASUB(2782)
BOWFIN (SS 287) Pacific Fleet Submarine Memorial Assn., Inc. 11 Arizona Memorial Drive Honolulu, HI 96818 (808) 423-1341	**LIONFISH (SS 298)** USS Massachusetts Memorial Battleship Cove Fall River, MA 02721 (508) 678-1100
TORSK (AGSS 423) Baltimore Maritime Museum Pier Three Pratt Street Baltimore, MD 21202 (301) 396-3453	**SILVERSIDES (SS 236)** USS Silversides and Maritime Museum PO Box 1692 Muskegon, MI 49443 (231) 755-1230
USS MARLIN (SST-2) Freedom Park 2497 Freedom Park Road Omaha, NE 68110 (402) 345-1959	**ALBACORE (AGSS 569)** Port of Portsmouth Maritime Museum at Albacore Park 600 Market Street Portsmouth, NH 03802 (603) 436-3680
LING (AGSS 297) State of New Jersey Naval Museum PO Box 395 Hackensack, NJ 07601 (973) 342-3268	**HOLLAND BOAT #1** Paterson Museum 2 Market Street Paterson, NJ 07501 (973) 881-3874

CROAKER (SS 246) Naval and Servicemen's Park 1 Naval Park Cove Buffalo, NY 14202 (716) 847-1773	**GROWLER (SSG 577)** Intrepid Sea Air Space Museum Intrepid Square New York City, NY 10036 (212) 245-2533 ext. 7325
COD (SS 224) Cleveland Coordinating Committee for USS Cod, Inc. 1089 East 9th Street Cleveland, OH 44114 (216) 566-8770	**BATFISH (AGSS 310)** Muskogee War Memorial Park PO Box 735 Muskogee, OK 74402 (918) 682-6294
BLUEBACK (SS 581) Oregon Museum of Science and Industry 1945 Southeast Water Ave. Portland, OR 97214-3354 (503) 797-4000	**BECUNA (SS 319)** Independence Seaport Museum 211 South Columbus Blvd. Philadelphia, PA 19106 (215) 922-1898
REQUIN (AGSS 481) Carnegie Science Center 1 Allegheny Avenue Pittsburgh, PA 15212 (412) 237-3403	**CLAMAGORE (SS 343)** Patriots Point Naval and Maritime Museum 40 Patriots Point Road Mount Pleasant, SC 29464 (803) 884-2727
CAVALLA (AGSS 244) Seawolf Park Pelican Island 2102 Seawall Blvd. Galveston, TX 77550 (409) 744-5738	**THE NAVAL UNDERSEA MUSEUM** P.O. Box 408 Keyport, WA 93845 (360) 697-1129
COBIA (AGSS 245) Wisconsin Maritime Museum 75 Maritime Drive Manitowoc, WI 54220 (920) 684-0218	

FROM AROUND THE WORLD:

COUNTRY	NAME	YEAR	DESCRIPTION	LOCATION
AUSTRALIA	Otway S59	1966	Oberon class	Holbrook, New South Wales
	Ovens S70	1967	Oberon class	Maritime Museum, Fremantle
	Onslow S60	1968	Oberon class	National Maritime Museum, Sydney
BELGIUM	B-143	1960	Russian Foxtrot cl. (Project 641)	Maritime Theme Park, Zeebrugge
BRAZIL	Riachuelo	1977	Oberon class	Navy Center, Rio de Janeiro
CANADA	B-15	1964	Russian Foxtrot cl. (Project 641)	Victoria, B.C
	Onondaga	1965	Oberon class (not on display yet)	War Museum, Ottawa
CHINA	229	1964	Russian Romeo cl. (Project 633)	Naval Museum, Qingdao
DENMARK	S 359	1956	Russian Whiskey cl.(Project 613)	Nakskov
	Springeren	1963	Delfinen class	Marinemuseum, Aalborg
ESTONIA	Lembit	1936	Mine laying sub	Estonian Maritime Museum, Tallinn
FINLAND	Vesikko	1933	CV-707 Finnish/German	Suomenlinna, Helsinki
FRANCE	Alose	1904	Naiade class	COMEX company, Marseille
	Argonaute	1958	S-636 Arethuse class	Sci/Tech Museum, Paris
	Espadon	1958	S-637 Narval class	Ecomusée de Saint-Nazaire
	Redoutable	1967	First SSBN (opening in 2001)	Cité de la Mer, Cherbourg
GERMANY	U 1	1906	First German submarine	Deutsches Museum, Munich
	U 995	1943	Type VIIC/41	Beachfront, Laboe
	W. Bauer	1945	U-2540, Type XXI	Technikmuseum, Bremerhaven
	K-24	1962	Russian Juliett cl. (Project 651)	Peenemunde
	U9 S 188	1967	205 class	Technik-Museum, Speyer
	U10 S 189	1967	205 class	Marine Museum, Wilhelmshaven
INDONESIA	Pasopati	1953	Russian Whiskey cl.(Project 613)	Surabaya, Indonesia
ITALY	Dandolo	1967	E. Toti class	Naval Museum, Venice
	Toti S 506	1968	E. Toti class (not on display yet)	Leonardo da Vinci Museum, Milan
HOLLAND	B-80	1957	Russian Zulu class (Project 611)	Den Helder
	Tonijn	1965	Dutch Potvis class	Marinemuseum, Den Helder
NORWAY	Utstein S302	1965	Kobben class	Marinemuseet, Horten
RUSSIA	Narodovolez	1929	D-2 Dekabrist class	D-2 Museum, St. Petersburg
	S-56	1939	S class, XI series	Port, Vladivostok
	K-21	1939	K class XIV series	Severomorsk, Kola bay

	NAME	YEAR	DESCRIPTION	LOCATION
	M-261	1955	Quebec class (Project A615)	Park 40 let Pobedy, Krasnodar
	M-361	1957	Project 637	Naval Academy, Pushkin
	B-413	1968	Foxtrot (Project 641)	Ocean Museum, Kaliningrad
S. KOREA	Sang-o	1994	Captured North Korean sub	Beach near Kangnung
SPAIN	Peral	1888	First Spanish submarine	City square, Cartagena
	SA-51 & 52	1964	Tiburón-I class	Science Museum, Barcelona
SWEDEN	Hajen	1904	"Ubåt No1"First Swedish sub	Marinmuseum, Karlskrona
	U-3	1942		Technical Museum, Malmö
	S 194	1954	Russian Whiskey cl.(Project 613)	Kalmar
	Nordkaparen	1962	Draken class	Maritime Centre, Gothenburg
U.K.	Holland 1	1901	First Royal Navy submarine	RN Submarine Museum,Gosport
	U 534	1942	Raised German U-boat	Historic Warships at Birkenhead
	Alliance S67	1945	"A" class	RN Subm. Museum, Gosport
	Ocelot S17	1962	Oberon class	Historic Dockyard, Chatham Kent
	Onyx S21	1966	Oberon class	Historic Warships, Birkenhead
	B- 39	1967	Russian Foxtrot (Project 641)	Folkestone Harbor, Kent
UKRAINE	M-305	1956	Russian Quebec cl.(Project A615)	Battery 411 Memorial, Odessa

Appendix II

Article Index from Submarine Review by Naval Submarine League-Annadale, Virginia

April 1983

The Evolution of SubDevGroup Two
The Soviet Threat
Submarine Lessons of the Falklands War
Warnings from the South Atlantic
Submarine Museum-Library
Submarine Command in Transition to War
Statements to the House Seapower Subcommittee
Seabasing the MX?
Torpedo Boat or Missile Boat
Book Review: War Under the Pacific

July 1983

Arctic Submarine Warfare
Emerging Soviet Submarine Technologies
SUBACS
Weapons and the New Attack Submarine
Loss of the Thresher
Arrivederci Dace
Submarine Aviation
The Intrepid Museum's Submarine Gallery

April 1984

July 1984

October 1984

The Missing Element
Book Reviews: U-Boats Against Canada
Book Reviews: Electronic Warfare

July 1986

Maritime Strategy Implications for the Fleet Submarine
Concentration of Force by Submarines
Dolphin-An Autonomous Semi-Submersible
The "K" Boats-"K" as in Calamity
Submarine Losses of Naval Academy Graduates in World War II
SUBDEVRON Twelve
Submarine Tanker Update
Strategic ASW
Trident-A Major Submarine Command
The Marginal Ice Zone
Book Review: Submarine of the Imperial Japanese Navy
Book Review: Submarine Captain

October 1986

Admiral Crowe's Remarks Submarine League Banquet
The Science Submarine
Artificial Intelligence in the Art and Science of Submarining
Canopus
Soviet Naval Power in the Pacific
A Naval Man's War in the South Atlantic
Admiral Trost's Luncheon Remarks
Soviet Writings
Enough of This "Silent Service" Bunk
What's in a Name
Book Review: Silent Warriors and the Phoenix Odyssey
Book Review: Red Storm Rising

January 1987

VADM DeMars Speech at Submarine Symposium Lima, Peru
Fighting in Defended Waters

Submarine Anti-ASW Warfare
Same Problem-1,000 Feel Below or 35,000 Feet Above
Under Ice Flooding Recovery
Employment of Submarines in Shallow Waters
Submarine Related Space Systems
Pre WW III Foresight
A Swing Strategy?
A Requiem for the Silent Service
Father Separation and Crises Adaptation in the Submarine
     Family
Submarine Aggressor Squadron-Its time has Come
Stress in C3I Operations in Crises
Book Review: Shinano
Book Review: Submarine Warfare-Today and Tomorrow

October 1987

Fundamental Principles of Submarine Warfare
The Role of U.S. Submarines
The Soviets on Submarine Survivability
Submarine Sanctuaries: A Bad Idea
Nuclear Submarine Operations in Shallow Water
Incoming Ballistic Missiles at Sea
The Inner Layer of Submarine Defense
Automation?
Torpedo Expenditure Rates in WWII
Submarine Officer Selection for Promotion
The Strategic Defense Initiative Submarine
The Concept of Over the Horizon Targeting
Book Review: Wahoo

January 1988

A Submarine Operational Tactical System
Computer Literacy for Submariners
New Submarine Concepts

Zero Range submarine Detection
Voice Language-Code Translator Computer
Submarine Automation
Laser Communications with Submarines
Book Review: Strategic Antisubmarine Warfare and Naval
    Strategy

October 1988

An Exciting Time to Be in Submarines
Submarine Warfare
The Forward to Jane's Fighting Ships 1988-1989
An Economic and Technological Assessment of the Soviet Navy
    1986-1995
Minitruders
Dutch Submarines in Combat, 1940-1945
The Chinese on Submarine Combat Survivability
Penetrating a Minefield
Identification: Cooperative Effort
A Submarine Reserve?
Fundamental Principles of Submarine Warfare
Jules Verne! Where Are You?
Want to Study About Modern Submarine Design?
Book Review: Submarine Warfare in the Arctic
Book Review: ASW Versus Submarine Technology Battle
Book Review: The Cardinal of the Kremlin

January 1989

Strategy Planning for Submarines
The Credibility of Our SSBN Deterrence
SLCMs in Arms Control: The Verification Conundrum
Submarine Fleet Potential
Our subs Fly with One-Half a Wing
Tempo in Submarine Operations
Strategic Antisubmarine Warfare

Sonar Transducers: A History
Submarine Power-The Final Arbiter
SSN's and Low Intensity Conflict
The Morality of War
The Seawolf SSN-21
DARPA Pushes Submarine Automation in the Future
Soviet Views of the U.S. Submarine Role in Carrier Groups
SLCM Dilemmas: Foresight and Folly
Our Congressmen Must Explain Submarine's Advantages
Soviet Closed-Cycle Submarines
In Remembrance/Red Lawson
The Submarine Review
Book Review: Anti-Submarine Warfare
Book Review: Submarine Warriors

October 1990

Honorable H. Lawrence Garrett III, SECNAV (Speech)
Honorable Norman Sisisky, Member of Congress (Speech)
Honorable Charles Herzfeld, DDR&E (Speech)
Admiral Bruce DeMars, Director, Navy Nuclear Propulsion
        (Speech)
Continuing Roles for Strategic Deterrent Forces
SSN Roles and Needs in the Next Decade
Third World Submarine Developments
A Detached View of the Submarine Force
The Submarine Threat of the Future
Vice Commander Roger F. Bacon (Speech)
Rear Admiral Michael C. Colley (Speech)
CNO at Leningrad, 12 October 1989 (Speech)
COMSUBLANT at SUBGRU Six Change of Command 13 July,
        1990 (Speech)
The Bonefish Fire and the People Who Saved the Ship
Book Review: Memoirs Ten Years and Twenty Days

April 1992

July 1992

April 1993

Ft. Trumbull-A Navy High Technology Site
Launching of the Naval Undersea Museum!
Sub Guide: The Kilo
Drawbacks to Conventional Warhead Submarine Launches
    Ballistic Missiles
Fifty Years Ago, The Escape of the Casablanca
Grappling for U.S. Submarines
Wahoo's Third Patrol
Book Review: The U.S. Navy in the 1990s-The Alternatives for
    Action

July 1993
Admiral Alfred J. Whittle in Memoriam
As I remember Vice Admiral Levering Smith
Admiral Bruce DeMars (Speech)
VADM William A. Owens (Speech)
VADM Roger F. Bacon (Speech)
Mr. Ronald O'Rourke (Speech)
Peacetime Presence or Wartime Patrols
The Future Course of U.S. Submarines
Stay Engaged Through Innovation
Pacific Fleet IUSS-A Strategic Plan
AIP-A Historical Perspective from Walther to Sterling
Subguide: Down to One Nuclear Shipyard
The Personal Computer and submarine On Board Training
Fast Attack Import Crews
Submariners Must Support Base Closures
To the Bottom of the Sea-and Back
Periscope Operations for the Uninitiated
Book Review: Our New National Security Strategy: America
    Promises to Come Back
Book Review: The Rickover Effect
Book Review: Macarthur's Ultra

October 1993

January 1994

Submarine Paradigm Shifts
New Attack Submarine: Options for the Future
Downsizing to Dollars, A Recipe for a Hollow Force
The Soviet Submarine Operations in the Baltic 1944-1945
Russian Submarine Forces-90 Years
A Distorted Submarine
Rebirth of a Submarine: USS Requin SS 481
The Saga of Pogy SSN 647
Training Technology-The Force Multiplier
The Nuclear Arrow Belongs in the U.S. Quiver
Comment on Defensive Anti-War Warfare for SSNs
Combat Systems Commonality, and Obsolete Equipment
      Replacement
They Leave Us the Best
How the Laminated Battery Jar Really Originated
Parche-Second War Patrol Report
Book Review: Forged in War-The Naval-Industrial Complex
      and American Construction 1940-1961
Book Review: Dictionary of Military Abbreviations

October 1994

SUBLANT Address to Annual Symposium
The U.S. Submarine Production Base
The Future of Strategic Systems
Keynote Address-Submarine Technology Symposium
Watching the Rear-View Mirror
SECNAVs and Submarines part 1
The Holland VI-An American Pioneer
Nimitz as a Submariner
U.S. Submarine Operations During the Korean War
Underwater Acoustic Communications-Is There a Role?
A Farewell to Submarine Group Six
A Cruise on the Nevada
USS Tang-Fifth War Patrol

July 1995

October 1995
President's Letter to SEAWOLF Christening
For Our Children's Freedom
U.S. Strategic Command: Changes, Hopes, Challenges
Our People-The Most Precious Resource
Submarine Force Plans and Programs: Preparing of the
    Challenges of the 21st Century
The Submarine Building Program
Heroes Beware, and Widows Too
Technology vs. Training: Soviet Subs in World War Two]
Submarines in East Asia
Realizing the Potential for Drastic manning Reduction
Sharks of Strategic Designation
Unhinging the Japanese Grand Strategy
The Baker Submarine
RADM Lane-Nott, RN Addresses the Nautilus Chapter
Ex-Boomer as a SSRN
The Battlegroup Commander's Most Unused Asset: The
    Submarine
Book Review: Stealth at Sea
Book Review: In Irons: U.S. Military Might in the New Century

January 1996
The President's Message on the 40th FBM Anniversary
Thinking Outside the Box
Strategic Systems Program
Sea Control and Submarines in the 21st Century
Trident Submarine as a Special Warfare Platform
Information Overload
An Undersea Coastal Surveillance System
Submarines of the St. Petersburg Malachite Bureau
Looking Forward-Thermionic Reactors for a Revolutionary
    Electric Boat
FIDO-The First U.S. Homing Torpedo

Buildings Honor Submariners-Part I
C41: How Much is Enough? How Much is Too Much?
American Submarines from a Russian Point of View
Admiral Roy Benson
A Direct Line to SECNAV
Book Review: From Battlewagons to Ballistic Missiles Submarine
    Admiral
Book Review: Silent Running

April 1996

The Heart that Beats in the Shark of Steel
National Defense Authorization Bill for FY 1996-An Extract
Submarine Programs in the FY97 Budget
SSBN Security
Battle Stations 2000
Purple Submarines
Dominate the Battlespace
U.S. Navy Torpedoes-Part
Submarine Radio Communications 1900-1945
The New Jersey Naval and Maritime Museum
Buildings Honor Submariners-Part II
Battlegroup Employment of submarines
Yesterday's Silent heroes-Gone But Never Forgotten
When the Captain Found His Marbles
Book Review: Turning Point: The Solomon's Campaign of
    1942-1943
Book Review: The Japanese Submarine Force and World War II

July 1996

Requirements and the R&D Process
COMSUBLANT at the Annual SubLeague Symposium (speech)
Submarine Birthday Wreath Laying Ceremony
White Paper on the New Attack Submarine
Submarine Technology Assessment Panel

October 1996

July 1997

October 1997

On Decommissioning Cavalla
The Submarine Industrial Base Council
Start III: Do we Need Bangor?
The Submarine Message
Management by Inspection
Midgets and the Monster (1943)
U.S. Navy Torpedoes, Part Six
The Trouble with Torpedoes
Akula Russian Nuclear Attack Submarines
Guarding the Decibels
Aging Russian Nuclear Submarine
Sun Tzu and the Art of Submarine Warfare
Estimating Angle on the Bow
Proposal for U-Boat Base in British Honduras
U.S. Should Shift to Two-Crew SSNs Now
Should Navy Plan Blue and Gold NSSNs
Mooring ALPHA-End of the Line
1945 Impressions of Dropping A-Bomb
Submarine, Shipmate, Self
History of Charleston Naval Shipyard

January 1998

Tactics and Training: Keys to Command and Control and
    Solutions to Radio Communications
Restrictions
Long Range Procurement Rate
Defense Panel and Trident SSGN
NSL Awards and Grants Programs
Synthetic XBTs from Satellites
U.S. Navy Torpedoes, Part Seven
Little Guys, Lotta Guts: X and XE Midget craft
John P. Holland: Mechanical Genius
Alfa Class-The 1960's Dream machine

What is TLAM/N and Why Do We Need It?
Removal of Nuclear Strike from SSNs
Post Cold War Role of Nuclear SLCMs
Remembering VADM Charles Lockwood
A Little Known Atomic Bomb Test
Reunion for Crevalle's Women and Children
Book Review: Quarterdeck and Bridge
Book Review: Securing Command of the Sea
Book Review: War Patrols of the Flasher
Book Review: Shooting the War
Book Review: The Winning Edge

April 1998

2000-The Submarine Centennial
Nuclear Submarine Disposal and Recycling
NY Harbor to Submarine as Dayton to Airplane
Persian Gulf and Fulminate Marine Corrosion
The Sprint of Human Bombs
A Power Electronic Revolution
Turbulent Tubby Linton
Loss of Grunion Possibly Explained
U.S. Navy Torpedoes Part Eight
In Support of Two-Crew SSNs
Developing Real Anti-Diesel Tactics
Whatever Became of the Third Officer?
Submerge Backing Down
Some Data Points for the Millennium
Talk at NROTC Commissioning Ceremony
Book Review: U-Boat Far From Home
Book Review: Wolf U-Boat Commanders in WWII
Book Review: The Unsinkable Fleet
Book Review: Kangaroo Express

July 1998

October 1998

July 1999

April 2000

Saga of Pampanito
Back to Our Roots
The Enemy Below..the Brass Above
Save the Subs From DACOWITS Designs
Not in Our Submarines
Memorial Day Address
Book Review: Hellions of the Deep
Book Review: Seapower and Space

January 2001

Presidential Proclamation
Dedication of Centennial Memorial
Address to NDIA Clambake by VADM Grossenbacher
Submarine Force Multipliers
The Operator is Part of the System
WWII: Japan's Disinterest in Merchant Ship Convoying
A New Kind of Target Motion Analysis
A Little Dolphin History
Further Downsizing RDT&E
First Disaster
NAVINT News
Improving Sub Warfighting Endurance
The Dolphin Scholarship Foundation
USS Rasher
NSL Awards Program Reviewed
More About Hitler's U-Boats
Richard Knowles Morris
Capt Donald Keach
Getting Out...I'm from Philadelphia
WWII Sub Vets Memorial Service
An Ode to Lum
Book Review: Under Ice

April 2001

Remarks to Corporate Benefactors: Force Level
A Fleet to Fight in the Littorals
Acting SecNav's Address to Corporate Benefactors
Future Security Environment 2001-2025-Part 1
The Coming Threat
Retaining the Submarine JO
A Perspective on Sub Officer Retention
Don't Forget the Arctic
Dick Laning and Seawolf
NAVINT News
Sub-Par Sub-Pay
Gangway-The Electric Revolution is Coming!
New Submarine Survival Gear
Bowfin Submarine Museum and Park
Keeping the Legacy Alive
Submarines, Seagulls, and Sea Lions
Book Review: Subs Against the Rising Sun
Book Review: Big Red

July 2001

Remarks at Annual Symposium
A Pacific Update
Future Security Environment 2001-2005-Part II
Acquiescence is Agreement
Arabian Gulf as Model for Littoral USW
Darter and Dace at Leyte Gulf
Sinusoid of the Arms Race and American Strategy
U-2513 Remembered
Missing and In Action
Fast Attack Dilemma
NAVINT News
Submarine Reserve Status Report
A Submarine Internet Site

Deterrent Park Honors All Who Served—Buy a Brick!
A Dependents Cruise—On a Floating Dry Dock?
One Submariner's Sea Stories-Part 1

Appendix III

All Hands-April 2000-by USN-Submarine Centennial Issue-48page magazine-Entirely Submarine. Other monthly issues periodically contain submarine related stories-viewable on line at: http://www.chinfo.navy.mil/navpalib/allhands/ah-top.html including last 4 years archives

American Submariner-by U.S. Submarine Veterans Inc/USSVI-Quarterly Journal of the Subvets group-Since 1966

Annapolis-U.S. Naval Academy-Nimitz Museum-Thomas Paine Special Collection of Submarine Books-Some 3000+items

Articles, Essays, Profiles and Scholarly Papers-Clay Blair has listed some 6 pages of items he used in researching for his book: Hitler's U-Boat war

Ballistic Missile Defense Public Statements-by Dept of Defense-http://www.acq.osd.mil/bmdo/bmdolink/html/statements.html

Bibliographies-

Albion, Robert G. **Naval & Maritime History: An Annotated Bibliography. 4th ed.** Mystic, CT: Munson Institute of American Maritime History, 1972. 370 pp.

Allard, Dean C., Martha Crawley, and Mary Edmison. **U.S. Naval History Sources in the United States.** Washington: Naval History Division, 1979. 235 pp.

Anderson, Frank J. **Submarines, Diving, and the Underwater World: A Bibliography.** Hamden Conn.: Archon Books, 1975. 238 pp.

Published in 1963 by Shoestring under the title **Submarines, Submariners, Submarining: A Checklist of Submarine Books in the English Language, Principally of the Twentieth Century.**

Bayliss, Gwyn M. **Bibliographic Guide to the Two World Wars: An Annotated Survey of English-Language Reference Materials.** New York: Bowker, 1977. 578 pp.

Beers, Henry P. **Guide to the Archives of the Government of the Confederate States of America.** Washington: GPO, 1968. 536 pp.

Coletta, Paolo E. **A Selected and Annotated Bibliography of American Naval History.** Lanham, Md.: University Press of America, 1988. 523 pp.

Ellinger, Werner B., and Herbert Rosinski. **Sea Power in the Pacific, 1936-1941: A Selected Bibliography** ...Princeton, N.J.: Princeton Univ. Press, 1942. 80 pp.

Foreign Affairs Bibliography: A Selected and Annotated List of Books on International Relations, 1919/1932-. New York: Council on Foreign Relations, 1933-.

Bibliographies and Indexes in American History, No. 2. Westport, Conn.: Greenwood, 1985. 399 pp.
Harbeck, Charles T., comp. *A Contribution to the Bibliography of the History of the United States Navy.* Cambridge, Mass.: Riverside Press, 1906. 247 pp. (Reprinted 1970 by B. Franklin).

Higham, Robin, ed. *A Guide to the Sources of United States Military History*. Hamden, Conn.: Archon Books, 1975. 559 pp.

———. *Supplement I*. 1975. 300 pp.

———. *Supplement II*. 1986. 332 pp.

———. *Official Histories: Essays and Bibliographies From Around the World*. Manhattan, Kans.: Kansas State Univ. Library, 1970. 644 pp.

Official historical sections of the governments of the world are described and their more important publications listed.

Labaree, Benjamin W. *A Supplement (1971-1986) to Robert G. Albion's Naval and Maritime History: An Annotated Bibliography*. 4th ed. Mystic, Conn.: Mystic Seaport Museum, 1988. 232 pp.

Lewis, Charles L. *Books of the Sea: An Introduction to Nautical Literature*. Annapolis: U.S. Naval Institute, 1943. 318 pp. (Reprinted 1972 by Greenwood).

Lincoln, Charles H. "Material in the Library of Congress for a Study of United States Naval History." In Bibliographical Society of America. *Proceedings and Papers*. Vol. 1, pt. 1 (1904-1905): 84-95.

Mariners' Museum, Newport News, Virginia. *Dictionary Catalog of the Library*. Boston: G. K. Hall, 1964. 9 vols.

Merrill, James M. "Successors of Mahan: A Survey of Writings on American Naval History, 1914-1960." *Mississippi Valley Historical Review* 50 (June 1963): 79-99.

Millett, Allan R., and B. Franklin Cooling, comps. *Doctoral Dissertations in Military Affairs: A Bibliography.* Kansas State Univ. Library, Bibliography Series, No. 10. Manhattan, Kans.: Kansas State Univ. Library, 1972. 153 pp. (Reprinted 1973).

Morton, Louis. *Writings on World War II.* Washington: Service Center for Teachers of History, 1967. 54 pp.

National Research Council. Committee on Undersea Warfare. *An Annotated Bibliography of Submarine Technical Literature, 1557 to 1953.* Washington: 1954. 261 pp.

The National Union Catalog of Manuscript Collections. Various publishers, 1959/61-.

Neeser, Robert W. *Statistical and Chronological History of the United States Navy, 1775-1907.* New York: Macmillan, 1909. 2 vols. (Reprinted 1971 by B. Franklin).

New York. Public Library. *A Selected List of Works in the Library Relating to Nautical and Naval Art and Science, Navigation and Steamship, Shipbuilding, etc.* New York: 1907. 151 pp.

A Selected List of Works in the Library Relating to Naval History, Naval Administration, etc. New York: 1904. 145 pp.-*Submarines: A List of References in the New York Public Library.* Compiled by Mary E. Jameson, New York: 1918. 97 pp.

Notable Naval Books: The First 100 Years, 1873-1973." U.S. Naval Institute *Proceedings* 99 (October 1973): 151-158.

Paine, Thomas O., assisted by Frederic C. M. Paroutaud. *Submarine Registry and Bibliography*. Santa Monica, Calif.: Submarine Warfare Library, 1992. 828 pp.-A submarine registry listing approximately eight thousand boats of fifty nations with an annotated bibliography cataloging six thousand books and articles on submarines.

Patterson, Andrew, and Robert A. Winters, eds. *Historical Bibliography of Sea Mine Warfare*. Prepared by the Naval Studies Board for the Mine Advisory Committee, National Research Council. Washington: National Academy of Sciences, 1977. 137 pp.

Schultz, Charles R., comp. *Bibliography of Maritime and Naval History: Periodical Articles Published 1978-1979, With Cumulative Indexes for 1970-1979*. College Station, Tex.: Texas A&M Univ., 1982. 238 pp.

Smith, Myron J.-
———. *The American Navy, 1865-1918: A Bibliography*. American Naval Bibliography, Vol. 4. Metuchen, N.J.: Scarecrow, 1974. 372 pp

———. *The American Navy, 1918-1941: A Bibliography*. American Naval Bibliography, Vol. 5. Metuchen, N.J.: Scarecrow, 1974. 429 pp.

———. *Pearl Harbor, 1941: A Bibliography*. New York: Greenwood, 1991. 197 pp.

———. *The United States Navy and Coast Guard, 1946-1983: A Bibliography of English-Language Works and 16mm Films.* Jefferson, N.C.: McFarland, 1984. 539 pp.

———. *World War II at Sea: A Bibliography of Sources in English.* 3 vols. Metuchen, N.J.: Scarecrow, 1976. Vol. 1, *The European Theater;* Vol. 2, *The Pacific Theater;* Vol. 3, Part 1, *General Works, Naval Hardware and the All Hands Chronology;* Part 2, *Home Fronts and Special Studies.*

———. *World War II at Sea: A Bibliography of Sources in English, 1974-1989.* Metuchen, N.J.: Scarecrow, 1990. 304 pp.

———. *World War II, The European and Mediterranean Theaters: An Annotated Bibliography.* New York: Garland Pub., 1984. 450 pp.

Smith, Stanley H., comp. *Investigations of the Attack on Pearl Harbor: Index to Government Hearings.* New York: Greenwood, 1990. 250 pp.

U.S. National Historical Publications Commission. *A Guide to Archives and Manuscripts in the United States.* Edited by Philip M. Hamer. New Haven: Yale Univ. Press, 1961. 775 pp.

Writings *on American History.* Various publishers. 1902- An annual bibliography of books and periodical articles, including many titles on naval history. Since 1909 issued as a supplement to, or volume of, the *Annual Report* of the American Historical Assn. Published since 1950 by the U.S. National Historical Publications Commission. Not issued for the years 1904-05, 1941-47.

Britain Primary Sources (ADM=Admiralty)
> ADM1General RN Subject Files
> ADM 199Naval Historian's Files
> ADM 205First Sea Lord's Files
> ADM 217Western Approaches Command Files
> ADM 219Director, Naval Operational Studies Files
> ADM 239Technical Staff Monographs
> PREM 3Prime Minister's Papers
> PREM 4Prime Minister's Papers
> Churchill College, Cambridge-Captain SW Roskill Papers, Command HJ Fawcett Papers,
> Cunninghan of Hyndhope Papers, Sir Charles Goodeve Papers
> Imperial War Museum, London-GV Ball Papers, PGL Cazalat Papers, EH Chavasse Memoir,
> S. France Memoir, WJ Moore Papers, J. Moose Papers
> British Museum-London-AB Cunningham Papers
> Naval Historical Branch, London-Convoy and Anti-Submarine Warfare Reports, Annual

Electric Boat Technical Library and Records Vault, Groton, CT
> History of the Electric Boat Company
> Drawing Books
> Pattern Books
> Electrical Sketches
> Hull Plan Lists

Hagley Museum Archives, Wilmington, DE
> Elmer Sperry Papers
> Sperry Company Records

Janes Defense Weekly (World)

Janes Intelligence Review

Janes International Defense Review

Joint Force Quarterly (JFQ) Published quarterly by the Institute for National Strategic Studies for the Chairman of the Joint Chiefs of Staff

National Archives-Washington DC

 Record Group 19:

  General Correspondence of the Bureau of Steam
   Engineering 1911-1922

  Confidential Correspondence Regarding Research and
   Design of Radio and Other

  Communications Apparatus

  General Correspondence of the Bureau of Construction
   and Repair 1925-1940

  BurC&R-Correspondence Regarding Ships, 1916-1925

  BurC&R-Repair and Design Data for U.S. Naval
   Vessels, 1914-1927

  BurC&R-BurC&R Research Data 1913-1937

  Board on Submarine Claims 1918-1922

 Record Group 24: Personnel Records

 Record Group 38:

  Board of Inspection and Survey

 Record Group 45

  General Board Subject Files 1900-1947

 Record Group 80:

  SecNav Correspondence 1916-1926 & 1926-1940

  Compensation Board

  Records of SecNav Forrestal, 1940-1947

  Asst. SecNavy Alpha File

  Naval Consulting Board Correspondence Files, 1915-
   1923

  SecNav Confidential Correspondence 1927-1939

 Record Group 298:

  Office of Naval Research-General Correspondence of
   the Coordinator of R&D

Naval Historical Center, Operational Archives, Washington D.C.

 Bemis, Samuel Flagg-Submarine Warfare in the Strategy of
  American Defense and

 Diplomacy, 1915-1945

Biographical Files of Naval Officers
Documents on the Navy's Role in the Development of Atomic
     Energy, 1939-1970
Defense Technical Information Center Reports
Hearings of the General Board of the Navy (Microfilm)
Oral Histories:
     Arnold, Capt Henry
     Bethea, Capt James
     Hersey, John Brackett
     Horan, Frank
     Jackson, Harry
     Kern, Capt Donald
     Land, Emory
     Leonard, John S
     Leonard, John V
     Moore, RADM Robert L
     Mumma, RADM Albert
     Nardone, Henry
     Raborn, VADM William F
     Roseborough, Capt William
     Schevill, William
     Shugg, Carleton
     Smith, Capt Ralph
     Vine, Allyn
     Worzel, J. Lamar
Post 1 January 1946 Command File
Records of the Immediate Office of the Chief of Naval Operations
Strategic Planning Division Records
Submarines-Undersea Warfare Division Records
World War II Command File

Naval History by U.S. Naval Institute-by USNIP-This is a monthly magazine. In addition, many of the issues have been hardbound in book form. Some submarine articles of note appear in: Winter 1990-The Far East Odyssey of the UIT-24 (former U-511)

Summer 1990-Unseen Persuaders by RADM Broks Harral
Summer 1990-Buffalo's Home to USS Croaker
Spring 1990-Submariner in a Carrier
Winter 1991-Japanese Thunderfish: Torpedoes used at Pearl
    Harbor
Fall 1991-Forgotten Tragedy: The Loss of the USS O-9
Spring 1991-Nautilus's Permanent Home
Spring 1992-Passing Rickover's Muster
Spring 1992-The Seawolf's Sodium-Cooled Power Plant
Summer 1992-The Seawolf: Going to Sea
Fall 1992-Commanding Officer Breaking Down (WWII subma-
    rine skippers)
Winter 1992-The Mk-XIV Torpedo
Spring 1993-Young Warriors by Adm Yogi Kaufman
Spring 1993-Museum Report: USS Silversides
Summer 1993-Stand By For a Ram-Part 1 DD vs a U-boat
Summer 1993-A photographer catches the day at Electric Boat
Summer 1993-Museum Report-Baltimore's Fleet-Home to the
    USS Torsk
October 1993-Stand By For a Ram-Part 2
February 1994-Sonobuoy in WWII
August 1994-We Never Looked Back-The Tang in WWII
December 1994-Project 617: The Soviet "Whale"
August 1995-One Night of Hell: Japanese submariners torture
    survivors of the Liberty ship: Jean Nicolet
December 1995-We Got the Sonafabitch-The I-52 and it's gold
December 1995-A "Skate" shoot
December 1995-A Matter of Class by Morison, Samuel-A brief
    history and derivation of submarine
**Naval Studies Board Archive-National Academy of Sciences,
Washington, D.C.**
Basic Problems of Underwater Acountics Research
A Research Facility for Undersea Warfare

Subsurface Warfare: The History of Division 6, National
Defense Research Committee
New Concepts for Acoustic Detection at Very Long Ranges
Interim Report of the Panel on the Hydrodynamics of Submerged
Bodies, Committee on
Undersea Warfare
The Present Status of Long-Range Listening
Project Nobska: A Preliminary Assessment
Meeting of the Committee on the Hydrodynamics of Submerged
Bodies
Memo, Special Panel on Low Frequency Sonar
History and Activities of the Committee on Undersea Warfare,
1946-1956
A Survey of the Naval Reactor Program
Detection of the Submarines From the Surface and Below
Report of the Subcommittee on the Submarine Problem-
Colpitts Report
VADM Rickover's Presentation of 24 March 1960 on Naval
Reactors

Naval Submarine League Library-Annadale, VA
Naval Undersea Museum-Keyport, Washington-Large Research
library
Navy Laboratory Archives, David Taylor Research Center
EMB/DTMB 1899-1967 Personnel Subject files
Marvin Lasky Papers
Naval Weapons Center Oral History Collection
Naval Laboratories Biography Collection
Oral Histories:
Cummins, William E
Kelly, Capt Joseph P
Landweber, Ljouois
Lasky, Marvin
Records of Asst. SecNav James H. Probus

Records of Engineering Experiment Station, 1903-63 and Marine Engineering Lab, 1963-67

Navy News Service- http://www.chinfo.navy.mil/navpalib/news/navnews/.www/navnews.html

Navy Times Newspaper/Weekly

New London Day

Plastic Ship Modeler Magazine-Quarterly magazine for ship modelers. Mostly targets

Polaris-by US Submarine Veterans of WWII/SVWWII-Not a book but a journal/magazine continuously published for 45 years with many first person articles of WWII

Portsmouth Naval Museum-Portsmouth, NH

Sea Classics Magazine-by Challenge Publications-Monthly-Periodic submarine articles. Jan 2000, for example had articles on Karl Donitz and another on USS Tunny and early adventures with the Regulus missile

Sea Power-Journal/Magazine of the Navy League and in particular July Issues which are largely devoted to submarines.

Seizing the Enigma-by Kahn, David-ISBN 0760708630-This book has a bibliography of many sources of code breaking in WWII. There are 15 pages of references to many books of this part of the War.

St. Mary's Submarine Museum-St. Marys, Georgia-2nd Floor Library collection

SubCommittee-by Subcommittee-The premier R/C modeler magazine for Submarine Radio Control enthusiasts-Published quarterly-Contains actual photos of submarines and some actual history

Submarine Disarmament: 1919-1936-by Douglas, Lawrence-PH D Disser, Syracuse U

Submarine Force Museum and Library
Holland Collection
Electric Boat Collection (Individual Submarine Historical Files)

Submarine Museum-by Bastura, Ben-Private museum located in Middletown, Ct. Huge file collection on each submarine

Unpublished Resources-Clay Blair Jr has a list of sources of unpublished works at the Naval Historical Center at the Washington Navy Yard and later transferred to the ·NARA (Nat. Archives and Records Administration at College Park, MD. Many sources are detailed in his book Hitler's U-Boat War 1942-1945 on pp 823-830. Many U-Boat War Diaries are also here. Many more sources on Naval Intelligence, British sources, and various departments of the Navy at listed on pages 831-844 of the book above.

U.S. Navy History 1775-2001 Bibliography-
http://www.history.navy.mil/biblio/biblio1/biblio1.htm

U.S. Navy Operational Archives, Naval Historical Center, Washington D.C.
Hearings of the General Board of the Navy (Microfilm)
Strategic Plans Division Records
Submarines-Undersea Warfare Division Records

U.S. Navy Strategic Special Projects Office Technical Library/ Archives, Arlington, VA
Brief History of Navy Solid Propellant Fuel Experience
Fleet Ballistic Missile System: Polaris to Trident
An Historical Review of the Polaris Fleet Ballistic Missile Program
Record of visit to Lockheed Missile Systems Division, Sunnyvale and Sacramento
Records of the Special Projects Office Steering Task Group
Study of Navy-Contractor Relationships

U.S. Navy Websites-All reachable via www.navy.mil on the Internet and were current as of July 2001. This site contains links to over 500 Official Naval Web Sites URL: www.navy.mil

USSVI National Website-The SubVets National Website containing much information about the organization. Of note on this page is a huge listing of Memorials built across the country to memorialize submarines and a Building & Structures naming database. URL: ussvi.org

Washington National Records Center, Suitland, MD
Record Group 19:
BuShips General Correspondence, 1940-1945
BuEng General Correspondence, 1910-1940

Appendix IV

Ships' Deck Logs; Research and Copying

In Navy language, any kind of running record is called a "log." Many such logs are kept on board Navy ships. Most of these are not kept permanently. **Deck logs from commissioned ships are the only logs sent to the Naval Historical Center to be kept as permanent records** and, eventually, transferred to the National Archives.

> *Deck Logs: Ships that submit*
> *Deck Logs: Purpose, and Content*
> *Deck Logs: Location*
> *Deck Logs: Format, Research and Duplication*
> *What information is not found in deck logs*
> *Deck Logs of MSC/MSTS ships*
> *Merchant Ship logs*

Deck Logs: Ships that submit

Only deck logs from commissioned Navy ships are permanently retained by the Naval Historical Center and the National Archives. A ship "in commission" is a Navy command in her own right; she has her own administrative identity, and originates records in her own name. Annual command histories, written under a program initiated by the Chief of Naval Operations in 1952, are included in the active records of the Naval Historical Center. Deck logs are also held by the Ships History Branch of the Naval Historical Center. After 30 years, Ships History Branch transfers the deck logs to the Modern Military

Branch, National Archives and Records Administration, 8601 Adelphi Road, College Park, MD 20740-6001 [telephone (301) 713-7250].

Nearly all service craft are classified as "in service," rather than "in commission." They do not have their own administrative identity but are, in effect, floating vehicles operated by a parent command. Self-propelled service craft apparently keep a log of their movements for their parent command's administrative and legal purposes, but these are not sent to the Naval Historical Center and do not go into any permanent file.

Deck Logs: Purpose, and Content

A Navy ship's deck log is a daily chronology of certain events for administrative and legal purposes. Preparation of logs is governed by the current edition of Office of the Chief of Naval Operations Instruction 3100.7 (OPNAVINST 3100.7) series. This specifies the kinds of events to be entered:

- Absentees
- Accidents [material]
- Accidents/Injuries [personnel]
- Actions [combat]
- Appearances of Sea/Atmosphere/Unusual Objects
- Arrests/Suspensions
- Arrival/Departure of Commanding Officer
- Bearings [navigational]
- Cable/Anchor Chain Strain
- Collisions/Groundings
- Courts-Martial/Captain's Masts
- Deaths
- Honors/Ceremonies/Visits
- Incidents at Sea
- Inspections
- Meteorological Phenomena
- Movement Orders
- Movements [getting underway; course, speed changes; mooring, anchoring]

- Passengers
- Prisoners [crew members captured by hostile forces]
- Propulsion Plant Status changes
- Receipts and Transfers [of Crew Members]
- Ship's Behavior [under different weather/sea conditions]
- Sightings [other ships; landfall; dangers to navigation]
- Soundings [depth of water]
- Speed Changes
- Tactical Formation
- Time of Evolutions/Exercises/Other Services Performed

A deck log identifies a ship's location and movements daily. If the ship is underway, its latitude and longitude are to be entered three times each day in blocks provided for the purpose. Deck logs are not narratives, and do not describe or explain a ship's operations.

Deck Logs: Location

Held by The National Archives
Deck logs of commissioned U.S. Navy ships from **the earliest times through 1940** are in the Old Military and Civil Branch, National Archives and Records Administration, 700 Pennsylvania Avenue NW, Washington DC 20408 [telephone (202) 501-5385. **Logs from 1941 through 1969** are in the Modern Military Branch, National Archives, 8601 Adelphi Road, College Park MD 20740-6001 [telephone (301) 713-7250]. These logs are open for research. Requests for research appointments, and inquiries concerning log information, should go to the National Archives office holding logs from the time period of interest.
Held By The Naval Historical Center
Deck logs from 1970 to the present are in the custody of the Ships Deck Logs Section, Naval Historical Center, Building 57, 805 Kidder Breese Street SE, Washington Navy Yard, DC 20374-5060. All inquiries concerning research access to logs from 1968 and later years should be sent to the Ships Deck Logs Section.

Logs from 1970 through 1978 are held in paper form, stored in the Washington National Records Center, 4205 Suitland Road, Suitland MD 20746. Logs from 1979 through 1989 are on microfiche in the Ships Deck Logs Section. Logs from 1990 through 1993 are partly on microfiche in the Deck Logs Section, partly on paper at the Records Center. All logs from 1994 on are being retained on paper and stored at the Records Center. The logs that are classified must be sent to the proper authorities for declassification review before they can be researched or copied.

Deck Log: Format, Research and Duplication

Format: Deck logs are bulky documents. Into the 1980s logs were kept on oversized (10 by 15 inches) paper, a typical log consisting of two or more pages per day. In the 1980s, in keeping with a Congressional mandate to standardize on 8½ by 11 inch paper, deck logs began to be written, by hand, on pages of that size. This greatly increased the page count; we have seen single months' logs from recent years run to as many as 300 or 400 pages.

Under the old format, a ship's deck log might run 60 pages or more per month, or over 700 pages per year. (There are the inevitable exceptions, but this seems to hold fairly true.) Under the new format, logs can run from 100 to 400 pages per month or, say, from 1,200 to several thousand pages per year.

Research in Deck Logs at the Ships History Branch

The Ships Deck Logs Section staff consists of two persons. Given the number of inquiries received, the staff cannot read hundreds of pages in response to any one inquiry. Thus the Ships Deck Logs Section is unable to do extensive research in response to queries. Questions must be specific, and must be narrowed down to a particular time and/or place.

If a requestor wishes to search a log, this can be done at the Naval Historical Center (microfiched logs) or at the Washington National Records Center (paper logs). To arrange this, write to the Ships Deck Logs Section, at the address given above, at least two weeks in advance. Specify the ship(s) and time periods (month/year to month/year) involved and the date of the proposed visit.

Duplication of Deck Logs

Researchers using logs at the National Archives, or at the Washington National Records Center, can arrange to have pages copied there at the time they do their research.

The Naval Historical Center has no in-house capacity to do extensive copying. Small numbers of microfiche can be duplicated, and limited numbers of paper log pages can be copied on an office copier which is also used for other work.

Orders for production copying are sent to the Defense Automated Printing Service (DAPS). DAPS is a Defense Business Operating Fund activity under 10 USC 2208. It is not budgeted, but must pay its own way by recovering the cost of all work it does. Thus, any order for copying sent to DAPS must be paid for in advance. The Naval Historical Center has no funds to do this; for this reason, requestors must cover the cost of copying. The Ships History Branch will provide price quotes upon request.

Deck Logs: What information is not a deck log

Shipyard Work; Individual Work Assignments; Events Occurring Elsewhere

When a ship is being overhauled at a shipyard, the deck log records the ship's presence at the shipyard, but does not identify the work being done or the materials being used. These logs do not record day-to-day work assignments of individual crew members. A deck log records events taking place on board the individual ship or, if pertinent, in its immediate vicinity. It does not include events taking place elsewhere, such as the activities of crew members on detached duty.

Deaths and Injuries

In cases of deaths and injuries suffered on board ship, the log should record the simple fact of the death or injury and note whether medical treatment was given to the injured. It does not go into detail as to specific treatment given, and does not record other medical matters, such as visits to sick bay or injuries not suffered on board ship.

Medical Records

The Naval Historical Center does not receive medical records of any kind. *Individual medical records, as well as any existing medical logs from Navy ships,* are sent to the National Personnel Records Center (Military Personnel Records), 9700 Page Avenue, St. Louis MO 63132-5100. Under the records disposal schedule established by the Secretary of the Navy, in consultation with the National Archives, binnacle lists and morning reports of sick are not permanent records. They are kept until the information in them has been transcribed into the medical records of the persons involved, and are then disposed of.

Deck logs are not "Captain's Logs"

A deck log is not a daily diary written by the ship's captain. The "captain's log" was a dramatic device used by the creators of the television series *Star Trek* to introduce each episode, and does not exist in the U.S. Navy.

Deck Logs: MSTS/MSC Ships

Navy-owned ships operated by the Military Sealift Command (MSC), formerly the Military Sea Transportation Service (MSTS), are classified as "in service," manned by civilian crews. Inquiries concerning Military Sealift Command ships' logs should be sent to Commander (M0021), Military Sealift Command, Washington Navy Yard Building 210, 805 KIDDER BREESE SE, Washington, DC 20398-5540.

The identifying hull name of Military Sealift Command ships are prefixed by "T" followed by a hyphen and then the number. For example, the commissioned oiler USS *Platte* is identified as (AO 186), while the MSC-operated oiler *Pecos* is identified as (T-AO 197)

Merchant Ship Logs

There is no central repository for deck logs from merchant ships. Deck logs were traditionally considered to be the property of the ship owners to be held or disposed of according to their own record keeping prac-tices. After World War II, the deck and engineering logbooks of vessels operated by the War Shipping Administration were turned over to that agency by the ship owners, and were later destroyed, by the Maritime Administration, in the 1970s on the grounds that they were volumi-nous, costly to house and service, and very seldom used for research..

The National Archives has custody of the Official Logbooks, which were issued to American registered merchant vessels at the beginning of each voyage, and were turned in to the United States Commissioner at the port where each vessel ended its voyage. In these logbooks, mas-ters were required to keep information related to the health and welfare of crew members. These logbooks are not records of ships' operations, but are essentially records of personnel matters, collisions, emergency drills, and information on ships' watertight integrity. The Official Logbooks from U.S.-registered merchant ships are held by the Regional Archives of the National Archives closest to the U. S. port where each voyage ended. This port can be determined from the movement report cards which are part of the Tenth Fleet collection held by the Modern Military Branch, National Archives and Records Administration, 8601 Adelphi Road, College Park, MD 20740-6001. The movement report cards list the ports of call, the dates of arrival and departure, and the convoy designation, if the ship sailed in a convoy.

The Tenth Fleet records also contain the loss and damage reports for merchant ships, and folders about the individual convoys. Several other collections held by the Textual Reference Branch of the National Archives at College Park that are very useful for understanding mer-chant ship movement and operations are the Naval Armed Guard reports from each voyage and the Bureau of Naval Personnel's Naval Armed Guard Casualty reports. For the period of World War II, Naval Armed Guard detachments were assigned to U.S.-flag merchant ships, Army transports, and even some foreign-flag merchantmen.

Appendis V

FOIA

This page contains a repository of information to help FOIA officials process FOIA requests. *Information is available* on the different file formats used below.

The below are all links at the Freedom of Information Act page at: http://foia.navy.mil/resources.html

- *DoD Directive 5100.3, Support of the Headquarters of Combatant and Subordinate Joint Commands*
- *DoD Directive 5400.7-R, Sep 98*
- *DoD 5400.7-R, Department of Defense Freedom of Information Act Program*
- *DoD Freedom of Information Act Handbook*

FOIA HANDBOOK

Use this online FOIA HANDBOOK to find out how and where to make a request or file an appeal. It also identifies documents that already exist in the public domain; provides a *List of Commonly Requested Records*; and includes two publications: *A Citizen's Guide to the FOIA* and *Your Right to Federal Records*.

- *How to Make a FOIA Request*
- *Where to Send a FOIA Request*
- *Where and How to File a FOIA Appeal*
- *List of Commonly Requested Records*

- *A Citizen's Guide to the FOIA*
- *Your Right to Federal Records*
- *DoD Major Information Systems*
- *DOJ FOIA Guide*
- *Federal Acquisition Regulation Website*
- *FOIA Exemption (b)(3) Statutes List*
- *DoD Freedom of Information Act Briefing*
- *DoD Freedom of Information Act Program*
- *DoJ's Freedom of Information Act Guide & Privacy Act Overview*
- *Executive Order 12958, Classified National Security Information*
- *SECNAVINST 5211.5D, Department of the Navy Privacy Act (PA) Program*
- *SECNAVINST 5720.42F, Department of the Navy Freedom of Information Act (FOIA) Program*

This website is provided as a public service of the Department of the Navy's Office of the General Counsel in cooperation with the *SECNAV/CNO Freedom of Information Act Office.*

Appendix VI

The following is a partial list of articles published in the hard copy of PATROL. This was a magazine published by the staff at COMSUBPAC

April/May 1997

Maintaining the Force of the Future by RADM Jerry Ellis

Identifying the Problem Is the First Step in Correcting It by Force Master Chief Smutny

Birmingham Retires After 19 Years

Hospital Corps Force Master Chief Visits Independent Duty Corpsmen

Maintenance Aboard the Navy's First Submarine

Life Aboard USS Holland

Why is Maintenance So Hard?

Team Maintenance Maximizes Resources

'Dolphin Unique' Requires Unique Teamwork: AGSS 555

Forward Deployed Tender Provides Quality Maintenance to the Entire Seventh Fleet: USS Frank Cable

'Tough Old Girl' Fights to the End: USS Canopus

USS McKee Divers Exhibit "Excellence Under Pressure With Emergent Repairs

Regional Maintenance Will Carry Submarine Force Into the Future

Trident Refit Facility (TRF) PC Shop Boosts Productivity by 3000%

TRIEFFAC Enhances Fleet Operations

TRF Puts Progressive Repair to Work
Senate Bill No. S-652
Subase Pearl Harbor: 'It's Slightly Different Now'
Maintenance in the 21st Century
Intermediate Level Maintenance Now And in the Future
Indianapolis Visits Namesake by Video Teleconferencing
Indianapolis and SUBASE Pearl Harbor Boast Navy's Best Galleys
COMSUBPAC Selects 1997 Sea and Shore Sailors of the Year
1939 Article: USS Beaver Sails for Mainland

June/July 1997

People: Our Most Valuable Resource by RADM Jerry Ellis
Career Decisions Don't Come Easy by Force Master Chief Smutny
CNO Releases: Forward From the Sea 97 by ADM Jay Johnson
Why a Submarine? Story about the USS Alabama
There is Light At the End of the Tunnel: Retention and Downsizing
Man With a Mission: A Career Information Program Manager
Making the Toughest Job in the Navy a Little Easier: Navy Wives
Gold and Silver Anchor Awards
Weighing Gold in Los Angeles and Alaska: Career Counselors
Trident Refit Facility (TRF) Strikes Silver Again
HARP Duty The Secret is Out: Hometown Area Recruiting Program
A Chance to Train Our Reliefs: Midshipmen
Making the Change From White Hat to Khaki
Retention Over the Past 56 Years
Piped Ashore...Now What?
Force Multiplier For the Submarine Force of the Future
USS Houston Sailor named Sea Sailor of the Year for PacFleet
Columbus earns MUC for Cruise
USS H.M. Jackson wins Sterret Award for Combat Readiness
Bridge to honor ADM Clarey of WWII fame

Thoughts on Leadership and Command
Gold, Silver Anchor Winners Selected
Parents Take Active Role in Homeschooling
Ten Selected for Enlisted Commissioning Programs
Fly Away Team Conducts Successful Repair
Restorations Efforts at Jim Creek Ensure Future Salmon Stocks
Naval Radio Station Jim Creed Keeps SUBPAC Personnel in Touch with Subs Underwater
Honolulu Chiefs Run Honolulu Marathon
Ohio 'Discovers' Columbus
Around the World-the Gudgeon's trip in 1957-58

Appendix VII

The Following are articles of interest in "Undersea Warfare" Magazine

Fall 1998

Forward From Under the Sea by RADM Malcom Fages
The SSBN Security Program
The SSBN Security Program "Under Wraps" No More
Voices From the Deep: The New Age of Submarine Communications
Anti-Submarine Warfare
Submarine Legend: Dick O'Kane and the USS Tang SS-306
USS Augusta Gains Contact with New Sonar System
Trident Hull and Missile Life Extensions Approved
Submarine Rescue-Past, Present and Future
Unmanned Undersea Vehicle "Underway" for Testing

Winter 1998/1999

The Virginia Class: America's Next Submarine
Defense Science Board Supports Future Attack Submarine Development
USS Boise's 1998 Deployment
Virtual Reality Under the Sea
Welcome to the Goat Locker: New CPO's
An Interview With the MCPON James L. Herdt
Combined Crews Key to Henry M. Jackson's Successful ERP
Memphis Uses Gravity to Reach New Navigational Heights

Message to Today's Submariners by RADM Eugene Fluckey (MOH)

Final World War II Battle Flag of USS Barb SS 220

USS Hawkbill SSN-666 Completes SCIEX '98

PCU Connecticut SSN-22 Completes Sea Trials

Bottom Time-Thirty Years with Turtle and Sea Cliff

USS Tucson 1998 Westpac

Submarine Hero-Eugene Fluckey MOH

Spring 1999

Submarines in the New World Order by ADM Frank Bowman

COMSUBPAC Future Ideas Initiative

Water Balloon Shoots Weapons in Future Launching Systems: Elastomeric Ejection System EES

Innovation in the submarine Force Ensuring Undersea Supremacy

Submarines: American Innovation for the American Century

Submarine Force Year in Review:Special Insert

    Attach Submarine In Carrier Battlegroup Operations

    Intelligence, surveillance, and Reconnaissance

    Allied Engagement

    Mine Warfare

    Pins and Insignia

    E Winners

    Submarine Strike

    Special Warfare

    ASDA

    Sea Control

    Strategic Deterrence

Top Enlisted Leaders Benefit from Submarine Careers

Submarine Hero-TM2 Henry Breault

USS Asheville Leads the Way in High Frequency Sonar

Undersea Partners-The Mine Countermeasures Surface Force

East Sea ADCAP Torpedo Exercise

Shipmates Bid Farewell to USS Narwhal

Summer 1999
Interview with CINCPACFLT, ADM Archie Clemins
SCICEX-99: Undersea Science at the Top of the World
Naval Oceanography-A Submarine Force Multiplier
Silent Defense 1900-1940
1999 Photo Contest Winners
NR-1
Submarine Hero-Howard Gilmore
The Submarine Force of the Royal Australian Navy
SECNAV Addresses Naval Submarine League
New Undersea Recruiting Machine: Submarine Electronics
Computer Field
SubDevGru 2 SubDevRon 12 Celebrate 50 years
USS Michigan wins Omaha Trophy
SubLant Sailors of the Year

Winter 1999
The Case for More Submarines
60 Minutes and Andy Rooney Visits the USS Miami
Submarine Skills-Training Network
Silent Victory 1940-1945
U.S. Submarine Operations in the Atlantic during WWII
Namesake Outreach Builds Relationships
The "Big Gun's" Two-Theater TLAM Tally
Submarine Centennial
Submarine Stamps
SSGN: A "Second Career" For The Boomer Force
World War II Submarine Combat Veteran Retires From Active
Duty
Submarine Hero-Lawson "Red" Ramage
The Terrible Hours: The Man Behind the Greatest Submarine
Rescue in History

Appendix VIII

Websites containing further material
Websites change addresses frequently. If any of the below are
invalid, use an Internet Search Engine to locate them

A Brief History of Communications Intelligence in the United States-by Stafford, Laurance F-
(www.ibiblio.org/pha/ultra/SRH-149.html)
Chronological History of events leading up to World 1931-1944-421 pages (www.ibiblio.org/pha/events/index.html)
DOD Dictionary-606 pages and requires Adobe reader-
http://www.dtic.mil/doctrine/jel/new_pubs/jp1_02.pdf
Electric Boat Division of General Dynamics-(www.gdeb.com)
Historic Naval Ships Association-(www.maritime.org)
Japanese Monographs-(ibiblio.org/pha/monos/)-A series of 187 studies on Japan's role in WWII, written by Japanese participants in the events at the request of the US Government
Joint Electronic Library-
http://www.dtic.mil/doctrine/jel/index.html Joint Chiefs of Staff system
Library Of Congress Historical Collections-(memory.loc.gov/)
Military Search Engine-(searchmil.com)
National Archives and Records Administration-(www.nara.gov/)
National Cryptologic Museum-(www.nsa.gov:8080/museum/)
National Defense University Library-
(www.ndu.edu/ndu/library/library.html)

National Military Strategy-
> http://www.dtic.mil/jcs/nms/index.html

Naval Museum-Washington, D.C.-
> (http://www.history.navy.mil/branches/nhcorg8.htm)

Naval Postgraduate School-(web.nps.navy.mil/%7Elibrary/)

Naval Submarine League-(www.navalsubleague.com/)

Naval Undersea Museum-(http://www-num.kpt.nuwc.navy.mil/)-
> In Keyport, Washington

Naval War College Library-
> (www.nwc.navy.mil/library/default.htm)

Navy Department Communiqués and Press Releases Dec 10, 41 to
> May 45-(www.ibiblio.org/pha/comms/index.html)-630 pages

Navy Times-(www.onr.navy.mil/onr/pubs.htm)

New London Day-Daily newspaper-(www.newlondonday.com)

Newport News and Shipbuilding Co-(www.nns.com)

Nimitz Library at Annapolis-(www.nadn.navy.mil/Library/)

Nuclear Regulatory Commission Reference Library-
> (www.nrc.gov/NRC/reference.html)

Office of Naval Research On-Line Journal-
> (www.onr.navy.mil/onr/pubs.htm)

Pearl Harbor Attack Hearings-
> (www.ibiblio.org/pha/pha/index.html)

Prints & Photographs at the Library of Congress-
> (www.loc.gov/rr/print/)

Submarine Fleet-by Martini, Ron-Over 450 Boat pages written by
> individuals and the U.S. Navy in some cases of the later boats.
> In addition there are 100 pages that are classed as 'home' pages
> to individuals about submarines
> (wavecom.net/~rontini/fleet.html)

Submarine Fleet-by Harrison, Sid-Named the "Green Board". And
> some other links as well

Submarine History-by Harrison, Sid-One of the best overall collec-
> tions of submarines history on the net (http://www.uncle-
> sam.net/cny/history/hist-sub.htm)

Submarine World Network-by Martini, Ron-The author of this book's
Web site containing over 2000 links to submarine related mate-
rial-(wavecom.net/~rontini)

SubNet-by Don Merrigan-A very large source. He maintains a Fleet
page with information/picture and stats on a large % of the
U.S. Submarines every built (www.subnet.com)

Time Line of WWII-by U. of San Diego-
(history.acusd.edu/gen/WW2Timeline/1917-45.html)

Treaties, Declarations, Instruments of Surrender, etc.-
(www.ibiblio.org/pha/policy/index.html)

U-505 Website-(www.msichicago.org/exhibit/U505/U505home.html)
Location in Chicago, IL

U-boats-(uboat.net) The largest page on U-Boats in the world.

U.S. Gov. Printing Office On-line Bookstore for Military History-
(bookstore.gpo.gov/sb/sb-098.html)

U.S. Naval Institute-(www.usni.org)

U.S. Navy Websites-All reachable via (www.navy.mil) on the Internet
and were current as of July 2001. This site contains links to over
500 Official Naval Web Sites URL: www.navy.mil

U.S. Submarine Veterans Inc Website-by Harrison, Sid & Martini,
Ron-This is the official Web site of the SubVets National
Organization-USSVI at (ussvi.org)

USS Bowfin Museum-(http://www.aloha.net/~bowfin/) in Hawaii

USS Cod Website-(www.usscod.org) in Cleveland, Ohio

USS Pampanito Website-(www.maritime.org/pamphome.htm) in
San Francisco, CA

USSVI National Memorial Page-by Harrison, Sid & Martini, Ron-A
very large listing of places with memorials to submariners and
submarines around the country. Many pictures. Listed by Boat
name, by state and there also is a page that lists all other struc-
tures/buildings and named for submariners.

VMI On-Line Military Library-(www.vmi.edu/library/)

Appendix IX

Naval Proceedings Magazine articles.

Naval Proceedings is the magazine branch of the U.S. Naval Institute. The Naval Institute is a company which has been publishing naval works, including many books listed in this bibliography, Naval Proceedings magazine, Naval History magazine and other materials.

In 1874, the Institute started publishing the Naval Proceedings with one issue. It reappeared with single issues again in 1876 and 1877 and two issues in 1878. It became a quarterly in 1879 until 1913. In 1914 it was issued six times per year for three years until it became a monthly in 1917 and has remained such since.

The Naval Institute published a book in 1982 titled U.S. Naval Institute Proceedings Cumulative Index 1874-1977. The book is difficult to find and I have therefore ask and received permission of the Editor-in-Chief to list the articles pertaining to submarines in that book. In addition, I have included the articles of interest in the 1996-2001magazine editions. The listings below will indicate the month/year of the issue the article appears with the exception of the early days when the magazine was a quarterly and I will then indicate by 1st/1894 for example. I will list the month/year in the format 2/41 indicating Feb 1941 as an example and 10/19 indicating Oct, 1919.

A list of librarys where the Naval Proceedings are archived is at the end of the listing.

Women Should Not Serve on Submarines 8/95, 11/95, 2/96, 3/96, 12/99

World Navies in Review 3/2001

Repositories of Naval Proceedings Magazine. This information was correct in 1978. Check with each prior to going there for research.

US Air University Library, Maxwell Air Force Base, Alabama

US Naval Postgraduate School Library, Monterey, CA

U. of California Library, Berkeley

U. of Colorado Library, Boulder

Yale, New Haven, CT

US Library of Congress, Wash., D.C.

US Navy (Circular) 1st/1888

US Navy Dept Library, Wash., D.C.

US Naval Research Library, Wash., D.C.

US Command and Staff College, Ft. Leavenworth, KS

US Naval Academy Library, Annapolis, MD

US Navy and Nuclear ASW Weapons 12/84

Peabody Institute, Baltimore, MD

Boston Public Library, Boston, MA

Harvard U. Library, Cambridge, MA

MIT, Cambridge, MA

Mass. Historical Society, Boston, MA

Detroit Public Library

New York State Library, Albany

Buffalo Public Library, Buffalo, NY

Cornell U, Ithaca, NY

New York Public Library, NY, NY

Columbia U. Library, NY, NY

Engineering Societies Library, NY, NY

US Military Academy, West Point, NY

Dartmouth College Library, Hanover, NH

Cleveland Public Library, Cleveland, OH
US Artillery and Guided Missile School, Fort Sill, OK
American Philosophical Society Library, Phila., PA
Lehigh U. Library, Bethlehem, PA
Franklin Institute Library, Phila., PA
Carnegie Library of Pittsburgh, PA
Vanderbilt University Library, Nashville, TN\
US Army Engineer's School Library, Ft. Belvoir, VA
Mariners Museum, Newport News, VA
US National War College Library, Ft. McNair, VA
Seattle Public Library, Seattle, WA

Appendix X

The Clay Blair Papers

The following is a description of the Clay Blair Papers. These items dates 1945-1998, with a few items in Spanish from 1575 to 1626, were given to the American Heritage Center at the University of Wyoming by Clay Blair, Jr. in several accretions from 1973 to 1999. The Collections official name may be cited as: Clay Blair Papers, 1575-1998, Accession Number 8295, Box Number..., Folder Number..., American Heritage Center, University of Wyoming and was last edited in August of 2000

The complete listing is available from the University of Wyoming, American Heritage Center, PO Box 3924, Laramie, WY 82071-3924 and comprises 166 pages and cost $22.60 as of August of 2001.

Mr. Blair died in 1998. He and his wife Joan were working on a book about the history of the Code and Signal Section within the Office of Naval Communications, the OP-20-G, at the time of his death. Many of those materials are in the Collection.

The following is a brief description of the Collection condensed down from the 166 page inventory of the 368 boxes of material in the collection.

Series 1. Research files, bulk dates 1575-1993. 38.6 cubic ft. (86 boxes). Arranged alphabetically. Notes, documents, newspaper and magazine clippings, photographs, periodicals and photocopies of books.

Series II. Research Interviews, 1970-1978. 4 cubic ft. (14 boxes). Arranged alphabetically. Audio cassettes of interviews for the books *Return From the River Kwai, The Search for JFK,* and *Silent Victory*

Series III. Hitler's U-Boat War Research Materials.

Sub-Series A. General Research Files, 1939-1998. 9.9 cubic ft. (22 boxes). Arranged alphabetically by folder title. Contains notes, documents, newspaper and magazine clippings relating to Blair's U-Boat and WWII research

Sub-Series B. U-Boat Research Files, 1943-1998. 3.6 cubic ft. (8 boxes). Arranged alphabetically by folder title and numerically by U-Boat number. Contains notes, articles and photocopies of documents relating to U-Boats.

Sub-Series C. Oversized Research Files, 1942-1993. 3.42 cubic ft (9 boxes). Arranged alphabetically by folder title. Contains the same type of material as Sub-series B, but in a larger format.

Sub-Series D. War Diary Notes, 1941-45, no date. 1.8 cubic ft. (4 boxes). Arranged chronologically by year of the diaries. Includes Blair's notes from the War Diaries he researched.

Sub-Series E. Maps, 1979-1989. 1.38 cubic ft. (5 boxes). Includes maps used by Blair for research. Some have his notation on them

Sub-Series F. Photographs, 1941-1997....9cubic ft. (2 boxes). Arranged alphabetically by folder title. Includes photos which were used in the book and others that were not published in the book but may have been used for research.

Sub-Series G. Index/Note Cards, n.d. 2.7 cubic ft. (9 boxes). In original order. Includes a name index and other notes roughly by year

Sub-Series H. Research Interviews, cassette. 1987-1998. 1 cubic ft. (1 box). Arranged alphabetically. Audio cassettes of interviews for both volumes of *Hitler's U-Boat War*.

Sub-Series I. Microfilm, 1939-1945. 1.5 cubic ft. (5 boxes). Arranged alphabetically by title. Contains research for *Hitler's U-Boat War*. Much of the material is War Diaries and other official documents from the National Archives and Records Administration (NARA).

Series IV. Cryptography Research Files, 1929-1998. 5.85 cubic ft. (13 boxes). Arranged alphabetically by folder title. Contains research material and notes relating to code breaking and cryptography during WWII. Some of this material was used for the writing of the *Hitler's U-Boat War*, but the majority of the files were to be used for a book about the Code and Signal Section of the Office of Naval Communications, OP-20-G.

Series V. Curtis Publishing Company, 1960-1966. 3.15 cubic ft. (7 boxes). Arranged alphabetically. Memoranda, reports, speeches, newspaper and magazine clippings about the management of the company and the magazine, *The Saturday Evening Post*.

Series VI. Professional Correspondence, 1953-1998. 3.15 cubic ft. (7 boxes). Arranged alphabetically. Correspondence between Clay Blair Jr., and his editors, publishers, colleagues, and attorneys regarding his books and articles

Series VII. Personal Correspondence, 1940-1998. 1.35 cubic ft. (3 boxes). Arranged chronically. Correspondence between Clay and Joan

Blair, their families and friends. Also includes sympathy cards and letters regarding Clay's death.

Series VIII. Speeches, 1985-1990. .25 cubic ft. (1 box). Arranged alphabetically. By Clay Blair, Jr. regarding U.S. military history.

Series IX. Biographical Information, 1930-1991. .25 cubic ft. (1 box). Arranged chronologically. School and military records, identification and membership cards, certificates, newspaper and magazine clippings, and memorabilia regard Clay Blair.

Series X. Time-Life Corporation, 1949-1957. 5 cubic ft. (12 boxes). Arranged chronologically. Rough drafts of articles by Clay Blair, Jr. for the corporation.

Series XI. Manuscripts, 1947-1997. 58.95 cubic ft. (131 boxes). Arranged alphabetically. Drafts of free lance articles and books by Clay Blair, Jr. and Joan and Clay Blair, Jr.

Series XII. Photographs, 1900-1970s. 1.59 cubic ft. (4 boxes). Arranged by subject and chronologically within a subject. Of Clay Blair, Jr. from birth through 1964. There are also files of relatives, professional stills and story assignments

Series XIII. Washington Times-Rev Sun Myung Moon, 1977, 1982. .38 cubic ft (1 box). Arranged by physical description. Book, promotion kits, newspaper clippings, analysis of a strategic bomber controversy, and story lists.

Series XIV. Publicity Files, 1954-1998. 1.8 cubic ft. (4 boxes). Arranged alphabetically. Regarding books and articles by Clay Blair, Jr. and Joan and Clay Blair, Jr. Correspondence, reviews, and promotional material.

Series XV. File and Video. 1957-1998. .75 cubic ft (2 boxes).
> A. Microfilm:
> Research for an unpublished history of the Spanish treasure fleets of the sixteenth and seventeenth centuries, 1957-1964, 10 reels
> B. Motion Picture Film:
> Publicity clips for the film Return from the River Kwai, 16mm, B&W, 3 ½ minutes, 1979, 2 reels
> C. Video Cassettes:
> Tapes of programs Clay Blair worked on or had an interest in, including *Ridgeway, The Unsung Hero, Omar Bradley* (for A&E), *Korea: The Forgotten War*

Series XVI. Scrapbook Material, 1940-1964, 1970-1980. 1.31 cubic ft. (2 boxes). Arranged chronologically. Articles by or about Clay Blair, Jr. Also includes three scrapbooks regarding *Silent Victory* and three newspapers.

Series XVII. Miscellaneous Files, 1965-1998. .9cubic ft. (2 boxes). Arranged alphabetically.

Series XVIII. Korean War Material, 1990-1998. 1.15 cubic ft. (3 boxes). Arranged alphabetically. Contains material relating to the Korean War, including several conferences, television documentaries, and information about the book *Black Soldier, White Army*.

Series XIX. Books, 1954-1973. 3.4 cubic ft. (8 boxes). Arranged alphabetically. Authored or co-authored by Clay Blair, Jr.

Series XX. Periodicals, 1988-1998. .90 cubic ft. (2 boxes). Arranged alphabetically by periodical title and chronologically within each title. Includes journals and newsletters relating to submarine veterans.

APPENDIX XI

CHARLES LOCKWOOD PAPERS

LC Control Number: mm 70048694

Type of Material: Archival Manuscript Material (Collection)

Personal Name: Lockwood, Charles, 1890-1967.

Main Title: Papers of Charles Lockwood, 1904-1967 (bulk 1940-1960)

Description: 7000 items.
25 containers.

Biog./History Note: Naval officer. Full name: Charles Andrews Lockwood.

Summary: Correspondence, memoranda, diaries (1935-1967), reports, mss. and tss. of books, articles, and speeches, photographs, newspaper clippings, and printed matter relating mainly to Lockwood's naval career during World War II as commander of the U.S. Submarine Force in the Pacific and his research and writings on submarines after his retirement. A substantial part of Lockwood's papers concerns the development of the submarine as an effective military weapon and includes technical data on electric-impact switches, hydraulic doors, night periscopes, radar and sonar instruments, and trial runs of submarines equipped with these devices. Includes diary of John Allison Fitzgerald, prisoner of war in Japan. Correspondents include Hans Christian Adamson, George T. Bye, Ralph W. Christie, Merrill Comstock, Louis E. Denfeld, Robert S. Edwards, Ernest M. Eller, Robert H. English, James Fife, Edward E. Hazlett, Bodo Herzog, Ben Hibbs, Alan G. Kirk, Francis S. Low, Stuart S. Murray, Chester W. Nimitz, Günter Schoemaekers, and Lockwood's wife, Phyllis (Irwin) Lockwood.

Notes:	In part, photocopies.
	MSS48694
Forms part of:	Naval Historical Foundation collection.
Finding Aids:	Finding aid available in the Library.
Source of Acquisition:	Deposit, Naval Historical Foundation, 1972. Converted to gift, 1998.
Subjects:	Adamson, Hans Christian.
	Bye, George T.
	Christie, Ralph W. (Ralph Waldo), 1893-1987.
	Comstock, Merrill.
	Denfeld, Louis E. (Louis Emil), 1891-1972.
	Edwards, Robert S.
	Eller, Ernest McNeill, 1903-
	English, Robert H.
	Fife, James, 1897-1975.
	Fitzgerald, John Allison
	Hazlett, Edward Everett, 1892-
	Herzog, Bodo.
	Hibbs, Ben, 1901-
	Kirk, Alan Goodrich, 1888-1963.

Lockwood, Phyllis
Low, Francis S. (Francis Stuart), 1894-1964.
Murray, Stuart S.
Nimitz, Chester W. (Chester William), 1885-1966.
Shoemaekers, Günter
Fitzgerald, John Allison
United States. Navy—History—World War, 1939-1945.
Electric switchgear.
Marine engineering.
Periscopes.
Radar—Research.
Sonar.
Submarine boats.
World War, 1939-1945—Campaigns—Pacific Ocean.
World War, 1939-1945—Naval operations, American.
World War, 1939-1945—Prisoners and prisons, Japanese.
World War, 1939-1945—Radar.
Naval officers.

Local Call/Shelving:
          0536G

Repository: Library of Congress Manuscript Division Washington (D.C.)

CALL NUMBER: 0536G

Container Nos.
1   Diaries
              Nov 1935-Jan 9, 1942 13v

                    Jan 10, 1942-1949 12v
                    Mar. 20, 1941-Mar. 22, 1942 (typescript)
                    May 19-June 12, 1491 (photocopy)
2   Diaries
                    1950-52 (3 vol)
                    1953-54 (2 vol)
                    1955-56 (2 vol)
3   Diaries
                    1957-58 (2 vol)
                    1959-60 (2 vol)
                    1961-62 (2 vol)
4   Diaries
                    1963-64 (2 vol)
                    1965-66 (2 vol)
                    1967 (1 vol)
5   Correspondence, 1927-67 and Undated
         Family
                    1927-40 (6 folders)
6   1941-44 (6 folders)
7   Apr. 1944-48 (6 folders)
8   General
                    1948-52 (7 folders)
9   1953-63 (7 folders)
10   1964-67 and undated (7 folders)
11   Official
                    1920-Mar. 1940 (6 folders)
12   Apr. 1940-42 (8 folders)
13   1943 (8 folders)(Torpedo information)
14   1944-Feb. 45 (7 folders)
15   Mar.-Sept. 1945 (8 folders)
16   Nov. 1945-1947 (7 folders)
                    Orders to duty, 1925-55 (5 folders)
         Subject File
17   Loss of navy transport, 1943

Recommendations for prisoners of war, 1955. Includes a copy
    of diary of POW John A. Fitzgerald 44-45
Strategic Bombing Survey, 1942
Submarines, 1927-66
    Battle of Midway
    Bluegill, USS
    Bonefish, USS
    Grounding and salvage of USS H-3
    Harder, USS
    History of USS S-5
    Interview relating to the USS F-4 disaster
    Interview with Oliver F. Naquin
    Japanese naval and merchant shipping losses
    Major Japanese submarine operations
    Manual of free escape from submarines
    Misuse of Japanese submarines during WWII
    Monadnock, USS
    Nuclear-powered ships
    Patrol Report of USS Snook
    18Report of helium oxygen mixtures for diving
    Report of the explosion of USS E-2
    Sinking of USS S-51
    Size and growth of submarine force
    Submarine accidents
    Submarine escape history
    Submarine oceanography
    Submarine patrol incidents
    Submarine warfare
    Submarine warning flag
    Submarines-Organization, disposition, tactics (2 folders)
    Theodore Roosevelt, USS
    Upholder, HMS
    Wahoo, USS
Speech, Article and Book File, 1924-67

Miscellaneous
    1930-55 (3 folders)
25   Printed matter-Misc. 1957-66
U.S. Naval Academy—dedication services for
    Navy-Marine Corps Memorial Stadium,
    1957

Appendix XII

RALPH CHRISTIE Papers

The papers of Ralph Waldo Christie (1893-1987), admiral and submarine commander, were deposited in the Library of Congress by the Naval Historical Foundation in 1984. The collection contains 150 items in .4 linear feet of shelf space. The papers span the years 1941-1945 and consist primarily of Christie's official correspondence while serviing as commander of Submarine Squadron Five, 1941-42, and as Commander of Submarines, Southwest Pacific Force, Seventh Fleet, 1943-45. The correspondence, newsclippings, and an essay concerning Christie's efforts to have a Medal of Honor awarded to Samual D. Dealey, the commander of the the submarine Harder. The submarine and it's commander were lost in action in 1944.

The collection consists of one box with 11 folders of correspondence and the Medal of Honor Award information for Dealey.

The Naval Institute Press is the book-publishing arm of the U.S. Naval Institute, a private, nonprofit, membership society for sea service professionals and others who share an interest in naval and maritime affairs. Established in 1873 at the U.S. Naval Academy in Annapolis, Maryland, where its offices remain today, the Naval Institute has members worldwide.

Members of the Naval Institute support the education programs of the society and receive the influential monthly magazine, Proceedings and discounts on fine nautical prints and on ship and aircraft photos. They also have access to the transcripts of the Institute's Oral History program and get discounted admission to any of the Institute-sponsored seminars offered around the country.

The Naval Institute also publishes Naval History magazine. This colorful bi-monthly is filled with entertaining and thought-provoking articles, first-person reminiscences, and dramatic art and photography. Members receive a discount on Naval History subscriptions.

The Naval Institute's Book-publishing program, begun in 1898 with basic guides to naval practices, has broadened its scope in recent years to include books of more general interest. Now the Naval Institute Press publishes about one hundred titles each year, ranging from how-to-books on boating and navigation to battle histories, biographies, ship and aircraft guides, and novels. Institute members receive discounts of 20 to 50% on the Press's nearly six hundred books in print.

Full-time students are eligible for special half-price membership rates. Life memberships are also available.

For a free catalog describing Naval Institute Press books currently available, and for further information about subscribing to Naval History magazine or about joining the U.S. Naval Institute, please write to:

Membership Department
U.S. Naval Institute
291 Wood Road
Annapolis, MD 21402-5035
Telephone: (800) 233-8764
Fax: (410) 269-7940
Web: www.usni.org

USSVI-UNITED STATES SUBMARINE VETERANS INC.

This organization is open to all qualified submariners who were honorably discharged. The Creed of USSVI reads; "To perpetuate the memory of our shipmates who gave their lives in the pursuit of their duties while serving their country. That their dedication, deeds and supreme sacrifice be a constant source of motivation toward greater accomplishment. Pledge loyalty and patriotism to the United States."

The group of some 8000 members in 2001 is organized into 3 Regions and 10 Districts and some 85 Bases (chapters) in the United States. Headquartered in Silverdale, WA, it's address is: USSVI National Office, POB 3870, Silverdale, WA 98383-3870. Further information of the group, it's particular locations, plans, and accomplishments plus an application is available via their Web page at; USSVI.ORG. Associate memberships are also available for those with ties or strong interest in the organization.

NSL-NAVAL SUBMARINE LEAGUE

The Naval Submarine League (NSL) is a professional organization for submariners and submarine advocates. Benefits of NSL membership include **association** with a dedicated group of submarine professionals, a **professional journal–THE SUBMARINE REVIEW**, an **annual directory of members, information** on submarine developments and issues to assist members in creating public awareness of submarine capabilities and value to U.S. defense, a **forum** for exchange of thoughts on submarine matters, and an **invitation** to Annual Symposium and Annual Meeting.

The primary mission of the Naval Submarine League is to PROMOTE AWARENESS of the importance of submarines to U.S. national security, yet remain an INDEPENDENT AUTHORITY on submarine matters so that its CREDIBILITY is unquestioned and its message retains its effectiveness.

The Naval Submarine League was founded and incorporated in Virginia as a non-profit organization in 1982. Today League membership stands at about 4000. Two thirds of the individual membership fees are tax deductible.

Further information is available on the Web at: www.navalsubleague.com or writing: Naval Submarine League, POB 1146, Annandale, VA 22003

About the Author

Served in U.S. Navy in 1960 through 1968 and was a trained electrical nuclear power plant operator and served on USS Catfish SS-339 and USS Patrick Henry SSBN 599. Website on submarines is at: www.rontini.com and email to: rontini@vcn.com. Currently retired in Sheridan, Wyoming.

Printed in the United States
3510